Groove Tube

Console-ing Passions

Television and Cultural Power / Edited by Lynn Spigel

GROOVE TUBE

Sixties Television and the Youth Rebellion

Aniko Bodroghkozy

Duke University Press   Durham and London   2001

© 2001 Duke University Press

All rights reserved

Printed in the United States of

America on acid-free paper ∞

Designed by C. H. Westmoreland

Typeset in Bembo with Benguiat

display by Tseng Information Systems, Inc.

Library of Congress Cataloging-

in-Publication Data appear on the

last printed page of this book.

To my mother,

Christel Pick Bodroghkozy

Contents

Acknowledgments

Real life is what happens while scholars are busy trying to write their books. The acknowledgments page is sometimes the only place where a book's reader can get some clues about the author, about how the book came into being, and about how the book's evolution and the author's life interconnect. A great number of major life events have gone on for this author in the close to five years it has taken for this project to evolve from a Ph.D. dissertation to the volume you hold in your hands. While working on this book, the author went from anxious academic job seeker in Madison, Wisconsin, to gypsy scholar in Montreal, to unemployed scholar in Toronto, to (finally!) employed assistant professor in Edmonton. With the vicissitudes of the academic job market of the early 1990s, sometimes the only thing that kept the author's self-confidence from utterly evaporating was her signed contract for this book. Other more positive life changes also punctuate the production of this book. The author went from being a single woman living alone to a married woman and from being religiously unaffiliated to a convert to Judaism. And perhaps most significant of all, as the author rushes this book into production, she awaits the imminent birth of her first child.

Along with all the major life events that have revolved around the production of this book, there are numerous individuals and institutions that have helped shape it. First, at the University of Wisconsin, I owe an enormous debt to John Fiske and Lynn Spigel, my Ph.D. advisers and mentors. The influence of their scholarship is everywhere in these pages. Other faculty members at the UW, both in the Communication Arts and in the Journalism and Mass Communication departments, who have been supportive and wonderfully helpful to me include Julie D'Acci, Michele Hilmes, Robert McChesney, and James Baughman. As a graduate student in the Communication Arts department, I benefited enormously from the comradeship of my fellow "Telecommies." My work has been influenced and strengthened by the feedback I received from my peers as much as from our extraordinary faculty. Thursday afternoon colloquia where we would present our works in progress and then share beer at the Red Shed afterward provided invaluable opportunities for productive comments, critiques, and questions. I still miss that camaraderie. Thanks to fellow Telecommies Pam Wilson, Jeff Sconce, Steve Claussen, Shari Goldin, Lisa Parks, Kevin Glynn, and Mike Curtin. Other Madison friends who helped were Lew Zipin and Matthew Weinstein. Special thanks and gratitude go to Jan Levine Thal for both intellectual and emotional support.

Here at the University of Alberta I've juggled the responsibilities of being a new faculty member along with the need to get this book out. I'd like to thank my colleague Bill Beard, the other half of our two-person Film and Media Studies Programme. One couldn't ask for a more generous and supportive colleague. Other U of A colleagues proved particularly helpful as I reworked material in this book. Thanks to my writing group—Sue Hamilton, Susan Smith, Lesley Cormack, Glenn Burger, Annalise Acorn, and Judy Garber—who read new chapters and provided great feedback when I really needed it. Students who took my course on American Film and Television of the 1960s provided more help than they can possibly imagine, especially as I wrestled with how to conclude this book. Many issues raised in the conclusion came straight out of discussions in that class. My students also convinced me of the usefulness of including in this volume a chronology of 1960s events.

Other individuals to whom I owe much include my friend, mentor, and colleague Henry Jenkins, who has been a great ally during good times and bad. He has read this manuscript more than once and provided very useful and constructive comments. William Boddy has also been through this work twice and given me careful and thoughtful feedback. William and Henry's feedback also helped me make the painful decision to delete a chapter on the rock music industry and its comparison with entertainment television. George Lipsitz, who read the first draft for another press, provided tough but much-appreciated insights.

Both the University of Wisconsin and the University of Alberta have been generous in providing financial assistance so that I could do the research necessary for this project. The UW Communication

Arts department and the Graduate School provided funding so that I could conduct research in Los Angeles and at the Library of Congress in Washington, D.C. Here at the U of A, very generous funding from the Support for the Advancement of Scholarship Fund and the Humanities and Fine Arts Research Grant allowed me to pursue new research in Los Angeles at UCLA and in Madison at the State Historical Society. I am very grateful to the Faculty of Arts for its demonstrated support of its faculty and their research initiatives.

The kind of historical research that goes into a project like this necessitates a great deal of archival work. I would like to thank the archivists and personnel at the State Historical Society of Wisconsin for maintaining such a fabulous collection of underground newspapers from the 1960s. One could not hope for a more comprehensive array of papers. The Historical Society remains the premiere site for historians doing research on the social movements of the 1960s. I would also like to thank Madeline Matz, reference librarian at the Library of Congress, Division of Motion Picture, Broadcasting, and Recorded Sound, for arranging to let me see dozens and dozens of 16mm copies of television programs from the late 1960s and early 1970s. The efficiency and helpfulness of the LC personnel made my two-week stint of going through seemingly endless film canisters quite pleasant. The staff at the UCLA Film and Television Archives were also wonderfully helpful during my first trip out there to do research on *The Smothers Brothers Comedy Hour.* I would like to thank Lou Kramer for transferring to half-inch video all seventy-some episodes of the show so that I could view them all at the UCLA Media Lab. Thanks also to Brigitte Coopers for allowing me access to the bound scripts of Smothers Brothers shows at the UCLA Arts Library, Special Collections Division, during my first research trip and then to the papers of Tony Barrett and other television industry personnel during my second visit some years later.

I owe a special debt of gratitude to Tom and Dick Smothers, who generously opened their offices to me on my first research trip to Los Angeles, allowing me to go through all their papers and to photocopy anything I wished. Office manager Cathy Bruegger was especially hospitable. On my second research trip Tom and Dick again welcomed me into their offices and allowed me to borrow any photographic material I wished in order to provide illustrations for this book. Office manager Wendy Blair was very kind and helpful. The

Smothers Brothers exemplify the kind of invaluable receptiveness to scholarship about television and entertainment media that I wished other entertainment industry personnel shared.

Big thanks are also due to Ken Wissoker, my editor at Duke University Press, for his enthusiasm about this book and for his help in guiding a first-time author through the complexities of academic publishing. I'm also grateful for his patience in giving me the time to get this book right.

The pursuit of an academic career is a precarious endeavor at best, requiring great investments of time, money, energies, and hopes with uncertain rewards. My mother, to whom this book is dedicated, never wavered in her confidence that her daughter, the seemingly perpetual student, would make a success of this life of the mind. More recently my husband and partner, Elliot Majerczyk, has shown me that there is more to life than the world of the rational mind. He has cooked innumerable dinners while I was hammering away at this project. While I was immersed in 1960s television, Elliot, with his expertise in American popular music, gave me a deepened appreciation for sixties musical luminaries Bob Dylan and Brian Wilson. Okay, sweetheart, the book's done. Let's listen to *Pet Sounds* and give birth to this baby. . . .

Groove Tube

Introduction

Turning on

the Groove

Tube

In 1967 I was seven years old and enchanted by hippies. Living in a squeaky-clean Canadian suburb, I had never actually seen any real, live hippies—except on television. Yet those video images were powerful because I knew I wanted to be a hippie; I wanted to dress like them; I wanted to be around them. In the summer of that year, the so-called Summer of Love, when the hippie phenomenon burst like a psychedelic firecracker onto the North American mass media, I got my wish. Our family took a trip to Toronto, and, to satisfy my parents' curiosity and my own abiding fascination, we decided to drive through the city's much-publicized Yorkville district, a hippie haven that was Toronto's version of Haight-Ashbury. As our car inched along the congested main drag, my father demanded that we keep the windows rolled up. Outside our respectable Pontiac the sidewalks were jammed with the oddest and most bizarre examples of human wildlife my seven year old eyes had ever seen. The stoops and outdoor staircases of once-elegant houses were overrun with freakish-looking youths strumming guitars and bumming change. I remember seeing one young man sauntering down the street sporting a big, shaggy mane of red hair radiating in all directions, a fringed vest with no shirt underneath, and the biggest, craziest looped earring hanging from one ear.

I was terrified. Sliding down on the backseat, I was too distraught and afraid to look anymore. These frightening, filthy, bedraggled specimens didn't look at all like *my* hippies. My hippies were cute and sweet and childlike. What I saw outside the car window were not flower children, certainly not the flower children I knew from television. I didn't know what they were, but I wanted nothing to do with them.

My traumatic introduction to the hippies of Yorkville did not, however, fundamentally challenge my childish fascination with the idea of hippies. On Halloween I would dress up in headband, flowers, and funny vest to go trick-or-treating as a flower child. I begged my parents to buy me a flowered miniskirt (which I got) and plastic white boots (which I didn't get) so I could enhance my hippie, go-go girl appearance. I asked my mother to part my hair in the middle rather than on the side so I would look more like hippie girls.

What image of hippies was I trying to emulate? With the hindsight of some thirty years I recognize that the only hippies I encountered on a regular basis came from our family's unreliable and often-on-the-blink Magnavox color television set. *My* hippies were TV hippies. Throughout the later 1960s they came to play with me from shows like *The Monkees, The Mod Squad, Laugh-In,* and *The Smothers Brothers Comedy Hour.* In my TV-addicted suburban world these were the "real" hippies.

Television hippies gave me not only a way of dressing and parting my hair, however. They gave me a politics. A taken-for-granted antimilitarism and support of movements for social change have formed my core-belief structure for as long as I can remember. I did not come by these beliefs from my parents. My father, a fervent anticommunist, despised any form of social and political turmoil. For someone who had survived World War II, a Russian prisoner-of-war camp, and the dislocations of being a political refugee from communist Hungary, this may have been understandable. Our divergent "structures of feeling" began clashing heatedly and passionately in the early 1970s as I moved into rebellious adolescence—and yet another television show served as the terrain on which our differing beliefs battled. Arguing over the politics of *All in the Family,* my father and I played out our own painful generation gap. My mother, on the other hand, remained politically quiescent during the sixties. But when she separated from my father in the mid-1970s, she discovered the women's liberation movement. Among her favorite shows during this time were the feminist-inflected *Mary Tyler Moore Show, Maude,* and *Rhoda.*

This book grew from my desire to understand how prime-time television figured in the social and cultural dislocations provoked by the student and youth movements of the 1960s. Scholarly pursuits often have their basis in personal questions and autobiography, so part of my motivation here includes a desire to understand the extent to which my voluminous childhood television watching helped shape my political consciousness as a "child of the sixties." How did video representations of the youth counterculture and student rebellion allow space for me, from a very early age, to align myself with the values and politics of that oppositional movement?

Much commentary about prime-time television in the 1960s suggests that the turmoil and social dislocations of the period were absent from the "Vast Wasteland." Sixties TV ran amok with flying nuns, suburban housewife witches with twitchy noses, Okies in Beverly Hills, campy superheroes in tights and capes, and bumbling espionage agents talking into their shoes. As one broadcast historian has argued, sixties programming "meant offering evenings of avoidance. At a time of racial turmoil, political murders, and a massive military intervention in Southeast Asia, Americans viewed relentlessly escapist entertainment and rigorously 'neutral' news programming."[1] To some extent this is true. Network television was a conservative medium in the business of delivering the largest bulk audiences possible to corporate advertisers. Those bulk audiences comprised largely adult and older Americans generally unsympathetic to the political and cultural insurgencies of the nation's youth. Preadolescents and children like myself, too young to have formed political allegiances, made up the other major bloc of television watchers. The teens and young adults fomenting all that turmoil were often the least likely to be watching.

Nevertheless, the childhood memories that provided the impetus for this work, and the research that grounds it, suggest something more complicated. The products of the entertainment industry, in order to be popular, must engage at some level with the lived experiences of their audiences: they need to be relevant.[2] Popular relevancy proved tricky in the United States during the late sixties and early seventies, however. As this book argues, entertainment television could not, and did not, manage to ignore or repress the protest, rebellion, experimentation, and discord going on in the nation's streets and campuses. Prime-time programming grappled with and confronted (often in highly mediated ways) many of the turbulent and painful phenomena of the period. Prime time explored the hippie scene and its attendant drug culture; numerous shows attempted to engage with the explosive issue of draft resistance; countless shows dealt with campus upheavals in one way or another, often featuring at least one almost ritualistic scene of demonstrators clashing violently with police. Later in the 1960s and into the early 1970s, prime-time dramas embraced particularly touchy issues such as fictionalized versions of the My Lai massacre, the Kent State University killings, and Weatherman-type urban guerrilla bombers. Other types of television programming such as variety shows and talk shows became the sites of on-air political confrontations.

This book will trace how the American media industry—specifically entertainment television—engaged with manifestations of youth rebellion and dissent. At the level of production, how did television networks, executives, and producers respond to the challenges associated with their strategies for representing aspects of a youth revolt that were just too colorful and too dramatic to ignore, despite attendant threats posed by an entertainment medium trucking with oppositional politics? At the textual level, what kinds of ideological negotiations can we uncover in the prime-time programming that resulted? How did this most culturally conservative of entertainment media, notorious for its "lowest common denominator," "offend no one" approach to program creation, suddenly find itself turning the most incendiary political material into prime-time series fodder? At the level of reception, how did insurgent young people respond to the texts produced? As the first generation to grow up with the new medium, how did movement-affiliated youth make sense of their relationship to television? How did they respond to the programming that tried to portray their movement's preoccupations? How did they respond to the culture industry disseminating that programming? Many disaffected baby boomers in the 1960s may have preferred just to ignore television's attempts to depict their antiestablishment politics and activities, focusing their attention on the products of another arm of the culture industry, the rock music business.[3] However, evidence from the pages of the movement's underground press suggests a spirited and active process by some in the countercultural and radical student enclaves in struggling over the mechanisms of mass-media incorporation. Engagement with popular media texts—frequently in an antagonistic way—assisted some sixties rebels in thinking through their movement's fractious relationship to the dominant order and helped them to understand the workings of that order. And although politicized sixties youth were overwhelmingly hostile to the television industry, the industry did not, necessarily, return that antagonism. In its attempts to lure baby boomers back to a medium that had significantly shaped their childhoods, prime time attempted to turn itself into a "groove tube," incorporating significant amounts of (admittedly simplified and sanitized) countercultural and campus politico values and critiques. The procedure proved anything but smooth for the networks or their audiences. In the late 1960s and early 1970s, prime time turned into an arena of culture clash, political controversy, generational battle, and ideological upheaval as did so many American institutions during that tumultuous era.

Making Sense of "the Sixties"

Writing about America in the 1960s is nothing if not complicated. For instance, when we refer to "sixties youth" or "rebellious, disaffected, insurgent young people" or simply "the movement," what are we actually talking about? Certainly not all those who were in their teens and early twenties in the mid to later 1960s participated in the activities, politics, and lifestyles discussed here. The category of "sixties youth" is often taken for granted as commonsensical, obvious, and not requiring definition. We all, supposedly, know who and what we're talking about. Things aren't that simple, however. We need to map out a working definition of the social/historical category of "rebellious youth of the 1960s."

Demographics provide one way to help define this phenomenon. In the immediate aftermath of World War II the United States, Canada, Australia, and New Zealand experienced a sharp and prolonged rise in fertility rates that only began to drop off by the mid-1960s. European countries, on the other hand, went through a birthing boom of only a few years immediately after the Second World War.[4] Thus, the baby boom was largely a North American phenomenon. "Baby boomers" formed a huge demographic mass and have often been defined precisely by their size. By their sheer numbers they have tended to shape and influence the social concerns dominant in society depending on their age at the moment. In the 1950s, when the first wave of the "boom" generation were children, concerns about family and child rearing were central issues within North American social, cultural, and political arenas. The 1960s, a period obsessed with youth, was literally awash with young people. Between 1960 and 1970 the population between the ages of eighteen and twenty-four increased by a spectacular and unprecedented 53 percent. Never had so much of the population been at the turbulent years of youth all at the same time. Historian of the baby boom generation Landon Y. Jones observes, "It is no coincidence, then, that the six years from 1964 to 1970 saw the outbreak of the most prolonged and dislocating domestic turmoil of this century. These were the same years that the first baby boomers massively entered the dangerous years." Jones presents the work of Norman Ryder, a pioneer of cohort theory in the field of demography, who argued that "throughout history the younger generation has challenged the older as it enters this life stage. The young are cultural insurrectionaries, *agents provocateurs* with no allegiance to the past. The task of the older generation is to control this 'invasion of barbarians' and shape their energies so they become contributors to society. Only then, by recruiting the young, can the culture maintain its continuity."[5] Jones goes on to argue that the vast numbers of young baby boomers overwhelmed their elders and made this process of social recruitment and continuity impossible.

This demographic definition of sixties youth has a certain explanatory power. Unfortunately it cannot account for the massive student and youth movements in countries that did not experience fertility booms. In France the youth rebellion of 1968 in alliance with French workers came very close to toppling the de Gaulle government and sparking a potential political revolution. The late sixties saw youth movements around the globe—in Japan, Mexico, Germany, and other nations.[6] On the other hand, the baby boom nation Australia was relatively quiescent during the sixties, experiencing few campus disruptions compared to the thousands on U.S. campuses.[7] Therefore, although an appeal to numbers and demographic determinism can help in defining rebellious sixties youth in the United States, it tends toward essentialism and must be used cautiously.

A baby boom definition is also problematic because not every person born during its first wave (generally considered to be between 1946 and the mid-1950s) actively engaged in campus politics (such as antiwar activity, draft resistance, or challenges to in loco parentis rules) or got involved with countercultural activities (psychedelic drug experimentation, dropping out, alternative lifestyles, acid-rock music fandom). The popular imagination tends to perceive baby boomers as generally white and middle class. Although working-class and African American couples participated in the fertility frenzy as much as did the white middle class, the first two groups tend to get erased from the picture. The working classes are often not seen as "a part of the sixties" at all except as adult reactionary hard hats responding violently and in disgust to the unpatriotic antics of the pampered and privileged children of the suburbs. Working-class baby boomers are practically nonexistent in the popular memory of the period. Typically this was not a cohort that went to university or participated in counterculture communities. Many boomer sons of the working class went to Vietnam, fought there, and died there. In the popular imagination, however, it is the disruptive activity of their luckier stateside brothers and sisters that defines "sixties youth."

John Clarke, Stuart Hall, Tony Jefferson, and Brian Roberts have delineated in their work on youth culture the differences between working-class subcultures and middle-class countercultures. Although their work focuses on the British context of youth activity, their observations make sense of the U.S. scene as well. In comparing the two groups, they observe that working-class subcultures tend to operate as a form of "gang," whereas middle-class countercultures are more diffuse, individualized "milieus" rather than the tightly knit leader-oriented subcultural group:

> Working-class sub-cultures reproduce a clear dichotomy between those aspects of group life still fully under the constraint of dominant or 'parent' institutions (family, home, school, work), and those focused on non-work hours—leisure, peer-group associations. Middle-class counter-culture milieux merge and blur distinctions between 'necessary' and 'free' time and activities. Indeed, the latter are distinguished precisely by their attempt to explore 'alternative institutions' to the central institutions of the dominant culture. . . . During the high point of the Counter-Culture, in the 1960s, the middle-class counter-culture formed a whole embryo 'alternative society',

providing the Counter-Culture with an underground, institutional base. Here, the youth of each class reproduces the position of the 'parent' classes to which they belong. Middle-class culture affords the space and opportunity for sections of it to 'drop out' of circulation. Working-class youth is persistently and constantly structured by the dominating rhythm of Saturday Night and Monday Morning.[8]

Because class is so much more hidden in the United States, subcultural youth activity may be more difficult to "see" than it is in Britain. But the structural differences set out by Clarke et al. are useful in defining aspects of a counterculture (which in this instance would include more directly political and insurgent youth groupings that often are separated off and distinguished from definitions of "the counterculture"). The point is that this is fundamentally a middle-class form of rebellion. Consequently, our definition of "sixties youth" must be limited by class.

It must also be limited by race. African American youth were highly politicized and insurgent in this period and, unlike working-class whites, were, to some extent, aligned with radicalized young middle-class whites. The civil rights and black-power movements had enormous influence on the evolving character of campus-based white youth insurgency. But although most campus politicos drew inspiration from the black movement and fought for the causes of racial equality and black empowerment, the segregationist structures so deeply embedded in American society manifested themselves here as well. The hugely influential New Left Students for a Democratic Society (SDS) had very few black members. In 1965 the Student Nonviolent Coordinating Committee (SNCC), the major student civil rights organization, asked all its white members to leave the organization.[9] Although blacks participated in antiwar activism (with Martin Luther King Jr. coming out strongly against the war in 1967), they tended to organize separately from campus-based student groups. In relation to the hippie-oriented counterculture, many of the distinctions Clarke et al. laid out for working-class subcultures could be applied to African American youth groupings as well. But unlike working-class youth subcultures, black youths were highly politicized and dangerously insurgent. Clearly these attributes attracted many middle-class white youths to the phenomenon of black uprisings and dissent. Ultimately, however, these were two different and separate movements. This book focuses primarily on the white, middle-class youth rebellion.

Even among white middle-class baby boomers of the period, we have to limit our field of vision. Those who participated in demonstrations and alternative lifestyles always formed a minority. However, at the time and since, this colorful lot has come to stand in for the larger category of "the youth of the sixties." This portion of the baby boom formed the leading edge for the generation—its avantgarde. And it was this segment of the baby boom that proved so fascinating to the culture industries. Television, music, cinema, even advertising showed little interest in exploring the lifestyles, values, and politics associated with the "silent generation" of baby boomer youth who remained on the sidelines or on the opposite side of all the social, political, and cultural ferment precipitated by their more vocal cogenerationists.[10] The silent generation of boomers was, at best, a rhetorical ploy for conservatives and Republicans to use as contrast to the long haired, draft-dodging, pothead freaks. Conformist sixties youth were too dull and colorless for the popular culture arena.

We also need a working definition of "the youth rebellions of the 1960s." Most historians and commentators of the period agree that the white, middle-class youth movement consisted of two distinct but inexorably related components: a politicized, universitybased mobilization often called the New Left or "the movement," of which SDS was a key element; and a more diffuse, less overtly "political" phenomenon of drug-oriented, alternative, antimaterialist, community living called the counterculture. Young people at the time tended to see the two phenomena as separate. Campus politicos despaired of the "do your own thing" hippies, who eschewed engagement and struggle with established power structures, whereas the hippies tended to criticize student activists for not dropping out to engage in the only fundamental change possible: psychic transformation. The underground press, a crucial alternative institution that allowed the decentralized and often amorphous youth movement a sense of coherence, consisted mostly of papers that spoke to one or the other tendency within youth circles. Hippie-oriented papers tended to feature stories on hallucinogenic substances, spiritual matters, and rock music. Politico-oriented papers tended to feature coverage of demonstrations, establishment repression, political theorizing, and rock music. However, these delineations are rather arbitrary and do not properly suggest the merging between these two tendencies. Activist students embraced many of the aspects of countercultural "lifestyle politics," such as drug use, engagement with the burgeoning youth music scene, and experimentation with different modes of living. Hippies, especially after becoming recipients of law-and-order disciplining, tended to move into more confrontational directions. So, although I think it important to distinguish between these two modes of youth rebelliousness in the 1960s, I think it is equally important to emphasize their common roots.

Making Sense of Sixties Youth Audiences

One of the key issues this book explores is audience reception practices. I want to reconstruct how countercultural and radical sixties youth struggled with, and attended to, their popular cultural representations in prime-time television. How does one go about doing that kind of historical reconstruction? One can, of course, interview numerous baby boomers, but I am wary of problems associated with the kinds of memory texts oral history would produce in this instance. Until very recently most attempts at "making sense of the sixties" have been initiated by individuals who participated in the period, often as active participants in the social movements that so defined the era. The memoirs and participant-observer histories that have appeared with great frequency since the mid-1980s are of enormous use, but almost inevitably the authors still have axes to grind, personal demons to exorcise, and unresolved battles to wage.[11] The era is still very much a contested terrain for boomers who, not surprisingly, will remember their youthful past in ways that help to make sense of who and where they are now. Oral histories are a less crucial resource for historians when other documents are available. One of my main resources for reconstructing the discourses circulating within youth movement circles about mass-media representations of youth dissent comes from evidence culled from the underground press.

Beginning in the mid-1960s a growing plethora of alternative newspapers, run on shoestring budgets with nonprofessional writers, began appearing in major cities and college towns. They were hawked on the streets of youth ghettos and on university campuses to readers

primarily in their teens and twenties. As what came to be called
"the movement" assumed the characteristics of a provisionally coherent political conglomeration of disaffected young people, papers that
spoke to and for that youth movement became a crucial information,
communication, and community-building forum. By 1969 over five
hundred underground papers had sprung up throughout the country, distributing anywhere from 2 million to 4.5 million copies to
"radicals, hippies, racial minorities, soldiers, and curiosity-seekers."[12]
The *Los Angeles Free Press,* one of the first and most widely circulated of these papers, reached a readership of almost one hundred
thousand. The counterculture-oriented *East Village Other* and *Chicago Seed* reached sixty-five thousand and twenty-three thousand respectively. Although some of that readership comprised adults "slum-
ming" safely in hippie and radical student spaces or lascivious types
drawn to the *Free Press* and other papers' notorious sex ads, the vast
majority of readers were aligned with the movement. Their reading
of the underground press provided one way to indicate that association.

Those who wrote for the underground newspapers saw themselves
not as observers of youth activism and lifestyles but as participants.
David Armstrong observes in *A Trumpet to Arms: Alternative Media in
America* that "*Berkeley Barb* founder Max Scherr saw the *Barb* as a propaganda vehicle and organizing tool fully as much as he did a newspaper of record. . . . The *Barb* covered most of the happenings of the
middle and last sixties from the instigators' points of view."[13] Journalistic notions of objectivity, distance, balance, and the like had no
place in underground press articles, which were advocatory to the
extreme and often not overtly concerned with accuracy of detail.

The underground press is a particularly rich source of historical
material precisely because its writers were members of the very community they covered. The voices that speak from these documents,
although not unmediated reflections of readers' perspectives and experiences, serve as compelling historical documents. Like any other
kind of popular press, the underground papers performed an "agenda
setting" role. Issues raised in the underground press most likely resonated in some fashion among those in the youth community who did
not write about their perspectives. If numerous underground press
articles made causal connections between television as a medium and
the rebelliousness of young people and used the theories of Mar-

shall McLuhan to explain why, then we can assume that these ideas had some currency at the time and must have circulated beyond the articles themselves. If underground papers like the *Free Press,* the *Seed,* and the *East Village Other* came to the defense of the embattled and summarily canceled Smothers Brothers variety show with petitions and letter writing campaigns, we can assume that the show was of some cultural importance to significant numbers of movement youth.

How can we make use of the kind of knowledge provided by these sources? Television historian Lynn Spigel has studied popular women's magazines and the clues provided by their articles and advertisements about the introduction of television into postwar suburban homes. She shows how these magazines engaged their readers in a frequently conflicted dialogue about the meanings of this new technology. Advertisements had to try to adopt the point of view of the potential consumer and thus can offer clues to the fears and hopes about the new medium. The knowledge provided by such documents is partial and mediated because we have no access to the everyday lives of the women who grappled with the social and familial changes wrought by television.[14]

The documents I use bear a closer relationship to their potential readership. If the underground press endorsed readers' points of view, it was not because the papers were trying to sell a product (beyond the paper itself) but because the generators of these documents did, in fact, share that viewpoint. However, underground press articles display frequently conflicted responses to questions of media co-optation. By reading underground newspapers we can see how discordant and diverse movement responses to the medium could be. There was nothing monolithic or singular about the points of view offered—even within the pages of one paper. Thus an exploration of the conflicts, anxieties, and contestations that went on within the papers themselves suggests that these issues seized the energies of radical and countercultural young people at some level.

Although these documents provide partial and always mediated access to a larger totality to which we have, finally, no real access, there remain fundamental gaps and silenced voices that reverberate in their muteness. Certain viewpoints do not speak from the pages of the underground press. The voices of women within insurgent youth groups are marginalized, if not totally absent, in the pages of the underground press, as they were to a large extent within the movement itself.[15] The majority of writers for the underground press were young, middle-class, white males. Male perspectives prevailed in a movement that frequently made sense of its rebelliousness as a means to assert *manhood*. Macho posturing and appeals to physically aggressive acts in order to signal militancy became more prevalent in youth activism as it entered its more confrontational and revolutionist phases in the later 1960s. Although women participated in insurgent youth politics and in countercultural communities in equal numbers to men, the language of the papers frequently evacuated the presence of women. The papers' layout and visuals also tended to marginalize, demean, and silence women. Many papers were littered with images of naked, sexualized young nymphs—"hippie chick" types who represented a fantasy of feminine sexual availability in these new "liberated," "permissive," and "open" times. These images often graced the covers of underground papers to boost circulation. The *East Village Other* regularly ran its own version of a "page three girl" called "Slum Goddess." Each week the paper would feature a photo of a young woman from the neighborhood—frequently only semi-clad. The very popular underground comix served up in the papers were notoriously misogynistic in their depictions of female bodies. R. Crumb's renderings of hypersexualized nubile nymphs particularly offended early women's liberationists. Many papers also featured pages of ads for porno films advertised with masturbatory representations of buxom and beckoning feminine flesh. When women writers, in the wake of the emergent women's liberation movement, began insisting on coverage of feminist issues, male editors found ways to ridicule content they couldn't censor. An article in the *Barb* about Berkeley women who were organizing carried the headline "The Women Are Revolting." A feminist manifesto on the politics of female orgasm in the *Rat* bore the title, "Clit Flit Big Hit."[16] Although these "politico"-oriented papers could not entirely overlook the uprising in feminist politics among movement women, the more countercultural papers did their best to ignore the whole thing. The *East Village Other* showcased a scathing denunciation of women's liberation positions penned by one of its few female writers, Renfreu Neff.

Because the underground papers largely obliterate the voices of women and make little acknowledgment of their gendered experiences and meaning-making endeavors, there is the threat that the historical narrative I construct will perpetuate that obliteration. In order to avoid such further silencing, this book interrogates questions of female representation in the mass culture texts discussed in the chapters that follow. For instance, I examine how young women were depicted in ways that defused the "threat" of youth rebellion. I explore how they functioned as "mediating" figures between archetypically *male* rebels and *male* establishment figures. However, this textual analysis cannot suggest how countercultural and New Left women may have read these texts. The silences in the underground press documents make it next to impossible to reconstruct how young women may have engaged with these mass-mediated constructions of themselves.

Making Sense of Theory and Method

In an article that has proven enormously influential on my thinking about this project, Stuart Hall argues for the need to situate popular culture within a historical process of social transformations.[17] Audiences for mass-produced popular culture are not passive and inert vessels that function merely to be filled with dominant, capitalist ideology inevitably encoded in such texts. Neither are these texts the straightforward property of dominant groups or classes. What we see in mass-produced popular texts, according to Hall, is a "double movement of containment and resistance."[18] Although the culture industries that produce these products have the power to "rework and reshape what they represent; and, by repetition and selection, to impose and implant such definitions of ourselves as fit more easily the description of the dominant or preferred culture," this power can be resisted, refused, and negotiated.[19] Popular culture can, therefore, function as an important site where cultural hegemony is fought for, won, rewon, and occasionally threatened. Todd Gitlin, writing about entertainment television, has argued that "major social conflicts are transported *into* the cultural system, where the hegemonic process frames them, form and content both, into compatibility with dominant systems of meanings. Alternative material is routinely *incorporated*: brought into the body of cultural production."[20] Although I argue with the smooth-running characterization of Gitlin's model—

one that leaves no room for hegemonic crisis or the *resistance* half of Hall's model—I do agree with his argument that social conflicts are brought into the sphere of popular entertainment.[21] With increasing urgency throughout the late sixties and early seventies, weekly television programs and other popular-culture sites worked on the conflicts and disturbances associated with youth rebellion. By charting a process of "incorporation," I want to explore, by looking at these texts, how that process worked. I also want to determine whether, in fact, the threatening character of this rebellion could be made to conform easily with "dominant systems of meaning." By tracing changing representations of youth disaffection and protest over a five-year period, roughly 1966 to 1971, I argue that these television programs are clues pointing to some important shifts in hegemony at the level of the social and cultural. These texts, therefore, serve as a kind of historical evidence, suggesting something about changing "structures of feeling," to use Raymond Williams's term for a culture's sense of life, its patterned way of thinking and feeling that can be located at the level of lived experience. Williams argues that we tend to notice changes in structures of feeling by the contrasts between generations:

> One generation may train its successor, with reasonable success, in the social character or the general cultural pattern, but the new generation will have its own structure of feeling, which will not appear to have come "from" anywhere. For here, most distinctly, the changing organization is enacted in the organism: the new generation responds in its own ways to the unique world it is inheriting, taking up many continuities, that can be traced, and reproducing many aspects of the organization, which can be separately described, yet feeling its whole life in certain ways differently, and shaping its creative response into a new structure of feeling.[22]

Although the elder generation did not smoothly train sixties youth "with reasonable success" to assume a pattern of social life already established, Williams's model can help describe a subtle process of social and cultural change. He argues that it is in "documentary culture" that we can most clearly get a sense of a previous culture's structure of feeling. Television, which is embedded in the everyday experiences of people within modern technological societies, is therefore a particularly useful place to trace this kind of change. These texts form a site for showcasing transformations as the structures of feeling associated with a new generation begin to be felt within the popular culture.

This study also benefits from Antonio Gramsci's theories about hegemony, particularly his argument that in order to maintain consent, hegemonic forces must, to some extent, accommodate and accede to positions associated with various subordinated formations whose consent is desired. Thus part of the hegemonic impulse is the perpetual attempt to incorporate positions, discourses, and practices that, although not necessarily in the interests of the socially and politically dominant, do not threaten their leadership positions.[23]

Particularly useful to me is Gramsci's idea of a "crisis of authority." During such a crisis the ruling elites are no longer able to naturalize their power, no longer able to lead. In effect they can only dominate, using coercive means rather than consensual methods attributable to a smoothly functioning hegemonic order. Subordinated groups no longer participate in validating the ruling classes in their positions as rulers. Dominant ideology is no longer accepted common sense. According to Gramsci, "the crisis consists precisely in the fact that the old is dying and the new cannot be born."[24] Nothing could describe what happened in the United States in the 1960s better than this. With increasing militancy as the decade progressed, young whites (both on campuses and in countercultural communities), young African Americans (both in ghettos and on campuses), women, Latinos, gays and lesbians formed insurgency movements that struck at the heart of the dominant social and political order—"the establishment"—questioning its legitimacy and revealing as myth many previously held tenets of what "America" was all about. The social order in the United States appeared to be unraveling, coming apart at the ideological seams. We can see examples of this in the steady dismantlement of prowar sentiment in the Lyndon Johnson White House or later in the increasingly antagonistic relationship between the Nixon White House and the mass media. Hegemonic forces in the political sphere no longer successfully asserted common cause with the cultural sphere. Universities as the intellectual sphere were in such disarray that they found themselves incapable of performing their ideological chores. Increasingly—as we will see especially in chapters 3 and 4—consensual strategies gave way to coercive tactics of a hegemonic system in peril. Television was intricately bound up in all this chaos. The crisis of hegemonic authority and legitimacy that wreaked havoc through the universities, the ghettos, the military complex, and the political process also manifested itself within the popular-culture industry. If, as cultural studies scholars argue, popular culture is one of the key ideological sites where hegemony is negotiated, then during a crisis of authority television can provide a showcase of ideological breakdown and reconfiguration. By examining television during this period—as an institution, a body of texts, and a group of audiences— we can also explore the extent to which the hegemonic process, in attempting to reassert a new form of cultural leadership, needed to acquiesce to the discourses of the dissenting subordinate. How did popular television figure into the overall turmoil of the period? What was its role in hegemonic breakdown and in hegemonic reframing? [25]

Chapter 1 looks at the introduction of television into suburban homes at the very moment that the baby boom was demographically exploding. How did this relationship influence the ways sixties young people made sense of themselves as "the television generation"? The chapter considers the various ways these young people made sense of their alienation and rebellion by their suggestion that television had turned them into freaks. We look at how the theories of Marshall McLuhan were mobilized by young people in empowering ways to make sense of the generation gap. The chapter also discusses the various dissident uses of televisual technology—from trip toys to guerrilla television.

Chapter 2 examines the representation of hippies on prime-time television, charting the strategies used by the medium to "domesticate" the phenomenon after an initial period of television hippie hysteria. One particular strategy we will explore involves "feminizing" the counterculture in the figure of the "hippie chick." We will also look at how writers for the underground press reacted to these portrayals and how countercultural communities responded to the media spotlight that so intensely shone on them.

Chapter 3 looks at the most media-obsessed and teleliterate group within the burgeoning movement: the Yippies. The chapter analyzes how the Yippies believed they could actually organize disaffected youth through manipulating the media. We will also look at how contentious the Yippies' media tactics were within the movement. The chapter focuses particular attention on the televising of the Chicago Democratic Convention riots and how Yippies, network newscasters, Chicago's mayor, and movement youth struggled over the meanings of that all-too-public moment of crisis and disarray. We will then look at how some activists saw television talk shows as a potential site to further manipulate the media and televise the struggle.

Chapter 4 documents the rise and fall of the only prime-time series to garner demonstrable youth movement support, *The Smothers Brothers Comedy Hour.* We will look at how the folksinger-comedian brothers began aligning themselves and their show more and more with antiwar and counterculture politics and how the threat this posed to network television led CBS to censor and then finally pull the show off the air. Like the televising of the Chicago Democratic Convention mêlée, we will examine how the confrontations around the Smothers Brothers show served as another venue for the playing out of an accelerating crisis of authority. The chapter examines the significant amount of attention the Smothers Brothers received in youth movement circles, the support, as well as suspicions, their case engendered.

Chapter 5 looks at another significant prime-time attempt to garner a countercultural youth audience and to appeal to youth politics—*The Mod Squad.* We look at the contentious development and production of the series and the suspicion, outrage, and, at times, grudging support the show generated in movement circles. As network television's initial attempt to do "socially relevant" dramatic programming by incorporating aspects of rebellious youth discourse, the series was part of an ideological process of negotiation. We will also look at the ways in which highly contentious and explosive issues like draft resistance and the My Lai massacre got massaged and mediated in fictionalized form in particular episodes of *The Mod Squad.* What can we say about the cultural politics of such mediations? Are they "victories" of a sort for the movement?

Chapter 6 examines the so-called Season of Social Relevance, the 1970/71 broadcast year, when all three broadcast networks tried to lure young, politicized viewers in an attempt to reconfigure the demographics of the viewing audience. We look at how the networks, working with *The Mod Squad* formula, performed acts of ideological negotiation by incorporating even more dissident youth discourse into entertainment programming. The chapter examines how and why "social relevance" appeared to fail and how it ultimately succeeded wildly when applied to the sitcom genre.

Chapter 7 considers the legacy of "social relevance" and the lasting impact that the sixties youth movement has had on American prime-time television. Has entertainment television lurched to the left? Have the social-change values of the 1960s become entrenched in popular entertainment, as many conservative critics have charged? In the 1980s and 1990s, how did prime time negotiate with the specter of the 1960s?

Because the chapters are not rigorously chronological and because not all readers will be equally familiar with the trajectory of events of the sixties, I have put together a narrative chronology of the years 1966 to 1971, the period under consideration in this book. I have also included in the chronology the airdates for most of the television shows discussed in these pages so that the reader can contextualize these examples of televisual culture with the social and political phenomena they were mediating.

So, without further ado, let us now turn on and tune in to the "Groove Tube."

"Clarabell Was the First Yippie"

1 The Television Generation from *Howdy Doody* to McLuhan

In 1949 an enormous RCA Starrett television set arrived in the home of writer Donald Bowie. In his "confessions of a video kid" Bowie, who was four years old at the time, describes the momentous occasion and how the installation of the set drew children from around the neighborhood to his house. As the delivery men fiddled with the knobs, a picture came on. There was Buffalo Bob, a grown man in cowboy raiment talking to a boy puppet in similar garb. And there was the clown Clarabell squirting liquid from a seltzer bottle right into the face of "father figure" Buffalo Bob.[1] Remembers Bowie: "My friends and I were hypnotized on the spot." From the vantage point of adulthood Bowie hypothesizes that this children's series, *Howdy Doody,* "was leading us, while we were still in our single-digit years, toward adolescent rebellion."[2] Surely the lessons for the juvenile audience could only be a celebration of antisocial behavior and disrespect for adults.

Another baby boomer writer, Annie Gottlieb, also remembered bonding with television. Like Bowie, she, the members of her generation, and the new medium of television moved from "childhood" to "adolescence" together. She observed, "Television was growing up with us, slowly gaining skill at delivering the images that would make us one organism with a mass memory and mythology. When Ed hosted Elvis in 1956, TV entered its inhibited, yearning puberty along with us. I was ten, and, watching the famed manoeuvres of the

Howdy, Buffalo Bob, the Princess, and Clarabell
with his subversive seltzer bottle.

Pelvis — primly censored just below the waist — I felt the first stirrings
in my own."[3]

These baby boomer memories suggest a potentially subversive relationship between the medium and the first generation to come
of age watching it. Bowie and Gottlieb described a symbiotic association: a television childhood learning antiestablishment values, a
puberty sharing an interest in verboten sexuality. Television, as Gottlieb implied, forged baby boomers into a special community — one
that recognized itself as such by the way its members all shared a
common television culture.

Aging boomers reminiscing about their childhood from the vantage point of the 1980s were not, however, the only commentators
who reflected on the special relationship between television and its
first young viewers. A number of popular-press writers in the late
1940s and early 1950s pointed out the connection between TV and the
tots. *The Nation* in a 1950 piece observed, "No Pied Piper ever proved
so irresistible. If a television set is on at night and there is a child
at large in the house, the two will eventually come together."[4] Television critic Robert Lewis Shayan also used the Pied Piper analogy in
his *Saturday Review* piece about children and the new medium published that same year. He went on to characterize television as a genie,
with its young viewers as Aladdins. Television would grant any wish,
fulfill any dream — all at the touch of a dial. According to Shayan, one

of those wishes was access to the adult world. "The child wants to be 'in' on the exciting world of adult life," he argued. Television provided "the most accessible back door" to that world.[5] For these adult critics, then, the connection between fifties children and television was a cause for anxiety. There *was* something unprecedented in the relationship. But what did it mean, and where would it lead?

From the moment of television's introduction into the American home, it was discursively linked to the children. Television, a postwar technological phenomenon, and the baby boom, a postwar demographic phenomenon, both led to profound political, social, and cultural changes in the landscape of American life. Arriving in U.S. homes at about the same time in the late 1940s and 1950s, these electronic and anthropoid new members of the family circle seemed allied in fomenting social revolution.

In the 1960s the phrase "television generation," which had first been coined in the mid-1950s, would function as a site of semiotic struggle over the meanings of youth in revolt. Diverse voices — from within the rebellious youth movement itself; from academic ranks, both administrators and professorial theorists; from the television industry; and even from the nation's vice president — all attempted to make sense of young people's rejection of dominant institutions and values by examining the generation's link to television. All agreed that television was important, but few agreed on how or why. Reflecting the deep generational divide and the seemingly unbridgeable gap between the ways the disaffected young constructed the world and the ways their elders did, the discourses about the meaning of the "television generation" were equally irreconcilable. "Television" became a sign, another marker of a generational battle that ripped apart the smooth functioning of adult and establishment power in the postwar social order of the United States.

Coming of Age with Television

With the end of the Second World War and with the promise of prosperity not seen since before the stock market crash of 1929, Americans embarked on a procreation blitz that confounded demographers and social planners. The birth rate, which in the United States had been going down steadily since the 1800s, suddenly began to rival

birth rates in some Third World countries. The Great Depression had
seen birth rates plunge because of the era's profound economic uncer-
tainty. By the Second World War most able-bodied American men
were in uniform, and many women were taking over the jobs those
men had left. When war rationing was added to the picture, the situation did not prove conducive to the formation of families.

When the war ended, everything changed. Government propaganda and the advertising industry promised a return to normalcy,
to stability. Women were encouraged to leave—or were forcibly removed from—the well-paying, often industrial, jobs they had held
during the war effort. Government-sponsored advertising campaigns
encouraged them to embrace domesticity and traditional modes of
femininity along with maternity.[6] Yet couples in the postwar period
largely embraced a domestic ideal of rigid gender roles and focus
on family building as a response to the severe dislocations associated
with the Depression, world war, and the new terrors of nuclear an-
nihilation. Paired with a cold war policy preoccupied with the containment of a (communist) threat was a domestic preoccupation with
containing myriad other threats to stability. "In the domestic version of containment," writes historian Elaine Tyler May, "the 'sphere
of influence' was the home. Within its walls, potentially dangerous
social forces of the new age might be tamed, where they could con-
tribute to the secure and fulfilling life to which postwar women and
men aspired."[7] In facilitating the creation of such homes, the federal
government offered low interest loans for returning vets to pay for
inexpensive, no-money-down bungalows in expanding suburbs. To
the largely white and middle-class beneficiaries of this largesse, the
brand-new subdivisions they moved into with their homogenous and
uniform character seemed tailor-made shelters from upheaval, social
struggle, and change. They also were tailor-made for the creation of
nuclear families. The white, affluent baby boom generation, which
precipitated so much upheaval, struggle, and demand for change in
the 1960s, ironically was nurtured in an environment that found such
turmoil anathema.

In the postwar period Americans linked the promotion of stability with the promotion of consumerism. If General Motors was
doing well, then (at least according to the head of GM), America was
doing well. American industry's return from a war-based to a consumer product–based market necessitated an expanding population

of buyers. As Vice president Richard Nixon's 1959 "kitchen debate" with Soviet Premier Nikita Khrushchev implied, American superiority over the Soviet Union lay in the U.S. population's ability and eagerness to purchase household appliances. So as "homeward bound" Americans moved into their ranch-style, prefab houses, their generation went on both a baby-making and a product-buying binge.

One of the products they bought was television. Ironically, however, this new purchase would not serve as a tool for stability. Television would prove to be a force for change and upheaval just as would the suburban boomer children who so thoroughly embraced and found themselves linked to the new medium. As birth rates skyrocketed, so did rates of first-time television purchases. In 1951 almost one quarter of American homes had televisions; by 1957 that figure had jumped to 78.6 percent. By the early 1960s the medium had achieved a near saturation rate of 92 percent.[8] The single greatest factor in determining television purchase was the presence of young children in the household. According to statistics, between the years 1952 and 1954 childless families made up 19 percent of new television households; families with teenagers accounted for 23 percent; and families with young children made up the largest percentage. Parents with children under two made up 32 percent of television purchasers.[9] This latter group comprised the parents of baby boomers. Another study showed that although entertainment was given as the primary reason for the purchase of a set, pressure from young children was also a key factor.[10]

The introduction of television into postwar homes created cultural anxieties marked by both utopian hopes and dystopian fears.[11] Many of those hopes and fears revolved around the perceived effects of the new medium on children. Cultural historian James Gilbert has argued that in the 1950s mass media such as television became linked with anxieties about social and generational change. New forms of commercialized youth-oriented popular culture seemed to be erecting barriers to mark off a new youth culture incomprehensible and potentially hostile to adult society.[12] In both the pessimistic and the optimistic arguments about television and its effects, commentators and critics couldn't help but assume that some fundamental change to the nation's young would inevitably result.

In the utopian vision of the new medium, television would bring the outside world into the home. Television sets were promoted for their ability to be "your new window on the world" and to bring faraway places into the home theater.[13] Those touting the benefits of television for children echoed this theme. Douglas Edwards, a CBS news analyst writing in *Parents* magazine in 1951, proclaimed: "With television today, the children get a sense of participation, of belonging. Contemporary events are brought to them in their homes. Korea is more than a tiny colored nose jutting out of the broad Asiatic face into the blue sea shown on a map in a geography book. . . . The chances are thousands to one that when you were a kid you never saw a President of the United States being inaugurated, [or] the great political parties holding their national nominating conventions."[14] It is unlikely that Edwards, with his purple prose, could have imagined the impact on those same children two decades later, when television broadcast images of another war in a southeast Asian country and when the medium televised another national political convention— that of the Democrats in Chicago in 1968.

The theme of television providing children with "a sense of participation, of belonging" was particularly important. In the conformist 1950s, when fitting in and being part of the group were not only signs of proper personal adjustment but were also signs of good citizenship, having television meant fitting in. Edwards undoubtedly thought television allowed children to participate in the larger world of social and political events and that they would feel a sense of belonging to a world made smaller and more comprehensible through the new medium.

However, in the 1950s this notion of "belonging" through the purchase of a television set implied necessary and successful conformity. Baby boom children conformed by becoming television children. The advertising industry helped to construct the concept of a television generation by manufacturing parental fears that children without television would carry a "bruise deep inside."[15] One notorious ad campaign pictured woebegone children who didn't have their own TV sets. The bruise that such children bore meant being "set apart from their contemporaries."[16] In the social climate of the 1950s nothing could be worse. Thus television became one means by which to link this segment of the population together. Baby boomers would not only have their huge numbers in common; they would also have their shared rearing with the television set to knit them together. Television, according to social scientific research of the period and according to the discourses of the advertising industry, was primarily something for the children. Children without television were pitiful outcasts among their peer group. Therefore, being a well-adjusted, "normal" child in the 1950s meant possessing and watching one's own television set. And so the television generation was born.

Even as television was touted for its ability to set off a new generation of youngsters as more worldly and sophisticated than their parents' generation, the medium was also promoted as facilitating family togetherness. Rather than setting children off as different and incomprehensible to the older generation, television would unite all its members into a unified nuclear unit characterized by harmony and shared activities. Lynn Spigel, in her examination of advertisements for early televisions in women's magazines, shows how the industry attempted to speak to postwar Americans' desires for a return to "family values." "The advertisements suggested that television would serve as a catalyst for the return to a world of domestic love and affection." [17] This promise may have been all the more seductive considering the dislocations and tensions of the war years and the immediate postwar period. Television-inspired family togetherness could be particularly useful in knitting children and adolescents firmly into the family circle. Parents and children would bond over their shared enjoyment of programming, thus eradicating any generation gaps. Television would also prevent potential juvenile delinquency by keeping "problem children" off the streets. Audience research suggested that parents believed having a television in the home kept the young ones from trouble outside. Proclaimed a mother from Atlanta: "We are closer together. We find our entertainment at home. Donna and her boyfriend sit here instead of going out now." [18] Presumably without the television Donna and her beau would be prowling dark alleys, fornicating in the backseat of a Chevy, or mugging old ladies.

Despite these utopian visions of children's protoglobal villages and family TV circles, pessimistic fears abounded. Rather than bringing the young and their parental generation together, television, a frequently circulated anxiety asserted, created an unbridgeable cultural chasm between the two. Well-known social critic David Reisman acknowledged the gap in a *New York Times* article in 1952 but sided with the TV-molded young. He was quoted arguing that "refusing to consider the possibility that there can be anything of value in the average television program amounts to an announcement on parents'

parts that they live in a different psychological and cultural generation from their children. If they cannot in good conscience share television and discuss the programs with their children . . . they should
at least allow their youngsters the right to live within reason in their
own cultural generation, not their parents'."[19]

This notion of a cultural divide marking off the television
generation from its forebears is central to James Gilbert's book on
mass media and the juvenile delinquency panic of the 1950s. The
trend toward a separate, peer group–oriented, culturally autonomous
"youth culture," already developing at least since the 1920s, had by
the 1950s achieved an unprecedented degree of social coherence and
economic power.[20] The consumer product industry had discovered
youth as an identifiable market group, and, as baby boom historian
Landon Jones points out, these youngsters were the first generation
to be so targeted and courted by advertisers: "Marketing, and especially television, *isolated* their needs and wants from those of their
parents. From the cradle, the baby boomers had been surrounded by
products created especially for them, from Silly Putty to Slinkys to
skateboards."[21] This isolation could appear menacing to adults. Consumer culture and mass media encouraged and even fostered styles,
fads, language, and—by implication—values and attitudes that appeared to place young people outside the dominant social and moral
order. Gilbert notes a study on delinquency published in 1960 suggesting that this more middle-class form of delinquency "derived in
part from an emerging youth culture fostered by a communications
revolution and a burgeoning youth market following World War II.
Its characteristics were pleasure and hedonism, values that sharply
undercut the beliefs of parents. In other words, delinquency was an
issue of generational struggle."[22] Rather than bringing the postwar
family together into a harmonious circle in which adult norms and
values would be unquestionably accepted, commercial culture—and
television in particular—drove a wedge into that circle.

Television seemed to destabilize the family circle by threatening
parental authority and traditional parent-child roles. A frequently repeated worry during the 1950s was that television exposed impres-
sionable, innocent youngsters too soon to a world of adult concerns.
One study of children's viewing preferences found that by age seven
children were watching a large amount of programming aimed primarily at adults. Variety shows such as Milton Berle's *Texaco Star The-*

ater and situation comedies such as *I Love Lucy* were particular favorites.[23] Berle even began to sign off his show with exhortations to the young ones to go promptly to bed after the show.[24]

According to media accounts, many parents expressed concern about how children were interacting with this new "guest" in the living room. Dorothy Barclay, writing in the *New York Times Magazine,* discussed the fear that television would supplant parents as the ultimate source of knowledge for youngsters: "Children get a great deal of important and accurate information from television . . . but is it too easy? Is this kind of learning more or less apt to stick? Is it too easily accepted? 'I saw it on TV' is now a statement of authority competing strongly with 'My mother told me.' "[25]

Parental authority, therefore, would be usurped by a fun, new gadget that required of children no discipline, no work, no discrimination. Television revealed a world of adult concerns and adult entertainment previously hidden from innocent eyes, but it also, potentially, threatened the whole structure of adult knowledge and wisdom as the final legitimizer of parental authority.[26]

Pessimistic commentators also viewed television as a "loud-mouthed guest [who] had settled himself in a corner and [had] begun to tell raucous and unsuitable stories to the children."[27] Parental authority was threatened again because, as Barclay noted in another article in the *New York Times Magazine,* parents in the new permissive climate of child rearing were unsure how to intercede between their children and the raucous guest. Controlling a child's television choices seemed censorious, even undemocratic.[28]

These views suggest an alliance between young children and the new medium that excluded parental authority—and also that of the school system. One of the most pervasive fears (one that continues to this day) was that television took children away from their schoolwork. Time spent watching the box meant time spent not doing homework. Late evenings spent watching Uncle Miltie meant fatigued and inattentive days in the classroom.

Fears that television was exposing youngsters to an uncensored adult world and that traditional authority was being subverted by the children's relationship to the new medium led Joseph Klapper to suggest an added danger perpetuated by television. Television would result in "premature maturity."[29] Klapper, a media effects researcher from the Lazarsfeld school of communications study, worried that not enough popular attention was being given to this danger, which had child psychiatrists deeply concerned. He and other analysts worried that television gave youngsters a distorted view of adulthood or that it helped in "creating and building in the child the concept that adults in general are frequently in trouble, frequently deceitful, mean, and, perhaps most important, very unsure of themselves and in fact incompetent to handle many of the situations which descend upon them."[30] Such portrayals may have reduced the amount of time children viewed adults as omniscient and caused them to find the real world of their elders wanting and full of shortcomings.[31]

The idea of premature maturity held within it an essentialized notion of childhood innocence that television threatened. Children would no longer be real children. In this vision "real" children were submissive to adult authority, and the boundaries between the realm of childhood and that of adulthood were clearly marked and rigidly maintained. Television's intrusion blurred those boundaries. The other side to this argument was the fear that parents would no longer be true parents because traditional notions of adult authority were supposedly being undermined along with the very right of adults to be authoritarian. If the new medium threatened to rob baby boomers of their traditional childhood, what on earth would this do to them? Leo Bogart meditated on the danger of premature maturity: "One wonders: Will reality match up to the television fantasies this generation has been nursed on? These children are in a peculiar position; experience is exhausted in advance. There is little they have not seen or done or lived through, and yet this is second-hand experience. When the experience itself comes, it is watered down, for it has already been half-lived, but never truly felt."[32]

By the mid-to-late 1960s, when the first wave of baby boomers hit college campuses, numerous answers were offered up to explain how this generation was or was not dealing with a reality that proved so different from its television fantasies. For this generation had not turned out as expected. In 1959 University of California president Clark Kerr had asserted: "The employers will love this generation. They aren't going to press any grievances. . . . There aren't going to be any riots."[33] He was mistaken. Large numbers of middle-class, white baby boomers who came to adolescence and young adulthood in this period helped cause a social, cultural, and political crisis unlike anything seen in American history since the Civil War. Indeed, the

United States from around 1966 to 1971 convulsed through a generational civil war.[34] Over and over again the question arose: how had this happened? How had this generation—the most wanted, the best housed and fed, the best educated, the most economically privileged group of young white people ever raised in this most prosperous of nations—turned into such a raucous, riotous, disrespectful, distrustful, disaffected bunch of potential revolutionaries?[35]

One answer was television. Depending on one's point of view, television was to be either praised or blamed for causing or assisting in the disaffected nature of many sixties youth. Understandably, adult commentators despaired and raged at television's effects on youth— that concern went back to the 1950s. More interesting was the fact that a significant number of disaffected young people—activists at antiwar rallies, writers for the underground press, video "guerrillas" —were also making sense of their generation's rebelliousness through its relationship to television. As the next section illustrates, activist youth, seeing their generation in revolt, looked back to their fifties childhoods spent watching *Howdy Doody,* sitcoms, game shows, and other programming. That experience served as a powerful explanatory mechanism to account for their profound alienation from and revolt against the dominant social order.

Television: Revolutionary Instigator?

This sense of shared consciousness via television was poignantly demonstrated in a speech delivered at the 1967 March on the Pentagon. Thousands of mostly young antiwar protesters had managed to swarm onto the grounds of the Pentagon and found themselves face-to-face with bayonet-wielding federal troops of their own age group. Yippie activist Stew Albert tried to appeal to the soldiers. He suggested a link between the troops and the protesters by appealing to their presumably common (masculine) history:

> We grew up in the same country, and we're about the same age. We're really brothers because we grew up listening to the same radio programs and TV programs, and we have the same ideals. It's just this fucked-up system that keeps us apart.
>
> I didn't get my ideas from Mao, Lenin or Ho Chi Minh. I got

my ideals from the Lone Ranger. You know the Lone Ranger always
fought on the side of good and against the forces of evil and injustice.
He never shot to kill![36]

Albert presumed that, as the television generation, those on either
side of the bayonets shared a cultural link. Their childhoods spent
with broadcast media should have instilled in them similar values and
ideals, including a Lone Ranger who was essentially a nonviolent cru-
sader for social justice. Albert's vision of a generation united through
radio and television ignored, of course, divisions of class and race
and evacuated women from the process entirely. Television was the
great unifier, used by Albert as a rhetorical trope to reach across an
adult-created, artificial "system" that inappropriately divided media
brothers.[37] Albert and many other New Left activists refused to see
that the federal troops guarding the Pentagon, like the young men
most likely to find themselves in Vietnam, came from a very different
class position. They may have watched much of the same television
programming; however, they most likely formed very different interpretations of what they saw.

    Although it may seem odd that an antiwar activist would attempt
to persuade armed soldiers that they and their antiwar cogenerationists were on the same side because of television, the rhetoric wasn't
entirely absurd. We need to take into account one of the dominant
ways people in this period made sense of television as a medium.
Four years earlier television had provided four days of continuous,
uninterrupted coverage of the assassination and funeral of President
John F. Kennedy. The networks made much of their medium's ability
to keep the nation together in a collective, shared experience of grief
and loss.[38] One of the dominant circulated meanings of the coverage
emphasized the power of the medium to forge viewers together into
a unit. Nine out of ten members of the baby boom watched the coverage. As the first television generation, they were far more affected
by the death of a vigorous, youthful president and its presentation
on the medium with which they had grown up. The assassination
served as an experience that united the generation—and the uniting
process happened through the experience of watching television.[39]
Thus when Stew Albert appealed to his "brothers" on the other side
of the bayonets, his rhetoric took for granted the unifying powers of

broadcast communication to instill similar experiences and values in members of the TV generation, no matter what social roles its various members occupied.

Whereas Albert invoked the television program *The Lone Ranger* to explain the values all members of his generation shared, other youthful commentators used their exposure to fifties programming to slightly different ends. Some used television to explain how many in their age group had rejected the values and lifestyles of their parents and how seemingly innocuous shows had, in fact, served subversive ends in fomenting the later full-scale rebellion.

Jeff Greenfield, graduate of the University of Wisconsin, wrote an article for the *New York Times Magazine* in 1971 as a member of the "first television generation" looking back to the programming of the 1950s.[40] Confirming Klapper's fears about premature maturity, Greenfield claimed that television had a particularly subversive influence on the young "because of what it showed us of the way our Elders really thought and spoke and acted when not conscious of the pieties with which children are to be soothed and comforted." He argued that from *I Love Lucy* and *My Little Margie* his generation learned that domestic life was dominated by dishonesty, fear, and pretence; from shows like *The Price Is Right,* baby boomers learned about greed; from the quiz show scandals they learned about the commodity exchange of wisdom and the fraudulence of that wisdom.[41]

Greenfield's article appeared to confirm what Klapper and his fellow analysts had warned: television had helped to solidify for the youth of America a disdain of the adult world. From Greenfield's perspective entertainment television of the 1950s provided an accurate representation of the hypocritical values of the older generation. Fifties sitcoms and game shows were anything but innocuous, escapist entertainment. They were instructive pieces of information that young people could use to make sense of their world—a world they did not want to perpetuate.

Eric Bonner, writing in Atlanta's underground paper the *Great Speckled Bird,* also meditated on the impact of watching fifties television. Like Greenfield, he also stated that the subjection of American youth to mass media resulted in their premature development. But whereas fifties analysts like Klapper and Bogart feared the potential effects of this process, Bonner celebrated it. He hypothesized that

"Good boy" Howdy and "father figure" Buffalo Bob;
Howdy Doody, a terrain of contested baby boomer
meanings.

whereas the maturation process had taken a good twenty years for
previous generations, the youth of the sixties, through their exposure
to television, had completed the process by age ten:

> Television, a system so efficient that by age ten we had gathered "it" all
> (IT being everything necessary to function as Americans.) But Mum
> and Dud [*sic*] could not see that we had a better grasp of reality than
> they. "*Captain Video*"? Don't be ridiculous, go watch Tee Vee, kid. . . .
> So we did and the TV sucked up new information from the environ-
> ment and fed it to us, and we ate and ate until we burst. . . . WE WERE

FORCED INTO MATURITY YEARS BEFORE OUR CULTURE REQUIRED IT,
BY OUR ELECTRIC ENVIRONMENT. . . . [ellipses in original][42]

Whereas Greenfield believed that television destroyed the traditional
maturation process by providing subversive representations of the
world the young were to inherit, Bonner believed that television had
done too good a job: ". . . we had swallowed all the red, white and
blue myths that Miss Jane and Buffalo Bob could invent and we were
ready to spit them back out on the world. Little Marines all!!" Unfortunately there was no place yet for these prematurely grown-up
youngsters within the mature community. All they could do was to
continue watching television and continue being fed the same myths.
Eventually, according to Bonner's eccentric theory, having been sur-
feited, they burst forth in "Holy Revolt," presumably having discovered, unlike the older generation, that the myths were lies. Bonner
made sense of the youth counterculture as the result of those who,
through years of television viewing, had been made just "too hip, too
aware to 'take over' the old insane mess."[43]

Greenfield performed a markedly different reading, specifically of
the generational meaning of *Howdy Doody,* than Bonner—although
they shared a desire to appropriate the popular baby boomer children's show as a vehicle to explain why the members of the Peanut
Gallery were dropping acid, disrespecting police officers and other
authority figures, growing their hair long, and raucously protesting
their nation's war policy. For Greenfield *Howdy Doody* did not attempt to instill patriotism in its childish audience. On the contrary,
the primary theme of *Howdy Doody* was that "*the villain was always
a Grown-Up in Authority.*" Phineas T. Bluster and the Inspector were
law-enforcement villains and figures of baleful Authority. Howdy
Doody himself was a fink—telling children to wash and to listen to
their parents. The clown, Clarabell, on the other hand, was a figure
of liberation, embodying the spirit of freedom: "Clarabell, the first
Yippie, was the true hero of the show. Where did the War Baby generation get the inspiration to hurl marshmallows at Strom Thurmond
and a pie at Clark Kerr. From the works of Lenin? From a footnote in
Marcuse? Nonsense. From the inspiration of that genuine free spirit,
that revolutionary foe of authority and good conduct, from Clarabell."[44] Greenfield's interpretation echoes Donald Bowie's suggestion

that *Howdy Doody* was leading the young into eventual rebellion. From a different perspective Greenfield's rhetorical ploy echoed Stew Albert's argument about the significance of *The Lone Ranger*. Both were at pains to disavow their rebellion from connection with the hoary old leftist European tradition of Marxism, the Russian Revolution, or the thoughts of Chairman Mao. Their revolution did not come out of the books of leftist theorists. Their revolution sprang from good old American popular culture.

The meanings that some sixties youths made of their relationship to television directly challenged preferred views. The writers quoted above took many of the fears first expressed by child psychologists and popular-press writers in the 1950s and turned them on their heads. Would television affect children's deference to the authority of their elders? Yes, these baby boomers asserted. And how liberating that was. These young people took useful and empowering meanings from television as the medium, the institution, and the programming with which they had grown up. Television validated their right (even their need) to rebel. Television, from this viewpoint, had helped bring it all about.

Michael Shamberg provided another voice explaining how television delegitimized the adult generation. Shamberg, a "media guerrilla," was part of a movement of young activists who wanted to use video as a tool of the movement.[45] Discussing the gulf between the "media-children" and "pre-Media Americans" in his book *Guerrilla Television,* he explained how television as a medium subverted the whole notion of deference to authority for young people:

> We get too much news to accept authority based on restriction of information flow. Yet pre-Media-Americans are conditioned to trust authority because "the President knows more than we do." Nonetheless our video sense of death in Vietnam is no less vivid than the President's.
>
> Agnew's attacks on television are successful with pre-Media-Americans who are anxious because they know too much and yet believe that authority is based on someone knowing more than they do.[46]

According to Shamberg, television (specifically its corporate/capitalist structure) had succeeded in teaching the television generation to question all authority. Media-children's sophistication in "reading" television and seeing the gaps in the flow of information separated them from their elders, who believed what they were told.

Miller Francis Jr., in the *Great Speckled Bird,* also explored the subversiveness of television in relation to Vice President Agnew's diatribe against the medium. (Agnew delivered a widely reported speech in Des Moines, Iowa, castigating the network news media for their perceived bias against the White House.) [47] Francis explained the nature of the medium in a particularly provocative way:

> After a couple of decades of exposure to the medium of television, the Amerikan [sic] system of corporate capitalism finally sits up and takes notice of a subversive in its midst—a child it has taken for granted as its own. . . .
>
> TV is a problem child in this context [of Agnew's attack]; indeed, television and Law & Order make strange, if not impossible bedfellows. . . .
>
> Television is probably the single most crucial unruly thread that is unravelling the whole fabric of American power both at home and abroad. . . . Enter a freak, an electronic monster that grooves not on "reason," "unity," "objectivity," "responsibility," "the negotiating table," "normality," and least of all on "the politics of progress through local compromise" but instead perversely revels in "instant gratification," "querulous criticism," "challenging and contradicting," "controversy," "the irrational," "action," "excitement," "drama," and "brutality and violence." . . . [Francis's quotes were all taken from Agnew's speech.] [48]

Apparently following a strategy of "the enemy of my enemy is my friend," Francis embraced television because the Nixon administration despised it. Television, from this perspective, exhibited the same antiestablishment characteristics possessed by protesting youth —whom Nixon and Agnew also despised. Presumably the political power structure of adult America could make no sense of the two "freaks" in its midst. Born and raised together as "problem children," sixties youth and television appeared to embody the same basic values. Francis's use of television to think through the yawning ideological gap between antiauthoritarian youth and the adult power bloc was similar to Shamberg's. Both saw television as an active agent in creating the division between the generations. On one side of the TV line were those pretelevision lovers of law and order. On the other side were those reared on two decades of TV-disseminated mayhem, shoot-'em-ups, and instantly gratified pleasure. Francis seemed less concerned than Shamberg that television as a medium and an industry was controlled by the very same corporate/capitalist system that the Nixon-Agnew administration defended and represented.

For commentators like Francis—as well as Greenfield, Bonner, Yippies such as Albert, and others—television escaped the ability of those in power to control it, just like the nation's rebellious young were incapable of being controlled. They had been raised in their suburban neighborhoods to respect those in authority, to be obedient workers who wouldn't question hierarchy, and to reproduce the conformist, sterile world created by their parents' generation. Similarly television was supposed to be the great force for cultural indoctrination. An ideological hypodermic needle, it was supposed to inject its viewers with dominant views sanctioned by the social and political order. As Greenfield observed: "Television should have been a part of the pattern of increasing control of tastes and opinion; a source not of the greatest freedom of which rulers speak when a new tool for the amplification of their voice is discovered, but a new source of blandness, and imposed acquiescence to the will of the Elders."[49] But as Greenfield further noted, the first generation weaned on television didn't turn into a bland, acquiescent lot. This development could only mean that television wasn't doing what it was supposed to be doing—any more than many children of the baby boom were doing what they were supposed to be doing. Television and the children of the tube were both subverting the social order they were supposed to uphold.

Marshall McLuhan: Guru to the Television Generation

Members of the disaffected youth generation of the 1960s, such as those quoted above, were not without assistance in their attempts to make sense of their relationship to television. Marshall McLuhan, professor and director of the Center for Culture and Technology at the University of Toronto, found himself one of the most quoted and analyzed social theorists of the 1960s. His books, especially *Understanding Media: The Extensions of Man,* became best-sellers despite their often dense prose; NBC attempted an hour-long documentary to explain his theories; *Newsweek* put him on the cover of the magazine;

and the youth movement, especially those who aligned themselves more with the hippie counterculture than with the New Left, appropriated portions of his theories to validate themselves. Of all the social thinkers and theories influencing the youth movements of the 1960s, none was as pervasive as McLuhan. His name and his aphorisms, along with attempts to explain his theories, can be found generously sprinkled throughout the underground press. No other figure who was not of the movement itself received so much positive notice in the alternative newspapers that served dissident youth communities.[50]

Why McLuhan? A writer in New York's hippie-oriented *East Village Other* supplied one answer: "We, the underground, have found another wizard to enlighten our movement. Not that we give a fuck about more self-justification (our existence is justification enough) but just so we can give the establishment some food for thought, we can cram Marshall McLuhan down their throat and watch them vomit."[51] McLuhan was a weapon. An establishment-sanctioned and respected professor, McLuhan's theories — as mobilized by the youth movement — damned their elders and the entire established social system while praising insurgent youth culture and youth values as the inevitable wave of the future. Whether the movement wanted or needed self-justification is debatable. Its writers used McLuhan as though it did. To understand why McLuhan and his media theories were so attractive, we need to examine some of McLuhan's theories and how they were appropriated by sectors of the youth movement for their own ends.

McLuhan believed that the introduction of electronic media, television in particular, had radically altered all aspects of social life. Print-based Western culture, which had been dominant since the invention of movable type, had finally been replaced. The new electronic culture had more in common with oral-based, tribal cultures of the pre-Renaissance period. McLuhan's vision of electronic tribalism involved television and other media's shrinking of space and their helping to foster interdependence to such an extent that the earth would now function as a global village.

This idea of a new tribalism resonated strongly with many who identified themselves with the hippie counterculture. Hippies aligned themselves (often simplistically) with Native Americans and saw themselves as a tribe. When the hip community of the Haight-

Ashbury staged the first "Be-In" to bring together both hippies and Berkeley politicos, the organizers billed it as "a gathering of the tribes."[52] The event's famous poster featured a lone Indian astride a horse and carrying an electric guitar.

Robert Roberts's piece explaining McLuhan's importance to the movement in the *East Village Other* crystallized how hippie youth were taking up McLuhan's idea of tribes:

> We, the electric-age generation, have been the first to feel the impact of the retribalizing effect of the new multi-media environment. We grew up with television, which fed our brains with millions of black and white dots electronically arranged and rearranged into microsecond patterns and images. . . . We are in the age of gestalt and shape. We are no longer die-cast parts of a national mechanism. We are a tribe.
>
> We are the new breed of American Indian who smoke grass and hash and drop peyote as a tribal ritual. . . . We are the reincarnation of oral, pre-literate man. . . .[53]

The hippies and freaks of the East Village and of the Haight-Ashbury were, thus, harbingers of social and cultural change. Created by interaction with television, they were the shape of things to come. McLuhan had said so. They embodied not only the appearance of a tribe but the cognitive processes and values described by McLuhan as characteristic of the electronic age.

Critical for McLuhan was the distinction between the "message" of print media and the "message" of electronic media. Print was linear, one thing at a time, detached, rational, and visually motivated. Electronic media were everything-all-at-once, holistic, involving, irrational, and tactile. The dominance of one media form or the other shaped the culture as a whole, created its "bias."

Youthful appropriators of McLuhan eagerly latched onto this binary in order to make sense of their disaffection from dominant values. McLuhan, seeing his theory apparently manifesting itself concretely in the guise of the youth movement, was more than happy to provide the appropriate explanation. In *The Medium is the Massage,* a picture-filled, bite-sized overview of his major theoretical points, McLuhan observed: "Youth instinctively understands the present environment—the electric drama. It lives mythically and in depth. This is the reason for the great alienation between generations."[54]

The adult generation remained print-mired. We have already seen McLuhanite media guerrilla Michael Shamberg work with this binary. At another point Shamberg noted: "The 1960s were a Pearl Harbor of the senses. Whole new technologies conditioned us from birth to relate to a world which was not that of our parents' childhood. It came as a sneak attack because print-man, impervious to his own bias, was unable to perceive that any time there is a radical shift in the dominant communications medium of a culture, there's going to be a radical shift in that culture."[55] The radical shift in the culture was a shift toward "Orientalism."[56] Irrationality, non-linearity, holistic approaches to constructing reality—all these both McLuhan and counterculture youth attributed to Eastern cultures. Sixties youth, in their rejection of the corporate-consumerist culture of Western late capitalism, embraced versions of Eastern philosophy. Particularly among participants in the psychedelic community, those philosophies seemed to provide a more appropriate way to make sense of a hallucinogenic experience.

Of crucial importance here is the neat fit between McLuhan's description of the new electronic culture and the hippies' perception of their drug-inspired counterculture. Although not all those who aligned themselves with the youth movement embraced the psychedelicism of the hippie lifestyle, it is no exaggeration to assert that youth culture as a whole, from the SDS politicos on the campuses to the suburban "weekend hippie" in middle America, identified drug use as a key component of youth culture.[57] Pot, magic mushrooms, peyote buttons, mescaline, Orange Sunshine LSD—all these mind-altering drugs were a defining element of what the youth rebellion meant. More to the point, drug use facilitated the rejection of Western rationalism. The essence of an LSD trip for many acidheads was the embrace of irrationalism, the heightening of one's tactile sense, the feeling of being at one with the world and one's fellow trippers. Drug culture heightened for young people the very cultural attributes McLuhan believed television had ushered in. A female student at Columbia, quoted by *Newsweek,* clarified the connection by explaining that reading McLuhan was like taking LSD: "It can turn you on. . . . LSD doesn't mean anything until you consume it—likewise McLuhan."[58]

Tactility was one of the new cultural attributes McLuhan believed television had ushered in. With almost perverse logic McLuhan

claimed that television, as an "extension of man," extended one's sense
of touch, not one's sense of vision.[59] Miller Francis Jr. seized on this
notion to differentiate his generation from the previous one: "A generation raised on assimilation of the electronic experience of television is not a visual (Marcuse's 'one-dimensional man') generation
but is instead a generation plunged into a depth relationship with
every facet of their world."[60] Robert Roberts also saw the empowering qualities of tactility over vision: "We are a tactile generation who
groove on touching. . . . We grow our hair long because we don't
need visual distinctions any longer."[61]

Another writer for the *Bird* zeroed in on McLuhan's observations
that television was moving society away from print culture and all
that it signified. The writer, Dennis Jarrett, examined the issue by
quoting the ponderings of John Densmore, one of the members of
the rock group the Doors. Densmore noted that today's young people
were not a reading generation; they dug what was happening because
"they just take it, like McLuhan says—the whole thing." Jarrett went
on to explain:

> That means two things: 1) That we're not a reading generation, and
> 2) that we accept irrationality in language without fussing around
> for hidden meanings. In this regard, Densmore points out that when
> Jim Morrison sings "meet me at the back of the blue bus," he doesn't
> know, literally, any more about that blue bus than you do. Yet the
> blue bus functions as an image. This is almost impossible for anyone of
> the Brooks & Warren generation (you know who you are) to under-
> stand. . . .
>
> McLuhan in *The Gutenberg Galaxy, The Mechanical Bride,* and *Under-
> standing Media* discusses, if that's the right word, exactly the kind of
> statement John Densmore made. Why are we getting away from the
> printed word? Why are we forming tribes? Why are we open to the
> irrational?[62]

It seemed that significant numbers of sixties youth were "open"
to all manner of things incomprehensible to the older generation.
McLuhan was useful because he explained the cultural and perceptual chasm that divided youth from everyone else in a way that appeared to favor youth culture and youth values and that proclaimed
that given time and a few more television generations, youth culture
and values would prevail.

But that was still in the future. In the 1960s the young people of the baby boom were still the only segment of the population molded by television into new tribal creatures. Consequently, they were mutants. Echoing Miller Francis's yoking together of television and its youthful progeny as freaks and problem children, Robert Roberts saw the children of the electric age as "hideous offspring, reared on a diet of super-technology, and now rejected as deformities. We are the mutants who've been bombarded by speed-of-electron media and metamorphozed [*sic*] into a tribal society that the establishment, ironically finds repulsive."[63]

The establishment did indeed find the tribalized youth movement repulsive. According to a Lou Harris poll, "college protesters" were the most despised group in America, more detested than prostitutes, atheists, and homosexuals.[64] Marshall McLuhan was in a small minority of authoritative adult voices who seemed to speak in positive tones about the nation's rebellious young people. Other critics also wanted to explain how the pampered tots of the fifties had turned into the hellions of the sixties. Many, like McLuhan, pointed to television. Their ideas, however, would have had few empowering possibilities for sixties rebels. We need to examine this discourse, however, in order to show how television could embody such contradictory meanings by differently situated commentators. This discourse also shows the many ways the medium was constructed as a culprit to explain youth rebellion, the generation gap, and sociopolitical upheaval.

Blaming Television

Many observers of the youth movement commented on the impact of television in creating rebelliousness among the young, but S. I. Hayakawa made a veritable career of it. Hayakawa was both a noted semanticist and president of San Francisco State during its bloody and violent four-month student strike. Ruthlessly prevailing over the strikers, Hayakawa, with his trademark tam-o'-shanter, became a national hero in some circles.[65] His opinions about how television had caused youth unrest circulated widely.

TV Guide, in two separate editorials, quoted from an extensively publicized speech he delivered at the convention of the American

Psychological Association in 1969. In the speech Hayakawa blamed the sheer volume of television consumed by young people throughout their lives for the mayhem they were wreaking on the social order. By the time they reached eighteen years American youth had watched at least twenty-two thousand hours of television, he proclaimed.[66] Other commentators picked up on this statistic as if it alone explained the problem. Hayakawa declared that all this viewing activity was essentially a passive experience. Young people sat absorbing rather than interacting. All that passive absorbing resulted in a generation that could not relate to parents, the older generation ("the establishment"), or anyone but themselves.[67]

Hayakawa's theory of television spectatorship and the young differed in notable ways from McLuhan's. McLuhan said that television was highly participatory—far more than print. With its low definition, television as a medium required viewers to fill in the gaps, make meaningful a random series of flickering dots. McLuhan and Hayakawa came to the same general conclusion—the experience of television watching had made young people rebel against the established social order. The difference was that one saw the experience as active and empowering, and the other saw it as passive and destructive. One saw the resultant rebellion as salutary to the culture, the other as frightening and regressive.

McLuhan and his young acolytes weren't the only ones who saw television watching as a participatory rather than a passive activity. John Sloan Dickey, retiring president of Dartmouth College, who had been evicted from his office during a recent student occupation of the administration building, took a generally positive tone. He said that young people became participants in knowing society's imperfections by seeing them on television. "Kids see this now and act in it. They're participants. Television makes it real, personal, not just book stuff. And that makes it much more important for them to act."[68] In a sense Dickey's view seemed more consistent and logical. Active spectators became active agents. Hayakawa's theory rested on the conclusion that an essentially dull, idle, and indolent state of being before a television set would result in frenzied, out-of-control turmoil in the streets.

Vice President Spiro T. Agnew, continuing his attack on television, also felt the need to explain how the medium had caused youth to take to the streets in demonstrations. In a special cover story in *TV Guide* Agnew quoted many "experts," including Hayakawa, to bolster his thesis. At one point he asked: "How much of the terrible impatience of so many young people—evident in the virulence of their protests—can be traced to the disparity between the real world and that Epicurean world inside the television set where the proper combination of pills and cars and cigarettes and deodorants can bring relief from suffering and instant gratification of all their material wants and desires?"[69]

Widespread was this idea that impatience for social justice and an end to the war in Vietnam (NOW!) emerged from the lessons of commercial television. Eliot Daley, a television producer, also pondered this point in *TV Guide.* The young were impatient because television had taught them that things did not take time: "Every problem had a solution. Every program had a conclusion. There were no alternatives to explore (no time for that). There were no human idiosyncrasies to consider (power or deceit will prevail). Opinions, rights, feelings of others? Irrelevant. Due process of law? What a laugh!"[70] On the one hand, television's ability to reveal realistically society's imperfections had galvanized young people into protest and rebellion. On the other hand, television's Epicurean fantasy world of instant solutions had done the same thing. For these commentators television as a sign held within its bounds some rather contradictory causative meanings.

One issue that brought unanimity to anxious adult commentators was the connection between television commercials and the youth drug scene. Many believed that implicitly (and often explicitly) advertisements broadcast messages of instant bliss through the consumption of a particular product—often a drug. For Hayakawa commercial television subverted the Protestant ethic of "study, patience and hard work in learning a trade or profession before you may enjoy what the world has to offer." But, paradoxically, commercial television had revealed that material possessions could not offer bliss and contentment. Thus, young people were turning their backs on America's consumerist paradise and seeking nirvana through mind-altering substances. Hayakawa found this a dangerous rejection be-' cause the young people were rejecting "not the culture itself but merely the culture as depicted by Madison Avenue and the networks."[71] Hayakawa wanted to have it both ways. He wanted to damn youth rebels for swallowing the message of instant gratification broadcast by commercial television, and he wanted to damn youth for rejecting a culture that manufactured such messages.

Whether embracing or renouncing those messages, young people had turned to drugs because of what television taught them, according to these critics. As we have already seen, McLuhan's theories, as used by some young people, suggested a link between the psychedelic drug experience and television as a perception-altering technology. For some acidheads this was an empowering way to make sense of their activities.

Other critics found the link more frightening. Eliot Daley blamed television more than the duped/doped youth, arguing that the medium was essentially a drug pusher:

> Teen-agers are the shock troops of a culture hooked on drugs. At a $100,000,000 annual clip, many TV commercials encourage us to expect miracles from drugs. The young apparently have been convinced. Soaring after Utopia or Nirvana or Ultimate Reality, their crash landings have made lurid news.
>
> . . . We thought we could buy temporary relief indefinitely and would never have to grapple with the roots of our dissatisfaction. Now we're all reaping the whirlwind.[72]

Hayakawa argued for a link between LSD and television viewing that, predictably, was diametrically opposite to that suggested by McLuhan: "The kinship of LSD and the other drug experiences is glaringly obvious: both depend on turning on and passively waiting for something beautiful to happen."[73]

This fear about television as a form of drug addiction was certainly nothing new. In relation to the young this theme goes back to the early 1950s. Lynn Spigel discovered a cartoon in a 1950 *Ladies' Home Journal* warning about "telebugeye." The cartoon shows a young child looking like she is strung out on heroin as she gazes at a TV western.[74] In the late 1970s Marie Winn, in her best-selling book *The Plug-In Drug,* argued for the need to wean youngsters from their television addiction. In a chapter on the first television generation, she attempted to show, as Hayakawa and others had before her, that too much television watching was symptomatic of rampant drug use among the youth.

For these critics television asserted a baleful influence on the

The Silent Majority

Adult America zoned out before TV images of war. An *East Village Other* comic of older-generation cluelessness.

youth of America. Adults, however, seemed to have escaped its mind-warping capabilities. Agnew, in an observation that suggested more about the validity of the generation gap than he may have intended, noted: "The adult who matured intellectually and went to work before television became such a pervasive presence in the home may still be able to take his prime-time TV shows as he does his movies — as a form of entertainment and escapism from the humdrum of daily life."[75] The vice president apparently missed the fact that the disaffected young people of the period were rebelling against everything that represented the humdrum of daily life within the dominant social order. Frequent cartoon representations of adult America appearing in the "comix" of underground newspapers depicted them zoned out in front of a television set. The image of a balding, beer-bellied suburban male sprawling before a television that spewed forth images of mayhem became almost iconic of the older, uncomprehending generation.

This brings us to an interesting paradox. As I have tried to show, young people aligned with the youth movement, as well as alarmed adults, used the perceived link between television and its first genera-

tion of young viewers to explain the current state of the TV generation. On the other hand, this generation had by this point abandoned
the medium to a considerable extent as a major source of information
and entertainment. (Yippies Abbie Hoffman and Jerry Rubin were
notable exceptions.) Harlan Ellison, noted science fiction writer and
regular TV critic for the Los Angeles underground paper the *L.A. Free
Press,* explained the situation this way:

> Walking down the streets these days and nights are members of the
> Television Generation. Kids who were born with TV, were babysat by
> TV, were weaned on TV, dug TV and finally rejected TV. . . .
>
> But their parents, the older folks, the ones who brought the world
> down whatever road it is that's put us in this place at this time—they
> sit and watch situation comedies. Does this tell us something? . . .
> The mass is living in a fairyland where occasionally a gripe or dis-
> couraging word is heard. . . . The mass sits and sucks its thumb and
> watches Lucy and Doris and Granny Clampett and the world burns
> around them.[76]

The kids had rejected the content of television, leaving it and its
irrelevant programming to their elders. Like teenagers and young
adults of previous and succeeding generations, they watched less
television than any other age group. For members of the student
protest movement or the hippie counterculture, art films and rock
music were the preeminent arenas of cultural consumption. Any self-
respecting head or campus politico would be looked at askance were
she or he to exhibit a too-hardy interest in the products of the Vast
Wasteland. Hip and activist young people rejected television as a
commercial, network-dominated industry hopelessly corrupted by
the values of the establishment. The censorship and heavy-handed
cancellation of *The Smothers Brothers Comedy Hour,* the only network
program to succeed in engaging these young people, provided tangible evidence of the medium's corruption.[77]

Groove Tube: Trip Toys and Guerrilla Video

The "message" of the medium may have been too unhip and too corrupted with the discourses of the established social and political order
for young people to engage willingly with its network-dominated

form to any great degree. The technology of television was another matter. As a stroboscopic aid to enhance an altered state of consciousness, contentless television was frequently celebrated within the hip community. At the same time, the development of low-cost, mass-marketed, portable video equipment allowed counterculture types, as well as politicos, to proclaim that the movement would finally be in a position to create its own (revolutionary) video content, bypassing establishment channels of distribution and control. Thus, as spectators, heads and freaks could use the tube for some psychedelic, subversive fun. As putative producers, "video guerrillas" envisioned using the medium for political organizing, consciousness raising, and community building.

Robert Roberts rhapsodized in the *East Village Other* about television's "millions of black and white dots" and their perpetual electronic rearrangements into patterns and images. This view of the medium eradicated content (and implicitly the ideological interpellations that went with it), allowing for a free play of video signifiers, unanchored by any final meaning or signification. D. A. Latimer, in the *East Village Other,* proclaimed television "the most potent consciousness-altering force in history" and, referencing McLuhan, argued that "any head who has watched eight hours of TV while stoned will bear [McLuhan] out: television is Cool, it involves the viewer on every level of consciousness; from verbal to nonverbal sensory conduits, visual and aural."[78] Television as television, therefore, could be the ultimate trip toy.

The *East Village Other,* reprinting a piece from the hippie-oriented *San Francisco Oracle,* instructed readers on proper freaked-out use of their television sets. The writer argued that through his readings of McLuhan he had discovered the meditational uses of television. To turn the set into a meditation device, one first had to eradicate the surfeit of content transmitted by the television industry. Once that was accomplished, the viewer would be able to perceive the stroboscopic nature of the medium and its mandala-like patterns so familiar to psychedelic substance users. He then provided concrete instructions:

In a darkened room, turn on your TV set. Find a full channel. Adjust the brightness control all the way to bright (to the right). Adjust the contrast control (to the left). Adjust the vertical hold and verti-

cal linearity controls all the way to the left or right. Tune the channel selector to an empty channel. Readjust for maximum brightness
as necessary—maximum retinal color results from maximum bom-
bardment of the retina. Concentrate on sending your meditations out
from your ashram to mine. Thank you. "We now return control of
your TV set to you."[79]

This detailed strategy to eradicate content in favor of foregrounding the visual components of the medium certainly seemed to indicate a rejection of television programming as information and entertainment. The offerings of the broadcast networks were what got in
the way of a useful engagement with the formal properties of the
medium. Tripped-out viewers' abilities to play with, distort, readjust
and finally deny broadcasters their power to impose their content
suggests a knowing refusal to be delivered up to the preferred viewing techniques of the medium.

A reporter for *TV Guide,* exploring the television habits of the hip
residents of the Haight–Ashbury, found similar practices. In an interview with Ed Sanders—poet, musician, and member of the band The
Fugs—this "spokesman" for the community talked about watching
Gunsmoke with the sound off and a Beatles or Fugs record playing.
Sanders called it "free mixed media." Poster artist Peter Max con-
curred that this was the proper way to watch television. "You've got
yourself a self-produced show. It's grand. The visual sense is pleased
by the screen, the aural by the records, the physical by the couch or
whatever you're on, while the taste buds are satisfied by whatever
you're smoking."[80] By turning TV into a "groove tube," Sanders and
Max were suggesting empowering ways by which hip youth could
use the medium for their own pleasures. As children of McLuhan,
Haight–Ashbury's young would predictably use it in a fashion that
turned the technology into an extension of their psychedelically en-
hanced perceptual senses.

This was only a first step in seizing control of the medium. As
EVO's D. A. Latimer pointed out, television was a "powerful psychedelic force," "emphatically a head gimmick, all of the best features of strobes and lights and hallucinations in one box." Television
was also a force with a "prediliction [*sic*] for mind-fucking"; therefore, the psychedelic community needed to use it for more humanity-
serving ends.[81]

Members of the hip community attempted such a project with an early venture called "Channel One." Created by Ken Shapiro and Lane Sarasohn, Channel One was a video theater and "psychedelic shrine" set up in the Lower East Side in 1967. The theater housed a number of black-and-white televisions and seating for about sixty, mimicking a theater-in-the-round set up. The environment was supposed to suggest the comforts of one's own living room. Shapiro and Sarasohn created short production pieces directly targeting a counterculture audience. "We concentrate on humor, psychedelic satire," Shapiro explained in Latimer's *EVO* piece. "The heads are a gorgeous subculture, with their own language, their own jokes—and since so little of it can be broadcast over regular media, drugs and sex and such, it gives us a whole world of totally new material to work with. We like to think we're providing heads with their own CBS."[82]

The potential for creating alternative video productions outside the dominant network media channels blossomed in 1968 with the introduction of portable half-inch video recording equipment into the U.S. market. The affordable Sony Portapak helped create a video art movement in the 1960s and 1970s. One branch of this movement flowered amid the high-culture art world of galleries, museums, performance art, and "happenings" and received funding from the Rockefeller Foundation and the National Endowment for the Arts. The other branch, without foundation money, blossomed amid countercultural and student politico groupings.[83]

Beginning in 1969 and continuing into the new decade, the underground press featured numerous articles rhapsodizing about the revolutionary possibilities of grassroots video production. Videotape as a technological tool would transform the social order, ushering in an era of true participatory democracy through "feedback" and "process." Video collectives began forming around the country with names like "Video Freex," "Video Free America," "Global Village," "Ant Farm," "Raindance," and others. Michael Shamberg, a founder of Raindance, found himself in the paradoxical position of having written the video revolutionaries' bible, *Guerrilla Television,* which was both theoretical tract and how-to manual, but having published it through the CBS subsidiary Holt, Rinehart, and Winston. In 1969 some CBS executives, including network vice president Michael Dann, exhibited a quickly aborted interest in the productions of the video guerrillas. The network provided Video Freex with a

Holt Paperback $3.95

The book cover of Michael Shamberg's
how-to manual for video revolutionaries.

$60,000 budget to produce some experimental programming for
the network. At a public presentation in a Greenwich Village loft
"stuffed with oodles of sound and video equipment," the CBS brass
encountered what *EVO*'s Allan Katzman described as "committed
chaos." Rather than taped programming filled with "information
and entertainment," the executives got "spontaneity and fun," along
with a complete disregard for standards of "professionalism." Dann
mumbled a "rather apologetic and tolerant thank you speech," and the
network representatives beat a hasty retreat.[84]

The incident merely reinforced to the attendant freaks and Freex
that their approach to the medium was antithetical to that of network television. In *Guerrilla Television* Shamberg warned, "It is the
very structure and context of broadcast TV which are co-opting. Instead of politicizing people with mass-TV, Guerrilla Television seeks
to media-ize people against it." Attempting to use the channels of
network television could only be counterproductive, resulting in

video guerrillas getting caught in the hegemonic signifying webs of institutional power. Shamberg went on:

> When I first began working in alternative television I predicted that about a year later we would have a chance to air some of our tape, but only after TV labeled it something like "Crazy Experimental Far-Out Videotape Makers" so that somehow it would [be] set apart from broadcast-TV instead of posing a real challenge to its structure.
>
> Sure enough, eighteen months after I said that, we were asked to contribute tape to a show called "The Television Revolution." [85]

As guerrillas, underground video politicos had to avoid and evade the dominant institutions and their strategic ability to label and, thereby, capture. Foreshadowing the theorizing of Michel de Certeau on the tactics used by the weak to negotiate imposed systems, Shamberg warned his fellow video guerrillas: "It's impossible to vary your tactics each time, which is classic guerrilla strategy, if the people you must work with have pigeon holed you in a pre-determined category. The legitimacy you need to build a base of community and economic support may be unattainable if an alien press has already manufactured your image. The moment you surrender control of your media image, you're captured" (33).

The movement's video makers ended up cultivating a thoroughly distrustful and suspicious relationship to network television. Network broadcasters shared this antagonism and refused to show independent video pieces, typically on aesthetic, political, and technological grounds. William Boddy notes that the exclusion from the airwaves helped to "unite diverse independent producers in common marginality, creating a surprisingly close-knit community which took up the tasks not only of production, but also of distribution, exhibition, critical exegesis and publicity of the new work." [86]

Patricia Mellencamp emphasizes the importance of decentralized systems of distribution and exhibition to the underground video movement. Process was privileged over product. The video collective Ant Farm was emblematic of the approach. A kind of communal family, Ant Farm comprised environmental activists, artists, builders, and actors, along with "university trained media freaks and hippies interested in balancing the environment by total transformation of existing social and economic systems." [87] Emphatically nonhierarchical, and devoted to collective work methods, the group used psyche-delic drugs to unleash creative energies. Ant Farm, like a number of other video collectives, took its show on the road, touring university campuses in a video-rigged van, which Mellencamp compares to the early Soviet agitprop trains that toured postrevolutionary Russia attempting to educate the peasant masses in communist ideas and principles. "Like the Soviets," Mellencamp notes, "but without Marx, projects [like Ant Farm] encouraged audiences to participate in productions, as well as preaching the new visions of society" (53). Ant Farm traveled the campus circuit in a "customized media van with antennae, silver dome, TV window, inflatable shower stall, kitchen, ice, inflatable shelter for five, solar water heater, portapak and video playback system."[88]

Both media historian William Boddy and theorist Patricia Mellencamp point out the prevalence of video utopianism among practitioners of guerrilla television. Mellencamp notes the technological determinism that animated the video collectives. As followers of McLuhan, whose media theories were wholly instrumentalist in approach, this should come as no surprise. Mellencamp explains video activists' idealism: " 'Video' would bring global salvation via access, circumventing institutions and going directly to individuals of conscience—the people" (53).

"Feedback" was the key. Network television provided unidirectional, one-way, hegemonic communication from the top down. Alternative television was two-way, easily accessible, and worked from the bottom up. An article in the *Great Speckled Bird* heralded the inauguration of the Atlanta Video Collective, a group of people who had scraped together some video equipment and wanted to get more people together, along with ideas, equipment, money, projects to tape, and places to exhibit the tapes. Articulating a utopian vision of the transformative possibilities of feedback, the article proclaimed: "Video tape is a start in the process of turning channels 2/5/11/17/43 upside down, but, like TV didn't turn out to be little movies in the home, video tape isn't just cheap, accessible TV. The difference is feedback; to see, hear, experience people (and ourselves) in struggle (life, play, revolution) and know that you have some chance of affecting what will be in the next cycle (video feedback). . . . [Video feedback] can be part of the liberation struggle; from sexism, racism, and imperialism."[89]

Many commentators emphasized the inherently revolutionary quality of video feedback, yet these same commentators tended to fall back on visions of guerrilla video as a tool in fostering participatory democracy. This concept, a cornerstone of the early New Left and Students for a Democratic Society, had by the close of the decade and the early 1970s been dismissed by many of the more radical revolutionists within student politico circles as fundamentally liberal and incompatible with revolutionary vangardism. Many of the video guerrillas mouthed the revolutionism of the Weathermen yet in their writings kept slipping back into less apocalyptic rhetoric. An article in San Francisco's *Good Times* first heralded videotape as "a new phase in the revolutionary process" for the TV generation, who were described as "the revolutionary people." Yet later in the piece the author asserted that video recorders and tape would make possible true democratic participation and that feedback would lead to the return of the town meeting of ancient Greek democracies."[90]

Other commentators in the underground press assumed, with euphoric abandon, that the corporate colossus of mass media, along with the dominant social and political order, could be easily felled by the new technology. An *East Village Other* writer enthused: "Count to three and SHAZAM, society will be transformed—the establishment communications network will have been bypassed."[91]

Cable television also held out the promise of transforming the social order along decentralized, democratic lines. In a page-one story in 1971 the *Los Angeles Free Press* asserted the potential of community access cable allowing for cheap production by local groups and organizations. The proliferation of channels would give alternative, movement-oriented video collectives and political groups access to the airwaves, bypassing network dominance and allowing for a democratization of television. The article noted that because cable franchising was under the jurisdiction of local governments and because few cities had yet been cabled, it would be easier for local groups to exert pressure on the proposed franchises. Furthermore,

> if we force cable operators to install systems now that are technologically capable of meeting community needs, we can later go on to create a TV that will tear down the walls that the media barons build to keep out the dispossessed, the thoughtful, the angered.

Cable TV per se is not revolutionary, but real popular control of information is. Until we have the power to define our reality, we will never escape or destroy the image of reality created by the massive communications industry. Cable power to the people![92]

These video visionaries may have been a bit naive about the potentials of technology *as* technology to usher in fundamental social and political change. They were not at all naive, however, about the institutional powers arrayed against their projects of pluralizing mass disseminated televisual discourse. Over and over again these members of the television generation pointed out how the oligopolistic structure of network television limited diversity of expression and how the capitalist and corporate nature of the network system distorted and silenced the counterhegemonic discourses and actions of movement activists.

In the 1970s cable entrepreneurs appropriated aspects of video guerrilla rhetoric about democratizing the medium and seizing control away from network behemoths. Cable, they ballyhooed, would be interactive and two-way. More recently, of course, similar rhetoric has been used by Internet providers. Boddy observes:

> The rhetorical similarities between the technological visions of some video guerrillas and the entrepreneurs of the booming cable industry in the 1970s seem disquieting in retrospect. The wishful thinking about the autonomy of technology and the refusal of history and politics among independent video makers may have inadvertently enlisted them as the avant garde for an (un)reconstructed communications industry only too happy to lead a "media revolution" which would leave existing power relations untouched."[93]

Video guerrillas seemed to have assumed that by practicing their televisual counterpolitics outside the institutions of network television and by using two-way, feedback approaches this would somehow be enough to, "SHAZAM!," transform the dominant social order. Of course, it didn't happen. But on the other hand, the fact that the emergent cable industry felt a need to mobilize countercultural discourse in its appeals to potential subscribers suggests some form of negotiation with those positions on the part of the communications industry. Cable franchisers were forced to include community access stations as part of their packages. Certainly, these channels and their programming would never live up to the utopian visions of change

A comic vision from the *East Village Other* of how the revolution might appear on prime time's *The Mod Squad* and *Julia*.

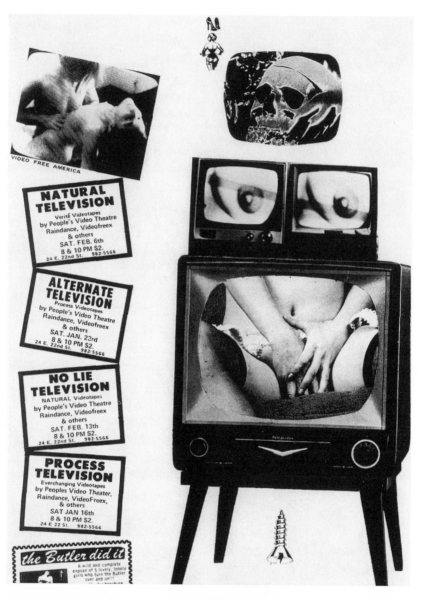

Just as many underground newspapers peddled female flesh in the name of sexual liberation, so too did video guerrillas. From an illustration in *Guerrilla Television*.

End page of Michael Shamberg's *Guerrilla Television*.
Smash the television, smash the State.

prophesied by those video revolutionaries. In the end, however, they
were correct to view television as a key site of struggle for the movement, even if many within the movement had long since given up
on the medium.

Herein lies the great paradox of the first television generation. Despite the clear recognition by many movement commentators that
coming of age with the medium had worked some fundamental
transformation on the ways that sixties youth constructed reality and
relations to authority, except for the video guerrillas, McLuhanites,
and Yippies (whose television activism will be discussed in chapter 3) most campus New Leftists and countercultural heads and freaks
tended to avoid engagement with television to any great extent.
Many of the era's young people actively rejected television as a useful
source of information, amusement, or edification. Some found ways
to eradicate network content and subvert "appropriate" uses of the
medium in favor of foregrounding its formal properties when they
did turn on the set — and themselves. Many also embraced their childhood histories with the medium and the ways in which *Howdy Doody*
and other programs had inadvertently promoted their rebelliousness.
Even as they turned the tube's programming off in droves, they still
recognized their inescapable link to the medium. Television, as they
saw it, was at least partly responsible for turning them into freaks,

for causing them to embrace the values of the East as they rejected the values of Western consumer capitalism, for pointing out that the adult social order was nothing to look up to or emulate. Even hostile critics such as S. I. Hayakawa and Vice President Agnew could not deny the power of television in molding the members of this generation. They would forever be the children of television. As such, many would also find it impossible to ignore how the medium constructed their movement, their social and political disaffection and subversions, their alternative lifestyles, their idealism, and their threat to the established order.

Plastic Hippies

2 The Counterculture on TV

In the mid-1960s American bohemia began to undergo a strange metamorphosis. The angst-filled, existential Beats began giving way to a new community of dropouts and rebels against the system. As Beat enclaves such as New York's Greenwich Village and San Francisco's North Beach began their gentrification process, new neighborhoods of nonconformists began popping up in low-rent districts like the East Village, the Haight-Ashbury, and in similar urban areas around the nation. These new bohemians shared certain common threads with their Beat precursors. Both were deeply critical of and disengaged from the values of white, middle-class, suburban family life. Both embraced philosophies and worldviews associated with Eastern mysticism. And both emphasized the importance of mind-altering drugs in achieving personal transcendence. The Beats, at this time primarily men and a few women well into their thirties at least, tended to look down on these new initiates into bohemia. The young kids, most still in their teens and early twenties, from comfortable homes, and with money either in their pockets or available from mom and pop via Western Union, weren't considered "hip" by the Beats. Derisively they were dismissed as "hippies."[1]

In the space of a few years, however, these new bohemians would bring into being the most widespread and influential counterculture ever to appear on the American sociocultural landscape. Hippie communities spread to almost every major American city—and to many smaller ones as well. Hippie slang, hippie dress, hippie lifestyle choices, along with hippie values and beliefs reverberated out from these enclaves to challenge a consensus of American social values cobbled together in the post–World War II era. The phenomenon of pampered baby boomers dropping out of the material world that so defined their childhood to embrace a footloose inner world of mystical and psychedelic experimentation fundamentally threatened a naturalized American "Way of Life." Historian David Farber has noted that hippies, far more than antiwar activists or black-power groups, served as "shock troops" in a "culture war" that challenged key values and cultural rules.[2] Rather than make lists of demands and organize protests, hippies enacted a radically alternative politics of everyday life—a radical way of *being.* Central to this way of being, of course, was the ingestion of LSD and other mind-expanding drugs. As we saw in chapter 1, youthful drug experimentation functioned as a site of fundamental moral panic for adults and for the social order in general. For acidheads, drugs had turned them into "freaks"—a new evolutionary species of human with next to nothing in common with the previous generation. For many in the adult generation hippie-freaks were destroyers of Western civilization.

Nevertheless, a surprisingly large amount of commentary about the hippie phenomenon during its heyday was tentatively positive. A largely sympathetic *Time* magazine cover story that ran in July of the "Summer of Love" concluded by arguing that "in their independence of material possessions and their emphasis on peacefulness and honesty, hippies lead considerably more virtuous lives than the great majority of their fellow citizens."[3] Although hippies may have been questioning the consumption ethic and middle-class morality, they were more nobly upholding traditional American ideals associated with Thoreau and even Thomas Jefferson.

This ambivalence about hippies was also evident in prime-time television representations of the phenomenon.[4] This chapter explores the at-times tortuous negotiations adopted by TV dramas and one notable news special in their attempts to make sense of the counterculture and its participants. Rather than circulate simplistic moral panics about sex-and-drug-addled, long-haired, out-of-control youngsters, many (but not all) television programs presented more complicated and ideologically tricky presentations. These presentations, like the *Time* cover story, frequently emphasized sympathetic portrayals. Yet if the hippie counterculture appeared to challenge postwar norms and values to a fundamental degree, why the attempt by these institutions of the dominant social order to portray sociocultural dissenters in ambivalently attractive light?

In the 1960s the postwar consensus of shared values, this hegemonic system of "normalcy," began to break down. The civil rights movement, beginning in the mid-1950s and gathering steam into the early 1960s, served as the first harbinger that all was not well in the social consensus. The movement of African Americans showed that not all members of the society were equally represented by a pluralistic common value system. The disaffection and disengagement of white, middle-class American youth, first manifest in the hippie phenomenon, was the second crack in the hegemonic armor.

In some ways this second challenge proved more frightening to the social order and to establishment power. Dominant social groups and institutions may never have had much need or interest in winning the ideological consent to dominance of the black population (coercion and force having been the traditional way American institutions worked on black bodies and communities). Nor have black Americans ever successfully been knitted into the liberal pluralist dream of American social democracy.[5] Such was not supposed to be the case with the pampered and fussed-over white, middle-class children of the baby boom. This group was meant to inherit and perpetuate the system of corporate capitalism, cold war militarism, consumer-oriented nuclear families, and rigidly defined gender roles.

Although American institutions and social elites may not have felt a great need to try winning the consent and allegiance of African Americans in revolt, those elites did feel a need to win back the rebellious and insurgent white youth. The remaking of a smooth-running social order depended on it. This process of rewinning consent was a largely cultural endeavor. Hippies were not fundamentally economic or political rebels—although their lifestyle behaviors and philosophical convictions had economic and political implications. Dropping out of the moneyed economy and the system of commodity accumulation suggested a rejection of capitalism. However, the parasitic hippie lifestyle of panhandling and scrounging for free stuff relied implicitly on an affluent, well-oiled capitalist system with lots of extra wealth to spread around. If the counterculture was a *cultural* form of Great Refusal, then the establishment society's response to that Refusal needed also to be primarily cultural. One area within which to fight this ideological battle was popular culture. In the case of the hippie phenomenon we cannot understand the social and cultural meanings of the counterculture and the dominant order's response to it if we don't pay attention to the hippies' representation within the popular media. This arena served as a key site where the dominant culture attempted to represent, understand, and thus "domesticate" the threat posed by the counterculture. On the other side, we also need to examine the extent to which hippies confronted, evaded, or exploited the spotlight shone on them by the media industries. This chapter also traces the frequently antagonistic relationship between members of the hippie counterculture and the television industry over the meanings and representations of *hippie*. The dominant order, through the workings of popular media, attempted to negotiate the ideological break effected by rebellious youth in their Great Refusal to support an exhausted and hypocritical ideological system. Countercultural youth, as the sophisticated media children we saw in the last chapter, recognized the mechanisms of hegemony in its process of attempting to reconfigure itself. They struggled against absorption and co-optation in order to evade ideological capture.

Television in the mid-1960s may have appeared an unlikely place for this kind of battle. Whereas the Hollywood film industry by 1966 and 1967 busily tried to capture youth audiences, having slowly come to the realization that unmarried young people formed the bulk of their ticket buyers, the television networks faced a quite different situation.[6] Television as a home-based entertainment medium constructed its audience according to concepts of households and families. Research has shown that young people, especially those in their college-age years, are the least likely to watch television regularly.[7] And as chapter 1 showed, members of the baby boom generation, as they reached their young adulthood, were rejecting television even as they embraced their formative relationship with the medium.

Nevertheless, between 1966 and 1967 the television networks announced their desire to revamp their programming schedules for "youth." Unfortunately "youth" was an amorphous and rather broadly defined category for the network executives. In the motion picture trade youth audiences meant those under twenty-five and unmarried. In television a youth audience could mean anybody between the demographic range of eighteen to forty-nine. This rather generous definition of youth, which certainly flattered those who would otherwise be deemed middle-aged, resulted in a certain amount of contradiction within the industry during this period. Early in 1966 *Variety* reported concern among television executives that viewing was up among the teenage and under-thirty-five age group and down among those in the thirty-five-to-forty-nine and over-fifty groups. Advertisers were most interested in reaching those between the ages of thirty-five and forty-nine, a demographic group considered the most lucrative consuming segment of the population.[8] Nevertheless, the networks, CBS in particular, also worried about their "geriatric" image. As early as March of 1967 CBS expressed concern about its position as video's "maiden aunt." According to a major story in *Variety,* the network planned a significant revamping of its schedule to better challenge NBC with the latter's supposed "command of young adult and juve viewership."[9] However, CBS was not the only network troubled about older viewers. One week after *Variety's* CBS story, the trade paper ran another piece, this time as a page-one banner headline report. According to the story all three networks were eager to serve youth audiences and were uninterested in "old folks."[10] But by using the Nielsen-inspired designation that "eighteen-to-forty-nine" meant youth, the networks found themselves hampered by a demographic that included two generations whose interests, tastes, and ways of interpreting social reality were radically different. The eighteen-to-forty-nine demographic encompassed the generation gap that would grow wider and wider as more baby boomers passed their eighteenth birthdays and entered into this unstable demographic.

The inherent contradictions in the networks' attempting to cater to "youth" so generously defined were noted by *TV Guide's* resident industry columnist Richard Doan early in 1967: "The paradox of the network's consuming passion for attracting young adult viewers is that the TV-ratings race continues to be paced by middle-aged-to-elderly stars."[11] Of course those at the higher end of the youth demographic were, in fact, middle-aged. And in matters of taste in entertainment, these middle-aged "young adults" had more in common with those in their fifties and sixties. According to Doan, the most popular television stars included the sixty-something Lawrence Welk, Ed Sullivan, and Bob Hope, and the fifty-something Red Skelton, Jackie Gleason, Lucille Ball, Eddie Albert, Buddy Ebsen, and Lorne Green. Television thus served as a marker of taste distinction.

Those who preferred these older performers occupied a cultural terrain very different from many in the baby boom, and this distinction became one means by which to point out generational conflict. Bob Hope, a television icon and also a highly visible Vietnam hawk, served as a potent reminder to the rebellious young that television was no longer their medium. It now represented—and was represented by—Hope and his elderly ilk.

It would take the television industry a number of years to figure out that what appealed to the older half of their "young adult" demographic was very different from what appealed to the younger half. It would also take a few years for the industry to decide that young baby boomers were, in fact, the most desirable consumer group.

Monkee Business

This does not mean that the networks had no interest at all in catering to teenagers. A number of teen-oriented programs popped up in the mid-1960s, including *The Patty Duke Show* and *Gidget,* that provided representations of wacky but clean-cut and eminently respectable teenage girls. There were also a few rock 'n' roll programs, like *Shindig* and *Hullabaloo,* that showcased fairly mainstream, top-forty bands and singers. *The Monkees,* which joined the NBC lineup in the fall of 1966, was part of this spate of teen programming, but it also differed in important ways. The show, which took its inspiration from the recent highly successful Beatles films *A Hard Day's Night* and *Help,* portrayed the adventures of a troupe of four wacky, long-haired musicians. Like the Beatles' films, *The Monkees* was not overly concerned with narrative continuity or logic, relying on frequent blackout sketches and musical interludes. The series was developed by producers Bob Rafelson and Bert Schneider, two young television mavericks who really wanted to make movies.[12] In a now-famous advertisement, they published a call in *Variety* for "4 Insane Boys, Aged 17–21" to play the parts of the Monkees. In a sly drug reference the ad also noted that applicants "Must Come Down For Interview." The fact that the group was prefabricated and thus not "authentic" plagued the show and the group throughout their popular-culture existence. As the "Prefab Four," they epitomized for many in the youth movement the mechanisms by which the entertainment industry commodified

The "Prefab Four." Early Monkees with
Beatlesque moptops. *(Author's collection)*

youth culture.[13] For the young actor-musicians who ended up with
the parts, the disdain from their cogenerationists was painful—especially for Peter Tork and Mike Nesmith, who came from the folk-
music circuit.

Reactions to the show by test audiences in its early development
and then by adult critics and network affiliates after it went on air
indicate that the series became a site for displaying the growing rift
between the tastes of the young and those of the older generation.
When screened for a test audience, the pilot did very poorly. According to Schneider, "the anti-establishment stance was too much of an
affront to [audiences'] sensibilities and attitudes. Those kind of testing services bring in the whole demographic, a typical TV audience,
so you're going to have all the older people in there as well as the
younger. Well, the older people just hated the kids—you couldn't get
past that."[14] The pilot needed to be retooled to make the long-haired
stars more palatable to audiences. Interviews with the Monkees were
tossed into the show to indicate that they were nice, regular guys

after all. For Schneider this would help resistant older audiences in getting to know the Monkees and "therefore buy some of their so-called anti-establishment." The strategy worked. The next set of tests was positive enough for NBC to air the series.

However, the gap between the tastes of the adults and the tastes of the adolescents continued to be an issue for *The Monkees*. Television critics writing about the new series tended to emphasize this rift. One newspaper critic asserted that although adults would "scream in outrage," the show would "delight the young."[15] Another critic noted, "Some adults may not understand The Monkees, but I think the teenagers will get the message loud and clear."[16] Adults may not have understood the message, but the representations of this new version of American youth (plus one Englishman) generated a great deal of anxiety. Press accounts tended to focus primarily on the actors' long hair and on the strange music they played. These ac-counts often carried a rather patronizing tone, as though the con-descending attitude could help to contain the cultural threat posed by these bizarre characters. As 1966 passed into 1967, cultural signi-fiers such as long hair, exotic clothing, rock music, and the drop-out lifestyle—all on display in *The Monkees*—increasingly served as indexes of hippiedom. An October 1966 *Newsweek* article indicates just how anxiety-producing these countercultural signifiers could be. The story pointed out that a number of NBC's rural affiliates refused to carry the show. *The Monkees* producer Bob Rafelson explained: "There is a grand resistance to kids with long hair. . . . The TV re-viewer on the Portland Ore. paper won't even look at the show. There's also conservative resistance by adults to the music."[17]

A 1967 story in *TV Guide* expounded further on the conflict be-tween the affiliates and the long-haired Monkees: "the affiliates are conservative, skeptical men known to be opposed in principle to any-thing long haired."[18] The situation degenerated when the Monkees engaged in a series of monkeeshines at a gala thrown by the network for its affiliates to introduce the new stars and shows for the fall sched-ule. The Monkees grabbed a stuffed peacock—the network's emblem —and played volleyball with it. Micky Dolenz playfully switched off all the lights in the room. Introduced by Dick Clark, the boys joked and kidded around but did not amuse their uptight audience. These hijinks so offended the sensibilities of some affiliates that a number of them—including at least five in key markets—refused to pick up the show. Despite the series' later popularity, this censorship permanently undermined its national ratings.[19]

A breakdown of the show's ratings also provided a site for the playing out of generational taste distinctions and struggles. According to *Variety,* the October 1966 TvQ ratings indicated that among viewers under eighteen *The Monkees* was among the most favored shows. Among adults the show was among the least favored. The series was number one with children ages six to eleven and number two with teenagers. For those above those age groups the show had little if any appeal.[20]

The troubled adult reception associated with *The Monkees* and the stark disjunction between its appeal to the young versus the not-so-young can tell us something about the breakdown of consensual taste values. And if taste distinctions are but a component of a larger ideological and hegemonic structure of normalized values, then a rift over taste can herald other rifts to come. The young fans of *The Monkees* were unlikely to be fully participative members of the counterculture, although the show's producers did try to court that audience by bringing on countercultural icons such as Frank Zappa. One should note, too, that the teenybopper *Monkees* fan of 1966 was quite likely to be a college student by 1969 and 1970. Although no television program, with the notable exception of *The Smothers Brothers Comedy Hour,* was ever able to garner any significant degree of youth movement support and regular viewership, *The Monkees* can be located within the same set of anxieties and moral panics that the burgeoning counterculture evoked among adult observers.[21] *The Monkees* may have been a decidedly scrubbed-down version of this counterculture, but enough signs of the new youth movement remained within the circulated meanings of the show to cause uneasiness.

It was not only the Monkees' hair and music, however, that indicated a breakdown in normalized values and tastes; the very style of the show suggested anarchy and uncontrolled youthful mayhem. The actors playing the Monkees didn't act or perform in any conventional manner: they "romped."[22] During preproduction Schneider and Rafelson, with rookie director James Frawley, decided they needed to ignore the rules of television production and shake things up. They set up a six-week improvisational workshop with Micky, Davy, Pete, and Mike where they perfected the zaniness that came to typify the series.[23] This spontaneous anarchism also reigned on the set. *TV Guide,* in a 1967 cover story, detailed the rather unorthodox methods used by directors Frawley, Rafelson, and others to film the series. Scenes were underlit or overlit, and the camera kept running after a scene was supposedly over. Schneider and Rafelson deliberately employed young, inexperienced directors because older professionals refused to work the ways the show's producers demanded. From Schneider's point of view, "it's impossible to reach into the same pool of talent where everybody else reaches because then you're not going to get innovators, you'll get imitators. Our attitude was 'we're jumping off the bridge here, there's no point in going halfway.' " [24] One disgruntled director grumbled: "If you don't care about your focus or your lighting, and if you're going to let four idiots ad-lib your dialogue, you don't need a director." [25] The bewilderment and contempt evident in this remark mirrored much of the adult response to the burgeoning hippie phenomenon with its antiauthoritarian, nonhierarchical, "let it all hang out" philosophies. *The Monkees* also refused to conform, refused to function within prescribed boundaries of professional competency and deference to authority figures. The series refused to play by the established rules. Adult audiences and critics expressed distinct unease with this. Professional, experienced television personnel did so as well.

Of all people, LSD "guru" Timothy Leary grasped what was going on with the series and in his 1968 book, *The Politics of Ecstasy,* tried to convince his hip readers of the show's psychedelic subversiveness:

> . . . the Monkees use the new energies to sing the new songs and pass on the new message.
>
> The Monkees' television show, for example. Oh, you thought that was silly teen-age entertainment? Don't be fooled. While it lasted, it was a classic Sufi put-on. An early-Christian electronic satire. A mystic magic show. A jolly Buddha laugh at hypocrisy. At early evening kiddie-time on Monday the Monkees would rush through a parody drama, burlesquing the very shows that glue Mom and Dad to the set during prime time. Spoofing the movies and violence and the down-heavy-conflict-emotion themes that fascinate the middle-aged.
>
> And woven into the fast-moving psychedelic stream of action were the prophetic, holy, challenging words. Micky was rapping quickly, dropping literary names, making scholarly references; then the sudden psychedelic switch of the reality channel. He looked straight at

the camera, right into your living room, and up-leveled the comedy by saying, "Pretty good talking for a long-haired weirdo, huh, Mr. and Mrs. America?" And then—zap. Flash. Back to the innocuous comedy.[26]

The Monkees did burlesque not only the shows that Mom and Pop watched but many of the values associated with the older generation. One episode, titled "The Chaperone," suggests how the show "monkeed" around with dominant values and institutions. In the episode, which aired November 7, 1966, the dreamy Davy falls for a lovely young blonde. Unfortunately her father is an authoritarian military general who runs his family like boot camp. The boys scheme to get past the general and into the girl's home. In one sequence Micky and Davy impersonate bomb shelter inspectors. Ringing the doorbell, they encounter the girl's father who bombastically informs them, "I'll have you know I was a *general* in the last war!" Davy looks up in mock reverence, "You were?" "Well," answers the general, loosening up, "that was a long time ago. I've put all that military nonsense behind me now." Catching himself, the general reasserts his military posture and bellows to the shuffling Monkees, "Stand at attention when you're addressing me! Dismissed!"

In another scheme the Monkees try to get the young girl past her father by throwing a chaperoned party—the only kind the general will allow her to attend. Calling the general on the phone, Micky impersonates a British colonel friend of his from the Battle of the Bulge and says he's throwing a chaperoned party for his son: "You know—twisting, frugging, cha-cha-cha—all that sort of rot. All the military families will be represented." The four boys gather around the phone as Micky does his over-the-top characterization. Behind them on the wall is a framed picture declaring, "Money is the root of all evil." Cut to the general's office. Behind him is a poster declaring, "Defend your country." In the foreground, holding the phone, we see the general, who, for no apparent reason, is decked out in full combat fatigues. On his helmet hang camouflage tree fronds. In his free hand he carries a riding crop. As he moves to his desk, the camera zooms back and we see a grouping of toy soldiers and tanks in combat positions assembled on the desktop. During his absurd conversation with "Colonel Dolenz" the general moves the toy soldiers around, at one point looking boyishly satisfied with the arrangement.

"Defend your country." Spoofing militarism;
the general playing with his toy soldiers.

The general agrees to allow his daughter to come to the party.
Micky ends up dressing in drag to impersonate their chaperone. Inevitably the general is smitten and refuses to leave the party. Cor-
ralled on a couch by the love-struck general, Micky notices a medal
on the general's dress uniform. "Oh, my late husband won a ribbon
like this for doing something to help shorten the war." "Oh, what
did he do?" "He deserted." The show contains an obligatory musical
number during the party. Young teens dance with great delight — one
young woman with bare midriff shimmying around the general — as
the Monkees deliver a somewhat trippy invitation to "Come with me,

Micky, in drag, fending off the advances of the
smitten general.

leave yesterday behind / And take a giant step outside your mind."
In the midst of all this the segment includes a muscle man striking
poses first to impress a thoroughly uninterested young woman. He
then succeeds in impressing a Mr. Clean impersonator sporting bald
head, gold earring, and very clean white shirt—thus extending the
homoerotic comic play already established between Micky and the
unsuspecting general. Eventually the general discovers he has been
hoodwinked. After the innocent rambunctiousness of dancing, the
general reasserts military discipline over the party-goers. Shouting
"*Hut*-two-three-four. *Hut*-two-three-four" over and over again, the
teenagers all begin marching like soldiers until they've all filed right
out of the Monkees' pad. Thus do military discipline and military
values destroy youthful pleasures.

The playful antimilitarism in this episode becomes more significant if we put it within the context of television programming that
surrounded it in 1966. In the mid-1960s prime time featured numerous comedies and dramas extolling the heroism of World War II
fighters. Most asserted that war was fun, painless, exciting, a good
way to meet lovely ladies, and a great way to bond with other heroic
men. In military comedies one did not laugh at the military as an
institution or at military men. Gomer Pyle was funny not because
he was a marine but because he was a slow-witted southern hick.
In *Hogan's Heroes,* the World War II prisoner-of-war comedy, only

the Nazis were portrayed as buffoons. The Allied prisoners, although funny, were heroes, always able to outwit the enemy Germans and assist the war effort. Television historian J. Fred MacDonald has observed, "There was in this escapism, however, a sociological dimension. These war stories and comedic encounters prolonged the inability of the American citizenry to confront the reality of war. TV showed stylized armed conflict in which virile Yank soldiers triumphed in the end and comedic farce stripped war of its brutal, violent, murderous nature."[27] The *Monkees* episode deviated quite distinctly from this war-is-good prime-time orthodoxy. In the show's attempt to speak with a counterculture accent, it depicted war and warriors as absurd. Militarism denied liberty and freedom; military discipline and military culture were anathema to youth culture. One couldn't dance while in parade march formation. The comedic antiwar position evident in *The Monkees* would not appear again in prime time until the Smothers Brothers battled with CBS to bring some of this discourse to the tube. Antiwar comedy would not finally really succeed in prime time until 1972, when the overtly antiwar *M*A*S*H* began its long and hugely popular run.

Dolenz, Jones, Tork, and Nesmith chaffed against their status as the Prefab Four. They disliked their bubblegum image and the fact that they were not allowed to play instruments or have much control over the production of their hugely popular record albums. They wanted to be taken seriously as a group by the counterculture. As their television show entered its second and last season, the Monkees attempted to display their "hipness."[28] Gone were the Beatlesque moptops. Micky adopted a wild and woolly Afro; Pete's blonde locks got considerably longer; Mike's sideburns turned into mutton chops. Their look-alike outfits gave way to love beads, Indian robes, and other psychedelic garb. They also used their show to deconstruct their manufactured status. In one famous episode near the very end of the series' run, titled "Monkees Blow Their Minds," rock put-on artist Frank Zappa appears with Mike, and the two argue over the artistic merits of Monkee music. Zappa adopted Mike's knitted cap, and Nesmith donned funny nose and fright wig to impersonate Zappa. The presence of Zappa, the very epitome of countercultural hip, seemed calculated to bestow on the Monkees a certain amount of perverse hip authenticity. During the exchange Nesmith-as-Zappa rails against the Monkees commercialization and political shallow-

The Monkees go psychedelic: longer hair, hippie garb, and attempts at deconstructing their manufactured image. *(Author's collection)*

ness.[29] The Monkees may not have been able to get out of their prefab box, but by pointing out its construction and critiquing it, they tried to show that they were not complicit with a commodity system that in fact created them. These anxieties about media co-optation and incorporation would be articulated again and again within counter-cultural circles as network television became more enamored of the hippie phenomenon in the years ahead. The Monkees may have been the first "plastic hippies," but plenty would follow. Few, however, would work so actively to subvert themselves.

Prime-Time Hippies

As the hippie scene in the Haight-Ashbury began to gain more and more media attention through 1967, both the networks and local public stations flooded the airwaves with news reports and documentaries on the new phenomenon. One of the first major network at-

tempts to explain what was going on with America's turned-on youth
was the *CBS News Special,* "The Hippie Temptation," reported by
Harry Reasoner and broadcast on August 22, 1967.[30] Reasoner's narration carried all the various moral panics about youthful chaos and
disorder. The "temptation" in the title referred, of course, to the lure
of LSD. The report focused almost obsessively on the dangers posed
by hallucinogenics, showing interviews with acidheads confined to
the psych ward and with psychologists who claimed LSD made interpersonal love impossible. Yet for a certain segment of the viewing
audience Reasoner's gloom-and-doom narration may have been subverted by the documentary's images. At the beginning of the report
Reasoner was filmed walking down Haight Street while speaking to
the camera. The correspondent walked stiffly in his dark suit, his face
arranged in serious lines, while all around him swarmed eccentri-
cally attired hippies, smiling bemusedly and glancing into the camera.
At another point in the program, the CBS cameras filmed the action
at the Avalon Ballroom, with its swirling, dancing bodies and hyp-
notic light shows. Reasoner's grim commentary admitted that it all
seemed highly exciting, "a veritable trip into Wonderland—until one
begins to wonder about destinations." However, the provocative and
tantalizing imagery kept escaping the anchoring function of the verbal description.[31] Some of the possible, perhaps preferable, meanings
evoked by the images were pleasure, bodily liberation, wonderment.
The commentary had to work just that much harder to deny those
meanings and to insist that this was all "dreamy narcosis," "lifestyle
without content," "grotesqueries."

In the end Reasoner, with the help of Dr. David Smith, head of the
Haight-Ashbury Free Medical Clinic, attempted to contain all this
documented behavior within a notion of pathology. Hippiedom was
a medical condition. The Haight scene was a symptom. Dr. Smith attempted to place the blame on middle-class society, but despite that,
his commentary assisted in constructing a discourse of the counterculture as "disorder"—both medical and social. Yet, on the other
hand, the documentary's tantalizing images kept spilling out and over
Reasoner's reasoned containment box of commentary.

This moral panic regarding turned-on youth also appeared in early
fictional representations of television hippies. Probably the first such
representation aired January 12, 1967, in the premiere episode of *Drag-*

net '67, producer and star Jack Webb's attempt to return his successful 1950s cop show to the airways. Entitled "The Big LSD," the episode drew on recent news reports about the hallucinogen (which
remained legal until October 1966), as well as stories about the Sunset Strip scene.[32] In monotone voice-over to images of Los Angeles,
Webb as Sergeant Friday declared, "This is the city." His voice-over
went on to discuss young people looking for something. Over shots
of churches, temples, and mosques, Friday said these were places to
find oneself. A college degree would be another means to find oneself. However, young people would find nothing in a capsule of LSD.
"When they try—that's when I come in. I carry a badge." *Dum-da-
dum-dum.*

Friday and partner Gannon were called to the scene of a weirdly
painted juvenile chewing the bark off a tree. The scene opened with
the cops finding the young man lying on the ground with his head
buried under leaves. As they pulled him up, there was a cut to a
shocker close-up of the young man's face—painted blue on one side,
gold on the other. Wide-eyed, he exclaimed, "Reality, man, reality. I
could see the center of the earth!" As Friday attempted to read him his
rights, the boy declared that he wasn't here, but there—and had green
hair: "I'm a tree!" Flipping out, he tore at Gannon's suit, then started
calling out various colors: "I can hear them all!" This hyperbolic representation has much in common with the wildlife on display in "The
Hippie Temptation." Friday and Gannon affected the same grim, stiff,
highly rational demeanor toward this drug-crazed, out-of-control
youth culture as would Harry Reasoner. Both fictional and documentary discourses focused on the sheer bizarreness of psychedelic
hippie culture and attempted to find conventional means to define
it—thus presumably to bring it under control. In the *Dragnet* episode
Friday and Gannon couldn't book the hallucinating youth for having
ingested a still-legal drug, so they held him for being "in danger of
leading an idle, immoral or dissolute life," according to Friday's voice-
over. Whereas "The Hippie Temptation" tried to contain hippiedom
as medical pathology, *Dragnet* contained it as social pathology.

Beyond its hyperbolic representations, the *Dragnet* episode exhibited a noteworthy difficulty in its attempt to depict the hallucinogenic state. When the law criminalizing LSD finally came down, Friday and Gannon eagerly went to work breaking up an acid party.
Garish red lights were used to suggest deviance and decadence. "Acid-

Hyperbolic hippie: acid–tripping Blue Boy looking
into the center of the earth; shocker close-up: the
face of hippie pathology.

heads" danced or lounged around languidly, suggesting an opium den
more than an LSD party. Friday and Gannon advised the kids to "try
to sober up and listen" as the detectives read them their constitutional
rights. Confronted with an alternative cultural phenomenon at odds
with dominant norms, Jack Webb was forced to make sense of it from
within the familiar categories and representational strategies used to
indicate drunken or narcotic states. The counterculture initially, at
least, evaded the dominant culture's attempts at fictional portrayal.
Documentary representations, as we saw, threatened to erupt out of
attempts to contain them within hegemonic definitions. Only when

Problems of representation: acid party as opium den;
more problems of representation: acidhead costumed
like a beatnik and sucking on a paint brush.

those aligned with the counterculture began circulating their own representations of the hallucinogenic state through creative works such as posters, underground film, and acid-rock music did the culture industries find a means to more closely imitate, co-opt, and incorporate a version of the counterculture. The political usefulness of these early depictions of rebellious sixties youth was precisely the ways in which these texts got it all wrong. How they got it wrong showcased a historically specific instance of establishment power's anxiety and weakness in the face of a phenomenon that defied strategies of definition—and thus containment.

Although *Dragnet* was clearly articulating the fears of the adult and parent generation, *Variety*, in its review of "The Big LSD," read the episode as appealing to those eighteen and under. Somehow, if the text dealt with a youth theme, it should appeal to youth. The review emphasized that in this year of the youth, "those shows that the kids have stuck with generally survived and those that have not passed muster with the teeners have fallen. It is this fickle and charismatic group that will determine whether 'Dragnet 1967' becomes 'Dragnet 1968.' "[33] *Dragnet* did indeed survive, with a run lasting until 1971, and it dealt frequently with themes of crazed hippies and demonstrating students. However, it is questionable whether the show appealed at all to a youth audience, specifically a countercultural one. On the one hand, the show—with its deadpan style of delivery, its obsessive attention to the minutiae of police work, its periodic "law 'n' order" lectures by Webb, and its consistently bad acting and writing—could have been read as camp. Certainly the show's current popularity in syndication relies almost entirely on its camp appeal. However, a review by Lawrence Lipton in the *Los Angeles Free Press* suggests that such a reading strategy may have been a difficult one to adopt at this moment in time. Lipton, an aging Beat now aligned closely with the more overtly politicized segments of the counterculture, assumed a tone of outrage after having viewed the *Dragnet* premiere. It should be noted that Lipton seemed to be perpetually in a state of outrage, and his column indicated an almost total absence of humor.

> "DRAGNET," DRUGS, DRAG-ASS DIRTY DISHONESTY: The debut of "Dragnet" as a TV series, another notable event on last Thursday night television. Cowardice, self-interest, fear, ignorance, these things are understandable, pathetic, human. Malice aforethought and deliberate falsification, these are evil and not even worthy of pity. . . . This series starts off as malicious mis-representation in every word, every scene, every prop even. Not one minute of the show bore any relationship to anything or anybody living or dead in the world of LSD. It was simply a mishmash of all the lying newspaper and police stereotypes.[34]

Lipton's palpable anger reveals an inability to step back from the image and take a knowing pleasure in its inept construction. The revolutionary potential of the counterculture and the youth movement in general to radically change the social order was still in its shiny and hopeful infancy at the beginning of 1967 for those involved. In such a politically charged atmosphere, it may have been impossible to make camp readings of the dominant culture's renditions of a revolutionary movement. The stakes were too high. The enemy was too clear. Camp readings may require a more distanced, detached, somewhat mocking critical stance. Such qualities were, of necessity, lacking in those participating in movements for radical social, political, or psychic change. The distance provided by a camp reading strategy could also insulate the reader/viewer from the painfulness of certain representations. Lipton's review, in all its fury and indignation, suggests that viewing such examples of the dominant culture's moral panics about youth may have been psychically wounding.

In the aftermath of "the Summer of Love" media extravaganza television hippies began popping up all over prime time, especially on law-and-order programs.[35] A number of themes recurred from one show to another, from one portrayal to another. These recurring themes provide clues to the contradictory nature of the dominant society's response to this dissident youth threat to prevailing norms and values. The contradictions in figuring the televisual hippie point to a growing crisis in the commonsensical acceptance of those norms and values. Villains, victims, and heroes no longer provided stable categories. Binaries of "good kids" versus "bad kids" were continually thrown into question. The only social category not up for serious excavation was the "Great White Father" as representative of the rational, benevolent institution of law and order.

Portrayals of middle- and upper-middle-class youth who were essentially and frighteningly duplicitous served as one site for the playing out of establishment anxieties about the younger generation. Surface markers provided no guide to indicate a crazed, out-of-control acidhead or a normal teenager. This theme appeared most hysterically in the widely acclaimed and highly rated *CBS Playhouse* drama, "The People Next Door," broadcast October 15, 1968.[36] The program was heavily promoted as the work of anthology drama veteran J. P. Miller, who wrote the play in response to his concern about his own son having dropped out and become a hippie.[37] The well-acted drama dealt with a middle-class suburban couple, their two children—the son a disaffected, guitar-playing rebel and the daugh-

ter a sweet, quiet, blonde, young teen—and the couple next door
with their clean-cut, honor-roll son. As the story unfolded, the first
couple discovered that their supposedly innocent daughter, Maxie,
was in fact a drug addict living a double life. She slept around and
hung out with unsavory characters in the East Village. The upstanding boy next door was the drug pusher who turned Maxie on—and
had done the same for most of the teens in the neighborhood. The
freaky-looking son, on the other hand, turned out to be the good
kid. The narrative attempted to explain Maxie's behavior by mobilizing the same discourse of hippiedom-as-medical-pathology evident
in "The Hippie Temptation." She ended up confined to a psych ward,
and doctors informed her parents that she had strong self-destructive
tendencies and would need to be in a "controlled environment" in-
definitely. The drama provided a few glimpses of Maxie's point of
view. The opening scene, a get-together of both families, provided a
series of pointed close-ups of the adults engaging in hypocritical activities as Maxie looked on. Her father fondled the neighbor's wife,
and all the adults drank and smoked excessively while railing against
youthful drug abuse. However, despite Maxie's later admission that
she had experimented with LSD to become a better person (unlike
her "phoney" parents) and because mom and dad had made her "uptight," Maxie's discourse never carried much explanatory power. In
the end there really was no reason for her deviance. Particularly noteworthy in the construction of this drama was Miller's attempt to
negotiate the dominant adult terror of rebellious youth. The youth
who looked and seemed to act in a deviant manner—the son with
his long hair, funny glasses, and guitar—was not deviant at all. The
clean-cut "good" kids turned out to be the truly frightening ones. On
the one hand, the drama painted the drug-oriented counterculture
as a highly contagious disease that could infect anyone's youngsters.
On the other hand, the text left open a reading of the counterculture
as essentially a smokescreen hiding some deeper pathology that had
nothing to do with the surface signifiers of the movement. Hippies
could, in fact, be good kids—provided they no longer did drugs. (In
a confrontation with his mother, who had found a joint presumably
belonging to Maxie, the son affirmed that he no longer needed drugs;
his music was turn-on enough.)

Harlan Ellison, television critic for the *Free Press,* did not find any
affirming meanings within this text. Adopting a reading position

similar to Lawrence Lipton's response to *Dragnet*'s "The Big LSD," Ellison railed against the drama's dishonesty and hypocrisy:

> It was the vocal statement of a man who is confused and terrified by the things young people are doing today, a statement that did not comprehend the blame lies in the venality and alienation of the older generations. . . .
>
> One can only conjecture what effect Miller's play had on the errant son. Were I he, it would have solidified once and finally my feelings that Dad was a phony intellectual, and a man to distrust simply because he knows not where it's at. Nor where it's going to be.[38]

An episode called "Trip to Hashbury" in the detective show *Ironside,* broadcast March 21, 1968, also mined the theme of youthful duplicity.[39] The narrative concerned a seemingly clean-cut girl, Barbara, whom Ironside and his young assistants found hanging around a hippie communal pad. She accused Ironside's assistant, Ed, of beating her; she then lapsed inconveniently into a coma and died. Clearly Ed would never engage in police brutality, so the wheelchair-bound detective needed to find out who actually did beat the young woman to death. As Ironside, Ed, Eva, and Mark delved into Barbara's story, it became clear that she, like Maxie in "The People Next Door," had been leading a double life. Barbara had told her father that she was "studying" the hippies and encouraging them to stop their drug use. In fact, she was totally caught up in the world of "Freddy's Pad," the name of the communal house run by a clearly evil middle-aged hippie leader. During his investigation of Barbara's background, Ironside obtained a diagnosis of the young woman's problem from her high school principal. She had low self-esteem and bad grades, which caused her to drop her academic courses. "Continued failure leads to lack of self-respect. That leads to Haight-Ashbury." Again, the hippie counterculture was a medical-social pathology, a recourse for those with inferiority complexes and low IQ's. As in "The People Next Door," a crucial villain of the piece was not a hippie but a clean-cut kid who masqueraded as a hippie on weekends. This villain, Barbara's boyfriend, David, initially appeared sporting short hair, a cardigan sweater, and exhibiting impeccable manners—the product of an opulent upper-middle-class household. In the end Ironside deduced that David had killed Barbara. The detective and company discovered the boy tripping badly on STP at Freddy's Pad and wearing a long-haired wig to cover his conservative appearance. Like the neighbor's boy in "The People Next Door," David had introduced Barbara to drugs and the world of Freddy's Pad.

The same essential plot recurred in an episode of *The Name of the Game,* "High on a Rainbow," broadcast December 6, 1968.[40] June Allyson played the status-conscious mother of a young girl caught up in the drug culture. The seemingly respectable college boy that Allyson had been pushing at her daughter turned out to be the drug pusher responsible for her descent into hallucinogenic debauchery.

We can make sense of these representations of seemingly "good kids" who were in fact deviant, evil Others from within a larger American cultural context of the fear of "the enemy within." A recurring trope of 1950s "Red Scare" narratives typically involved communists who looked just like upstanding, patriotic citizens. The moral panic revolved around the difficulty in differentiating the subversives from the good Americans. In the case of 1960s out-of-control, subversive youth and popular narratives about them, the return of this trope may suggest something about many adult Americans' anxieties at encountering rebellion and disaffection so close to home.[41]

All these programs also displayed a certain amount of criticism directed at the hypocrisy of the parental generation. The June Allyson character (played against Allyson's persona of the wholesome, bright, cheery all-American female) was shallow, destructive, and even violent, slapping her daughter after hearing the truth about what had happened to her. Barbara's parents in the *Ironside* episode were divorced, and one of Barbara's friends criticized them for being like all parents, incapable of recognizing their children's troubles. The friend, also immersed in the counterculture scene, asked how she could go home and fit into her mother's cookie mold, when she, the daughter, was bent?

Adults with power were also often portrayed as evil figures luring innocent or duped young people into psychedelic purgatory. "Trip to Hashbury" went to some lengths to emphasize Freddy's bald spot and paunch along with his far-out hippie costume and over-the-top slang. The teenaged hippies, on the other hand, shown strewn around the pad listening to a rock band, were portrayed mostly in a neutral manner with an emphasis on their bizarre costume but childlike demeanor. As Ironside's aides Eve and Ed moved stiffly and ill at ease around this assemblage trying to get someone to identify a photo of Barbara, the hippies appeared uninhibited and free in contrast to the detectives' strict formality. Hippies presented flowers to the law enforcement officers, which the establishment icons didn't seem to know what to do with. Scenes with Freddy, by contrast, played up his sinister quality. During an interrogation with Ironside, shots focused on Freddy's bald spot and on the outlandish, rectangular shades he never removed. When he was informed that Barbara had just died, his only response was "Poof!"

An episode of *Hawaii Five-O* featured a more obvious Timothy Leary figure, a college professor kicked out of his job for turning on half the student body.[42] Two of his victims were pretty, young females. One attempted to fly off a cliff, killing herself in the process. This episode showcases a recurring theme of young women as victims. In the context of a patriarchal discourse of women's essential weakness and malleability, these texts could forgive their female acid-heads to some extent and place the blame more emphatically on the evil, older male with power. The savior, however, usually turned out to be the good, older male with power—in this case state police official McGarrett.[43] By gendering the counterculture as feminine, these texts attempted to negotiate a representation of this youthful phenomenon that was not entirely negative. However, this strategy only reinforced sexist discourses.[44]

Many television portrayals of hippies contained these tortured attempts at negotiation. A certain amount of blame had to be meted out to the older generation, and the young had to be shown as not wholly to blame for their actions. Such concessions were unlikely to provide young people aligned with the counterculture a pleasurable way into these texts because they would not view their psychedelic practices and ways of being as problematic or as requiring the placement of blame. We can make sense of the negotiations going on in these texts by seeing them as preliminary and tentative attempts to shift and reconfigure the no longer "commonsensical" postwar system of conformity to and unquestioning acceptance of a suburban status quo. The drug culture remained taboo and the psychic and transformative possibilities offered by psychedelic drugs could never be negotiated in mass-mediated popular texts. Yet some of the values attached to drug and counterculture milieus were supported in these texts. Roland Barthes's theory of "inoculation" provides one means to explain this cultural process. Barthes argued that dominant formations will accept into the discourses they produce a small dose of that which threatens them precisely in order to strengthen their positions of power.[45] But were these doses of counterhegemonic discourse doing that job? They were certainly not succeeding in luring back the psychedelic young who were producing these challenges to the dominant system of norms and values. In fact, as we will see, some counterculture and radical youth actively deconstructed this very process of attempted incorporation and used these deconstructions as yet more weapons in their ideological struggle against capture. The most that we can say about these televisual negotiations was that older television viewers who may have been more ideologically aligned with hegemonic elites may have had selective aspects of their "common sense" questioned even as they were having some of their anxieties reassured.

This process of ideological realignment within hegemonic formations could be difficult and open to active resistance. One television viewer quoted by *TV Guide* provides a clue to the adult reception of all these prime-time hippies: "Having become satiated viewing TV coverage of dirty hippies, riots, drug users and ungrateful kooks and their insufferable behavior, it was encouraging and uplifting to see and hear the CBS presentation, 'Miss Teenage America Pageant.' It is good to realize that our country is not all delinquent and that refinement and good taste still have a place in our land."[46]

Domesticating Hippies

Although network television could not negotiate the phenomenon of psychedelic youth drug culture, many shows labored to find ways to portray the flower children sympathetically. The extent to which representations of the hippie counterculture could be separated from mind-altering substances determined the degree of favor or approval attached to those representations. Clearly the hippies of "Freddy's Pad" were constructed as dupes. However, the narrative attempted to focus the moral panic elsewhere. The hippies themselves evaded the disciplining and juridical mechanisms of law and order, and Freddy and David, who were not "true" hippies, ended up the recipients of discipline and punishment.

Other network offerings also tried to find tactics for dealing sympathetically with the social and cultural disaffection of their video hippies. One means to help defuse and disarm some dominant outrage about the counterculture's antiestablishment practices involved displacing the entire phenomenon into the future or into the past. *Star Trek* tried this with its space-age flower children in a February 21, 1969, episode, "The Way to Eden." *Bonanza* tried it with post–Civil War hippies in "The Weary Willies," broadcast September 27, 1970.

The *Star Trek* episode perpetuated the evil-adult-with-power narrative. The *Enterprise* intercepted a stolen spaceship commanded by a mad genius and his collection of colorful and eccentric young people. They were on a journey to locate the planet Eden, a pure, natural utopia far removed from the computerized, totally fabricated world of the twenty-third century. The *Enterprise*'s young guests sported hippie-inspired clothing, spoke a hippie-like slang, and carried musical instruments reminiscent of guitars and tambourines. They took an immediate dislike to Captain Kirk, who was depicted in this episode as rigid, officious, intolerant, and stuffy. The space hippies ridiculed him (the twenty-third-century slang for "square drip" being "Herbert") and staged a starship sit-in when initially refused free use of the *Enterprise*. Logical science officer Mr. Spock, on the other hand, responded quite sympathetically to the youths, engaging in a literally spaced-out jam session with them and using the *Enterprise*'s computer to try to locate the planet Eden. The episode is open to both positive and negative readings of these back-to-the-future hippies. They were clearly the dupes of an evil demagogue and finally highjacked the *Enterprise* to Eden. Arriving on the planet, they were promptly burned and poisoned by the "acid" that composed the vegetation on the surface. In the end their leader died from having eaten of the fruit of Eden; the young followers returned to "civilization" apparently contrite, chastened children.

More positively, the narrative opened a space for a sustained attack on conformist technological society. "The Way to Eden," unlike the vast majority of *Star Trek* episodes, questioned and challenged the benefits and superiority of the technocomputerized universe put into place by the supposedly utopian United Federation of Planets. Spock's position as ally to the space hippies, against a fairly unattractive Kirk, strengthened and, to some extent, legitimized that critique. By displacing the ideological dispute into the future and, for the most part, dispensing with the issue of drugs (except at the end—

and, even then, only punningly), the episode allowed for a reading of the counterculture and its rebellion against the dominant social order that was equivocally sympathetic.

The *Bonanza* episode about the "Weary Willies," whom the *TV Guide* synopsis described as "hippielike drifters who wandered through the West after the Civil War," also exhibited ambivalence in its portrayal but seemed, ultimately, even more supportive.[47] A trio of long-haired, guitar-playing young men wearing ragged Union and Confederate uniforms drifted into Virginia City and met revulsion from the townspeople, who saw them as lazy, shiftless troublemakers. Nevertheless, Ben Cartwright, patriarch of the Ponderosa Ranch, allowed them to set up camp on a portion of his land. He offered them work in the local mine, but the narrative made it clear that the Willies were totally disinclined to submit themselves to labor. The main Weary Willie character, Billy, played by Richard Thomas (soon to become familiar as John Boy Walton), became enamored with the local shopkeeper's pretty blonde daughter, Angie. The Weary Willy encampment soon resembled a hippie commune as large numbers of long-haired, bedraggled male and female Willies started congregating there, tearing down trees to make makeshift shelters. Ben Cartwright considered throwing them off his land, but Angie interceded, saying that the Willies were "good people." A romantic scene between Billy and Angie concluded with Billy trying to explain the Willy philosophy of life. He quoted a Walt Whitman poem: "What do you suppose could satisfy the soul except to walk free and know no superior." The townspeople continued to mobilize themselves against the Willies and against the Cartwrights. The narrative culminated with a vicious assault on Angie for which the Willies were blamed. Rampaging through the Willy commune, the townspeople burned it to the ground and pointedly smashed Billy's guitar. In by now a familiar narrative device, the bad guy was not a Willie but a supposedly upstanding young townsman whose affections Angie had spurned in favor of Billy. The true villain used his attempted violation of Angie as a pretext to launch an attack on the Willies.

As Billy stood amid the smoldering ruins of the commune, Little Joe and Ben Cartwright appeared. Ben offered to replace what the townspeople had destroyed if the Willies would stay on. Billy said no. Ben asked if he really thought things would be different in the next town. Billy, suppressing tears throughout the scene, replied that he hoped people would stop being suspicious, greedy, and violent.

> *Ben:* And be what—like you? The world full of people like you?
> *Billy:* Would that be so bad?
> *Ben:* No. The world isn't just going to stop, sit under a tree in the shade, dream about the future. You have to make the future.
> *Billy:* It ain't gonna be me, Mr. Cartwright, cause I don't like this world.
> *Ben:* Then change it, Billy. Don't withdraw from it. Become part of it. Make it better.
> *Billy:* Why should I?
> *Ben:* Because it's the only world you've got.

The paternalistic criticism of the Willies' disengagement from their post–Civil War social order may have been ideologically obligatory; however, more noteworthy was the episode's message of tolerance for a countercultural position. Such a message seems particularly remarkable because it appeared on a program that catered to a viewing demographic least likely to be open-minded about disaffected young people. Just as Spock in the *Star Trek* episode helped legitimize its space-age hippies, so the Cartwright clan helped to give sanction to its Civil War hippies. The episode also ventured a subtle antiwar position. Willies were returned vets from both the Union and Confederacy who could not integrate into postwar society and, thus, found comradeship with each other despite their former status as enemies. The undeveloped theme suggested that the experience of war itself had made social integration impossible. More developed was a theme of combating the fear and hatred directed by the socially dominant toward the socially disaffected. Ben Cartwright, as Great White Father, functioned to sanction the countercultural stance of the Willies, even while he offered an alternative position.

Televisual texts striving to negotiate more positive and less panicked representations of hippiedom had other strategies on which to draw. One recurring method involved focusing on the "hippie chick." Domesticating the counterculture might be an easier proposition if it could first be feminized.

Popular culture female hippies encompassed a series of apparent contradictions. They were both innocent and highly sexualized.

They were idealistically rebellious and malleable. They existed out-side traditional gender norms and structures and conformed to those norms and structures. Patriarchal myths of "the Feminine" informed the representation of the "hippie chick," at times making the figure threatening (because of its status as the Other) and at times mitigating that threat (because of its status as nonphallic).[48]

An episode of *Marcus Welby, M.D.*, broadcast early in 1970 typi-fies these contradictions. Titled "Madonna with Knapsack and Flute," the program suggested an updating of the virgin/whore myth to a counterculture context.[49] The narrative revolved around Dr. Welby's female friend Myra and her growing attachment to a waif-like, preg-nant young hippie, Tracy. The girl was an unmarried orphan who had just drifted down from the Haight-Ashbury. She had a bad case of mononucleosis, which caused her to faint regularly, but she was adamant about wanting to keep her baby and not be cooped up in any regulated environment. The narrative conflict revolved around Welby's attempt to control her activities for the good of the baby and Myra's attempt to mold Tracy into the image of her own deceased daughter. Used to being independent and free to come and go, Tracy continually wandered off, only to be found, finally, on the Sunset Strip in labour. As it turned out she had been looking for and had finally found the baby's father there. Myra's "sensible" plan involved Tracy and the baby coming to live with her. Tracy, however, wanted to move herself and the baby in with the unemployed hippie father. Welby, as the voice of patriarchal authority, sided with Tracy's plan, affirming to Myra, "Even though we don't approve, we'd better start to realize that these kids have some pretty different ideas of values."

On the one hand, Welby's pronouncement indicated a rather un-ambiguous validation of structureless, commodityless counterculture lifestyles. On the other hand, the validation wasn't all that radical because Tracy was being knitted into a nuclear family unit. At the end we see her fulfilling the "essential" aspects of femininity—loving mother and dutiful homemaker. The narrative emphasized that Tracy did not get pregnant because of promiscuity but rather through a love union that, although it may not have received the legal sanc-tion of a marriage license, nevertheless resulted in the constitution of the couple in the final scene. The ways that Tracy conformed to hegemonic notions of proper femininity helped to defuse much of the threat posed by her hippiedom.

The presence of the "hippie chick" could also be used to defuse an otherwise menacing representation of hippies in general. *Bracken's World,* a series that revolved around the actors, directors, and producers of a fictitious motion picture studio, dealt with this theme in the September 25, 1970, episode, "Murder Off-Camera."[50] The wife of one of the show's recurring characters, director Kevin Grant, had been murdered. Grant's son was found in the company of a hippie couple who claimed they found him bound and gagged by the side of the road. Eerie sitar riffs played on the soundtrack whenever the hippies entered a scene, and suspicion immediately fell on them. Much to Grant's alarm, the boy was completely captivated by the couple's charm. The male hippie appeared a threatening and aggressive character. The narrative suggested he wasn't what he seemed. The female hippie appeared far less ambiguous. She was all sweetness and light. Her costuming in a very short, lacy and frilly dress both emphasized her sexuality and evoked a little-girl innocence. The affection she lavished on Grant's now motherless son heightened her maternal qualities even as she and her more ominous partner displayed the qualities of rootless, rather parasitical wanderers.

As it turned out, the hippies were entirely innocent. Grant's housekeeper's nephew, a clean-cut boy who just happened to have a bad STP addiction, killed Grant's wife in a botched burglary and, seeing the hippies in the area, tried to pin the guilt on them. In the final scene studio head Bracken and Grant engaged in some liberal guilt about how, between the two suspects, they would have picked the hippies.

The denouement tried to negotiate the frequently negative representations of the hippies, especially the male one. His innocence ended up being affirmed mainly by the less conflicted representation of his female partner. Her childlike innocence was never in much doubt. Her gender made such a portrayal more readily acceptable given that the patriarchal feminine contained within it a naturalized notion of the essential childishness of Woman and of her existence outside the social realm. It was more problematic to attach these attributes to a representation of the male because the crossing or blurring of those gender markers could lead to certain amounts of cultural anxiety. Therefore, his apparent childishness (he was shown romping and dancing playfully with the female hippie) had to be subject to doubt. In the end the narrative could not really resolve the suspicions about the male hippie. His innocence was proclaimed almost by *deus ex machina*. Representations of the hippie chick carried no such dilemmas.

When the hippie chick refused to conform to notions of the patriarchal feminine, the situation was radically different. Maxie, in "The People Next Door," appeared initially to fall within the appropriate definitions as childlike, sweet, and ethereally blonde.[51] The revelation of her "true" identity was shocking because it totally subverted that image. Maxie was thus doubly othered. She was other to hegemonic social norms of middle-class behavior and she was other to hegemonic femininity. Hippie chick representations that did not subvert this second and crucial hegemonic category could thus mitigate and negotiate the threat of any challenge to the first category.

Popular culture hippie chick representations were premised on an unexamined acceptance of patriarchal definitions of femininity. Commonsense constructions of what it meant to be black and white were being exploded by the civil rights and black-power movements.[52] The counterculture was exposing as ideological construction the norms of middle-class family values. The final hegemonic construction to be exposed would be gender roles, but it wasn't happening yet in popular culture—nor was it happening yet in the milieu of the youth movement itself, at least not openly in any widely disseminated manner.[53]

"Death of Hippie: Son [sic] of Media"

On October 6, 1967, a procession wended its way down Haight Street. By this time the promise of the Summer of Love had turned into bitter dregs. Huge numbers of underage runaways peopled the neighborhood along with bad drugs, violent criminals who preyed on the young, and always, always more representatives of the media industry. The ritual ceremony, organized by the Diggers and other hip community stalwarts, was organized to proclaim the "Death of hippie, son of media" and the "birth of the Free Man."[54] The press release for the event declared:

> The media cast nets, create bags for the identity-hungry to climb in. Your face on TV, your style immortalized without soul in the captions of the [*San Francisco*] *Chronicle*. NBC says you exist, ergo I am. . . . and

the reflections run in perpetual anal circuits and the FREE MAN vomits his images and laughs in the clouds because he, the great evader, the animal who haunts the jungles of image and sees no shadow, only the hunter's gun, and knows sahib is too slow and he flexes his strong loins of FREE and is gone again from the nets. They fall on empty air and waft helplessly on the grass.[55]

The celebration of evasion poetically described here is a good example of de Certeau's theories of how the weak and disempowered use such tactical methods to prevent their ideological capture by the strategies of the dominant. However, the emphatically masculinist discourse of the press release needs attention. If popular culture representations of hippiedom tended to feminize the phenomenon as one means to negotiate its threat, then the answer from some self-styled countercultural spokespersons was to insist on its essential masculinity. The virile hippie "Free Man," unlike the hippie chick, could not be captured, contained, and turned into an image.

Fears of the prodigious abilities of the culture industries to contain and co-opt the counterculture circulated within the movement from the earliest days of its flowering. Those associated with the movement were conscious and sophisticated about the operations of the mass media as only the "television generation" could be.

Early in 1967 a letter writer to the *East Village Other* worried about the proliferation of frequently favorable representations of the counterculture and some of its well-known personages in the popular press:

> So what's it all signify? Obviously the transformation of many more squares to our side (rah-rah-sis-boom-bah) which is basically good; but this will also bring the pseudohip, who are already too numerous.
>
> . . . Now the Sanders, Kupferbergs, Zappas, Jones, Mekas, Ginsbergs, and others will have to realize the fact that preservation of this new, turned-on culture mustn't let "them" dilute it.
>
> Since this letter is going nowhere, I only plead that the now established establishment stay the hell out, unless they know what this is all about.[56]

Already—months before the Summer of Love—anxiety bubbled up about the media's ability to rework the discourse of the movement and to take away from its practitioners their capability to control the dissemination of meanings. Concerns about the pseudohip and the plastic hippie quickly multiplied.

In the aftermath of the Summer of Love, a writer in Madison's *Connections* seemed to validate the prophetic fears of the *EVO* letter writer. Preservation of the new culture was impossible, given the workings of the mass media industry:

> Incorporation, of course, was a pathetically simple process. The trappings were and are easily mimicked, for to the extent that they are outrageous and severe in their manifestations (color, taste, sound, touch) so are they easily assimilated. . . .
>
> . . . A mediocre, superficial, sick society has confronted a potential rebellion by slicking off its surface and selling it, swallowing it with dollar signs. It has ignored the real message of the hippies, because to do otherwise it would have had to confront its own paucity—an always uncomfortable process. And this particular challenge, because of its at least superficial emphasis on the surface manifestations of rebellion, did not really require any sincere soul searching. The society of buy and sell simply incorporated the costume and language, conveniently forgetting the soul. And it wasn't very difficult.[57]

The ideas of incorporation that surfaced frequently within youth movement circles were heavily influenced (consciously or unconsciously) by the media theories of the Frankfurt School, particularly Herbert Marcuse and his 1964 best-seller, *One-Dimensional Man*. Marcuse argued pessimistically that modern affluent, technological society made rebellion, social change, and the striving for freedom fundamentally impossible. Material abundance and the alleviation of physical misery could serve to refute any attempts at Refusal. If all one's vital needs appeared to be satisfied by the new technocratic State that succeeded in delivering the goods, opposition or nonconformity would be neurotic and irrational. Antimaterialist protests, such as the Beat scene or existentialism, however, were not seen as contradictory to the affluent, technological status quo. "They are rather the ceremonial part of practical behaviorism, its harmless negation, and are quickly digested by the status quo as part of its healthy diet."[58] Like Barthes's inoculation theory, the consuming of a bit of counterhegemonic discourse would only make the power structure stronger. For youth radicals working with this vision of mass-mediated society, rage and despair against popularly circulated representations of their rebellion and Refusal were inevitable. Counterculture youth critics had few other analytical paradigms with which to think through the cultural process at work.

Lawrence Lipton appeared to be subscribing to this position in a column written in October 1969: "Absorption by Co-option, a hair-of-the-dog-that-bit-you prescription, an Establishment panacea for dissent, are old remedies but more potent now than ever before because of the instantaneous blanket coverage afforded by the communications media. TV commercials are especially effective toward the end. By co-opting the language, slogans, dress, mannerisms and music of dissent the "revolutionary" sell is designed to disarm dissent while at the same time selling the product."[59] Another *Free Press* writer, also in 1969, basically blamed television for the demise of the Haight scene and the revolutionary possibilities it represented:

> . . . For the media principle at work is the exact opposite of censorship; don't quarantine the phenomenon but enhance it. Or to put it real raw, if you want to kill off a revolution, film it. The image media doesn't know about dialectics; it knows about INCLUSION.
>
> When the 'hippie movement'—to use the media's own tag—began to configure as a cohesive and potentially subversive social phenomenon in 1966–67, raising the possibility of mass defection of youth from society, image media rushed to the Haight Ashbury like Marines to battle. Every aspect of life there was exhaustively filmed and shown in a multitude of forms on TV and in theatres. Within a year the "hippie movement" had been institutionalized across America as a harmless lifestyle primarily concerned with sideburns and Nehru jackets. In its wake, Haight Ashbury became a death street, its life a popular subject for cheap horny flicks.[60]

These perspectives mirror, to a great extent, Todd Gitlin's argument about what happened to Students for a Democratic Society when the media spotlight turned on them.[61] Caught within hegemonic frames determined by the print and electronic news media, SDS was helpless, according to Gitlin, to control its mass-mediated image. Working with a generally top-down conception of Gramscian hegemony theory, Gitlin (as well as many others like him who participated and thought critically about the youth movement of the 1960s) ascribed almost total power to the formations of the power bloc. Like the duped masses of Frankfurt School theory, youth rebels—be they SDS members or counterculture freaks—appeared almost entirely passive in their relationship to mass media. Gitlin describes some of the ways SDS tried to seize control over its mass-mediated representations and their meanings. However, in Gitlin's narration mass-media strategies always seemed to triumph over SDS tactics.[62] Similar themes of defeat crop up in many articles written in the underground press that grappled with the relationship between the counterculture and its mass-mediated images in popular culture and the press.

This defeatism was not unconflicted or unchallenged, however. In the aftermath of the Death of Hippie parade, Lawrence Lipton pondered the likelihood of "peaceful co-existence during the period of transition between the phasing out of the old society and the emergence of the new." He went on to note: "We have not yet reached the full depth of depravity into which the society is sinking and the violence of which it is capable. The best I can foresee is a fake counter-reformation, using some of the slogans of the dissent and the 'other culture' of the underground to ABSORB IT, behead it and neutralize it. The masscom media are already trying to do just that. What we are seeing, however, is more polarization, not less."[63]

In the immediate aftermath of the Summer of Love, Lipton, as well as the organizers of the Death of Hippie parade, could still affirm tactical triumphs over the hegemonic processes of the media industry. The attempts to defuse the threats of a subversive youth movement did not appear to be working—dissent and conflict only grew sharper. By 1969, when more pessimistic perspectives began to appear, dissent and conflict were objectively still growing, but perhaps the euphoric sense of imminent revolution was being questioned. Certainly the utopian promise of the counterculture had shriveled.

Despite the palpable sense of rage and despair over the media industry's representations of the counterculture and youth dissent, it would be wrong to view the youth movement as passive, disengaged, or in any way duped by the workings of the process. Within the pages of the underground press, critical commentary about media proved a crucial resource for movement youth. If Gitlin's SDS in *The Whole World Is Watching* does, finally, appear passive and at the mercy of the dominant media, it may be because the author pays no attention to what was going on within the movement's own media outlets.

As this chapter and chapter 1 have shown, underground press pieces provided youth movement rebels with useful ways to think about and actively respond to, reject, or engage with popular media. Television could be evacuated of its objectionable content and turned into a trip toy with detailed instructions provided by an underground press article. A counterfeit counterculture could become the site of protest over the commercialization of the hip community, with the underground press disseminating information about the protest. The underground press could serve as a forum for consciousness raising about the means by which the counterculture could have its surface markers stripped off and made into fashion. Articles in underground papers could alert readers to particularly objectionable mass mediated representations of the movement.

The youth movement thus had resources on which to draw in its frequently antagonistic relationship with the culture industries. The youth movement did not rely for its validation on the media industry.[64] It had its own counter-media institutions. Those institutions built some defenses against recapture by hegemonic forces. The culture industry, as a major disseminator of naturalized consensual ideology, found itself failing badly in its attempts to win back this disaffected population. Evidence in the underground press indicates that those writing for the movement saw quite clearly the typically disguised process at work. If the point of hegemonic forces is to constantly attempt to win and rewin the consent of the subordinate, the process appeared stalled here with this crucial segment of the population.

"Every Revolutionary Needs a Color TV"

3 The Yippies,

Media Manipulation,

and Talk Shows

Although many in and aligned with the counterculture agonized and despaired over what the mass media was doing to their movement, one group of youth rebels embraced media, television particularly, as a tool of the revolution. As acolytes of Marshall McLuhan and as unconflicted members in good standing of the television generation, the Yippies confidently proclaimed their ability to manipulate mass media for their own ends. Jerry Rubin, one of the two most famous Yippies, proclaimed in the pages of Chicago's underground paper, the *Seed*, "You can't be a revolutionary today without a television set."[1]

Despite their assertions that "We Are Everywhere," the Yippies were actually a small cabal of movement people formed in the aftermath of the 1967 March on the Pentagon.[2] Jerry Rubin came to prominence with the influential antiwar Vietnam Day Committee in Berkeley; Abbie Hoffman had gone south to do civil rights organizing and was now a well-known East Village figure connected to the Diggers; Paul Krassner was the publisher of the popular and controversial underground satirical journal the *Realist*; Ed Sanders was an East Village poet and member of the Fugs. Nancy Kurshan and Anita Hoffman, Jerry's and Abbie's respective partners and two of the few female Yippies, were also important to the group, but, typical of macho-oriented youth movement groupings, their contributions received little public notice.

According to Krassner, the Youth International Party was concocted on New Year's Eve 1967 in Abbie and Anita Hoffman's East Village apartment as a group of activists gathered to smoke marijuana, plot actions for the upcoming Chicago Democratic Convention, and watch *The Smothers Brothers Comedy Hour,* all before heading off to a New Year's Eve party.[3] The confluence of pot, protest, and popular TV that evening seems a particularly apt inauguration for the new entity.

Under the charismatic, some would say clownish, leadership of Hoffman and Rubin, the Yippies became the most widely known figures associated with the youth movement of the late sixties and early seventies. They saw television as their conduit to a mass public. The medium, in turn, helped to make them both famous and infamous. Hoffman and Rubin became the first American radicals and left-wing revolutionaries to find themselves celebrities and household names — all through the magic of television.

The Yippies' obsession with television has been subject to much criticism — recently by media scholars and historians, as well as during the Yippies' heyday by their movement contemporaries. The underground press was rife with arguments about whether there was madness or method to the Yippies' media tactics. This chapter examines how Abbie Hoffman and Jerry Rubin attempted to articulate their tactical manipulation of television through their best-selling books, as well as through articles published in the underground press. The chapter also examines responses to the Yippies from within movement circles. Crucial to any exploration of the Yippie-television relationship is the August 1968 Chicago Democratic Convention. The saturation coverage of the confrontations between protesting young people, many encouraged to come to Chicago by the Yippies, and the city's police officers served as the Yippies' TV apogee. We will examine how this tumultuous event became a field of both enraged and exhilarated struggle for meaning with Hoffman and Rubin and their allies attempting to fill the signifier "Chicago" with revolutionary inevitabilities. The chapter concludes with an examination of another televisual terrain of struggle for youthful revolutionaries like the Yippies. Television talk shows, like the coverage associated with the Chicago upheavals, were treated seriously by Yippie-influenced movement youth. Many believed the frequent on-air clashes between talk show producers and militant guests served to unmask the power relations that supposedly had been revealed in Chicago. If nonfictional television could be made into a site of so much chaos and hegemonic disarray, perhaps the revolution could be televised.

Advertisements for the Revolution

Abbie Hoffman and Jerry Rubin premised their antic practices on the theory that "Yippie is a myth." The two pursued this idea in their books, Rubin with glib one-liners, Hoffman with more thoughtful substance.[4] "Yippie" was supposedly a blank page, an emptied signifier on which the reader/viewer constructed his or her meaning. The mass-mediated representation of "Yippie" was to be an open text demanding an active response. Hoffman and Rubin's conception of the mass media's process of turning "Yippie" into a polysemic text suggests John Fiske's idea of the producerly text—popular and accessible but relying on the viewers mobilizing their various "discursive competencies" on the text in self-interested, active ways.[5] Jerry Rubin celebrated the polysemy of Yippie meanings by claiming, "The left immediately attacked us as apolitical, irrational, acidhead freeks [*sic*] who were channeling the 'political rebellion of youth' into dope, rock music and be-ins. The hippies saw us as Marxists in psychedelic clothes using dope, rock music and be-ins to radicalize youth politically at the end of a policeman's club."[6] Rubin then asserted that only the right wing saw them for what they really were—thus producing a perversely preferred reading.

Abbie Hoffman also expounded on notions of myth requiring active meaning making. Comparing hippies and Diggers (the latter being his model for the Yippies), Hoffman claimed that the hippies were media manipulated, a myth created by the media. As we saw in the previous chapter, this was an issue that elicited anguished concern from within the hip community. Diggers, on the other hand, were a "grass roots myth created from within." The bottom-up process of mythification here meant that Diggers (and by extension Yippies) manipulated the media rather than the other way around. The trick in this grassroots myth was to evade definition, confound understanding, resist categorization and analysis. "If the straight world understood all this Digger shit, it would render us impotent, because understanding is the first step to control and control is the secret to our extinction."[7] Distortion and incomprehension by the established powers within the media industry were precisely what the Yippies wanted. As we have seen, when network television engaged in its frequently earnest attempts to understand the hippie phenomenon, many in the movement saw only a process of co-optation and hegemonic incorporation. The Yippies, keenly aware of this process, developed tactics they believed shielded them from the same fate.

Language was one weapon to avoid capture. Hoffman, drawing on Marshall McLuhan, claimed that the language of the rising revolutionary youth culture was incomprehensible to the older generation because it mirrored the qualities of television commercials—nonlinear, composed of images juxtaposed in haphazard ways. Thus Hoffman, in answer to a reporter asking why he was marching on the Justice Department, explained he was going to give it an enema. The answer was ludicrous, giving rise to an impossible image, short-circuiting journalistic strategies of rational sense making. However, to other children of McLuhan, the image would be evocative: "it means an act of violence or more specifically an act of revenge."[8]

The Yippie tactic was to evade ideological capture by confounding the media's attempt to explain, in suitably rational terms, what the Yippies meant, what they stood for, what was significant about them. Both Rubin and Hoffman insisted that Yippie mass-mediated antics were meant to demand active participation from viewers, no matter what that response would entail. By activating differently situated audiences to respond either in rage and disgust or in enthusiastic revolutionary revolt, the varied responses would heighten contradictions, sharpen dissent and polarization, and topple the power alliances just that much more quickly.

In his critique of Jerry Rubin's tactics, Todd Gitlin notes in *The Whole World Is Watching* that Rubin conceptualized "the revolutionary mass [as] just that: a *mass* to be 'turned on' by media buttons."[9] The suggestion is that the Yippies relied (consciously or not) on a "hypodermic needle" conception of communication. In this model the recipient is injected with the message and reacts appropriately to what the sender has communicated. This conception would seem to contradict the Yippies' stated desire to send a textually open message onto which the recipient would have to write his or her own meanings and then act on those meanings. Although Gitlin neglects this aspect of Yippie media thinking, his remarks do point to a certain

level of confusion and contradiction within the Yippie philosophy of
media manipulation.

This confusion is most obvious in the Yippies' arguments that by
attracting media attention, especially television, they were producing advertisements for revolution. Rubin proclaimed that the nightly
coverage of demonstrations inevitably resulted in a new wave of
younger members of the television generation who wanted to grow
up to be demonstrators. The experience of watching campuses blowing up on TV would cause high school kids to want to see the same
thing happen when they hit the colleges.[10]

Hoffman, as usual, was a little bit more sophisticated in his thinking but also seemed to take for granted that young people would
construct the appropriate meanings out of the televised texts. Both
Rubin and Hoffman claimed that coverage of youthful rebellion
was inherently exciting, would elicit a response, and, if the viewer
was young enough, would cause the viewer to want to participate.
Hoffman explained how this coverage worked as advertisements for
revolution by referring to theories in perceptual psychology about
figure/ground relationships.[11] In television boring programs such as
Meet the Press functioned as the rhetorical ground; exciting advertisements functioned as figure, chock-full of information and per-
suasive mechanisms. Stylistically, the programming was as dry, dull,
and lifeless as its actual content, but the advertising was characterized
by flashes, zooms, and appeals to the viewer's needs. Asked Hoffman:
"Do you think any one of the millions of people watching the show
switched from being a liberal to a conservative or vice versa? I doubt
it. One thing is certain, though. . . . A lot of people are going to buy
that fuckin' soap or whatever else they were pushing in the commercial."[12]

Hoffman applied the same theory to make sense of coverage of
demonstrations during the Chicago Democratic Convention.[13] Very
little of the televised coverage dealt with the youthful protesters.
William Small, head of CBS News in New York, emphasized that in
total CBS and NBC, the only two networks to provide live broadcasts,
devoted only about 3 percent of their entire coverage to the violent
disturbances on the streets.[14]

As far as Hoffman was concerned that tiny amount of coverage
was of no consequence in itself. The images from the convention hall
formed the "dull field of establishment rhetoric," the demonstrations

the exciting figure requiring involvement by viewers. Thus, as Hoffman logically put it: "*We were an advertisement for revolution.*" [15] Hoffman went on to explain that the gaps and omissions in the coverage helped to create the Yippie myth by forcing viewers to make things up for themselves, but his ultimate point was similar to Rubin's. If an advertisement worked because it successfully persuaded the viewer to buy the product on offer, then if the product offered was youth revolution, the viewer would buy that too. Youthful television spectators of the convention coverage were supposed to be active agents in meaning making, but the preferred meanings were somewhat limited. Alternative meanings were open to adults, and the Yippies were quite happy to let those meanings circulate because they would heighten conflict. However, Hoffman and Rubin apparently expected the young to construct fairly singular "correct" interpretations and expected those turned-on youths to then act up in the appropriate manner.

The Yippies' analysis of media reception processes may have been somewhat weak, but they were also criticized, at the time and since, for the very strategy of using mainstream media outlets for their advertisements. Michael Shamberg, who was deeply invested in fostering movement-oriented, decentralized, grassroots video projects to get information to the people outside the domain of the broadcast networks, was one such critic. Although Shamberg, as we saw in chapter 1, bore the imprint of McLuhan's theories as much as the Yippies did, he distrusted mainstream media profoundly. In his 1971 video primer, *Guerrilla Television,* he argued that it was structurally impossible for the Yippies to get a movement view across by using the establishment media. "No alternative cultural vision is going to succeed in Media-America unless it has its own alternative structures, not just alternative content pumped across the existing ones." [16]

More recently David Farber in *Chicago '68,* a wide-ranging analysis of the players and events that created the turmoil of the Chicago Democratic Convention, makes a similar argument. Farber states that the Yippies accepted the structures and institutions of cultural production within American society as without inherent meaning. Television, therefore, could be used to encourage a revolutionary consciousness already dormant among the young even as the State used the same institution for very different ends. Simulating revolution through an institution that authenticated notions of the real, the

Yippies would make "a revolution that looked like fun" available to otherwise apolitical youth.[17]

Todd Gitlin also pinpointed the Yippies' blindness to the workings of media institutions. The hegemonic processes of the media involved strategies such as a focus on flamboyance and elevated rhetoric to contain and marginalize dissident positions that could not be ignored. Rubin and the Yippies played into those strategies, constantly needing to heighten their outlandishness to recapture the media spotlight. The Yippies thus strengthened power bloc formations and demoralized a movement whose "spokesmen" were less and less accountable to a base of support because media exposure distorted the extent of that support.

All these positions have merit, yet they assume an analysis of power relations in which the dominant remains monolithic and all-powerful, whereas the resisting subordinate is structurally incapable of engaging in struggle anywhere on terrain controlled by the dominant. Recent media theorists have grappled with the question of whether radical discourse can ever be disseminated through media institutions such as popular television. Colin MacCabe has argued that any potentially radical discourse can be rendered reactionary by the realist impulses of television. He refers to the British television program, *Days of Hope,* which sympathetically depicted in fictional narrative the rise of the British labor movement and the 1928 General Strike. The aesthetics of realism deny contradictions, uncertainties, or any difficulties for the viewer in decoding the material, thus ensuring that the viewer will not suffer the kind of social/ideological/political discomfort necessary to activate the desire for social change.[18] MacCabe's argument falls within a tradition of deep suspicion about the workings of popular culture and the industries that produce those texts. Avant–garde works that deny the strategies of realism, that disavow pleasure, and that are produced outside the institutions and mechanisms of the dominant culture industries are seen as the only tactical means for fostering a radical sensibility among disempowered social groups.

John Fiske adopts a very different position, arguing that popular televisual texts can be progressive because they do not construct a unified spectatorial position but are open to different reading strategies based on the needs and positions of viewers. Although such texts are still infused with dominant ideology, for them to be popular alternative meanings must be available. Fiske questions whether popular television can serve radical political ends given that such politics do not and cannot exist within the realms of representation and symbolic systems. However, popular culture can serve progressive political ends because at the micropolitical level disempowered societal groups can use selectively chosen products of the culture industries in empowering ways. Although Fiske concentrates on these micropolitical tactics of everyday popular usage outside the context of a coherent macropolitical movement for social and political change, he does suggest that at certain moments popular culture can assist in radical movements: "Radical political movements neither originate nor operate at the level of representation or of symbolic systems. This does not mean, however, that when historical conditions produce a radical crisis the media and popular culture cannot play an active role in the radical change that may occur: what it means is that symbolic or cultural systems alone cannot produce those historical conditions."[19]

The Yippies wreaked havoc with all these theories about the radical, progressive or reactionary qualities of popular culture. Although the movement out of which the Yippies sprang did not originate from "symbolic systems," at some level that movement—as this book shows—did operate within those systems of representation. Although the larger movement's relationship to those symbolic systems was contentious, suspicious, and frequently hostile, many of the culturally circulated meanings of the movement operated within the realms of symbolic systems—those of the dominant culture industries as examined here, as well as within the movement's own symbolic systems, such as rock music, underground films, and comix. The Yippies took an entirely different tack. To a significant extent they operated within the representational systems of the dominant social order. However, their media tactics indicate an attempt to create disruptive representations that suggest the radical, avant-garde text far more than the popular realist text. The Yippies embraced bizarre, disjunctive imagery over verbal discourse. Understanding that television was primarily a visual medium, the Yippies attempted to subvert any attempts by the hegemonic forces of electronic journalism to bring them into the lingual economy. Jerry Rubin railed against radicals who appeared on television wearing suits and ties: "Turn off the sound and he could be the mayor! The words may be radical, but television is a non-verbal instrument! The way to understand TV is to turn off the sound. No one remembers any words they hear; the mind is a technicolor movie of images, not words." [20] Participating in verbal discourse brought one into the dominant order's regimes of power. By operating at the level of imagery, the movement could avoid having itself defined, normalized, and, thereby, disempowered.

The Yippies could not be constructed easily into a "realist text" and therefore cannot be theorized adequately using MacCabe's notion of "dominant specularity." Dominant specularity implies a reading position constructed by texts from which the world makes coherent, realistic sense. Gitlin's argument implies that the media, working within certain hegemonic frames, were able to assert that position of dominant specularity by using various strategies to represent not just the Yippies but the movement in general.

Over and over again, however, the Yippies attempted to destroy the realist impulse in televisual representation. They did not accept as "inherently meaningless" the structures and processes of the institutions. In their writings they tried to expose those processes for their readers. In their televised antics they did the same thing. Although it may be true that the Yippies were naive and misguided in thinking that they could mobilize youth to foment revolution via television, they were much less naive in their understanding about the workings of the medium. In the end it was probably inevitable that a generation so self-conscious about its relationship to television as in some ways formative of its radical disaffection would produce a phenomenon like the Yippies, which took that self-consciousness to its logical conclusion. If television had helped create a rebellious youth, then television could also help create a revolutionary youth.

Chicago, Czechago

The final week of August 1968, a week after Soviet tanks had rolled into Czechoslovakia, killing "Prague Spring," the Democrats staged their presidential nominating convention in the nation's second city, Chicago. The chaos, violence, shocks, and general pandemonium of those hot August days, broadcast live on national television, became a searing instance of hegemonic breakdown. Before an estimated viewership of 50,500,000 households who watched an average of nine and a half hours of coverage, the fiction of a benign democratic system operating consensually was ripped away to reveal the ugly violence and coercion on which that system rested.[21] Because the unmasking of hegemonic powers can be so potentially threatening to those who wield power and so liberating to those who challenge it, the different interest groups involved worked overtime to construct and circulate their meanings about the chaos of Chicago. Whereas Chicago mayor Richard Daley and other conservative forces were concerned to nail down interpretations to vindicate official violence and chaos, the Yippies were happy to let any discourse about Chicago circulate. The Yippies appeared to understand that any contentiousness about what Chicago meant only further exhibited their vision of a social order teetering on the brink of collapse.

The networks came in for the brunt of criticism over their coverage of the events. They sought cover in appeals to journalistic professionalism and to polling material that suggested, despite charges of prodemonstrator bias of news reporters, the majority of viewers believed that not enough police force had been used.[22] The implication was that because so many Americans supported Mayor Daley's police tactics, the news coverage was ideologically neutral.

Many in the movement, especially Yippie-allied participants in the demonstrations, made sense of the role of the journalists quite differently. They saw the news media as their willing or unwilling ally in the confrontation with State power. Lawrence Lipton at the *Los Angeles Free Press* explained the "method in [the Yippies'] madness" in their organizing around the Chicago demonstrations. Yippie tactics used a theatrical approach to exhibiting dissent and political rebellion. This was key to getting media attention. Lipton explained: "The theater of the absurd can be highly entertaining by all media standards. That it is also DEADLY effective is another matter. And don't for a minute imagine that the Power Structure and its political puppets in public office do NOT know it. What the Yippies contributed to the new revolutionary technique of the Left in Chicago was the technique of manipulating the media so that it provided at least a partial visual and oral report on what was happening."[23] Yippie media guerrillas played subversively to the media's appetite for entertaining, provocative imagery. Rather than being "caught" by a media strategy that (as Gitlin argues) merely marginalized and rendered unthreatening a serious political movement, the process ended up working in the movement's favor. By being journalistically bound to cover visually engaging material, the media found itself compelled to broadcast dissenting discourse. Movement-affiliated viewers could find pleasure in this coverage by witnessing how the broadcast media's traditional script for containing youthful protest could no longer function. Truth spilled out all over the place. Robert Gabriner wrote in Madison's *Connections* about watching the CBS television coverage. He noted this process at work and how the CBS correspondents were, willy-nilly, finding themselves on the side of the police-battered protesters:

> Tuesday night hinted at the Wednesday debacle. You could tell because my father figure [Walter Cronkite] was beginning to get angry. There was more talk about security, about the arbitrary authority of Daley, about mistreatment of the press. Then, it happened. Dan Rather of C.B.S. got slugged. Cronkite began to crumble. One could tell that the C.B.S. news team could not digest and regurgitate the spectacle. They were part of it, but they were in the wrong corner. Too many of them were ending up like the demonstrators outside. Cronkite's tone changed appreciably throughout the evening. He was mad with Daley and his police.[24]

Gabriner pointed out that Cronkite and the other reporters were being inexorably drawn toward the position of the demonstrators and away from Daley and his police. Gabriner gleefully noted that Cronkite referred to Daley's finest as "gestapo," to the situation as a "police state" and to the demonstrators as "those poor kids."[25] Gabriner's reading indicated a crucial rupture in power-bloc alliances. One ideological apparatus of state power suddenly revealed itself as deeply at odds with a repressive apparatus of the state. Of course such apparatuses (in this instance the news industry and an institution of law and order) are relatively autonomous; however, as Althusser has noted, they tend to reinforce each other and must do so for the state to function.[26] In 1968 the State was having a great deal of difficulty functioning with any degree of smoothness. As Gabriner saw it, "The scenario was now beginning to be improvised. The text was being torn up and replaced with whatever came up."

Gabriner conceded that by the end of the convention the CBS news team attempted to reassert the old text. "They had, in fact, recovered their cool. For a few relatively short moments C.B.S. and Walter Cronkite had turned the tube over to reality."[27] For those few days another text was in operation. According to a writer in the *East Village Other,* the script for Chicago had been written by the television generation: "They were the TV teeners and boppers who had grown into full blown media guerillas [*sic*]. They had sloughed off the prefabrications of TV and used it to create their own real live drama."[28] In the struggle for control over its televisual representation Chicago presented a moment in which the movement felt in command. Forming a tactical alliance with news reporters who had been beaten and battered by Chicago's police just as the long-haired, freaky kids had been, the Yippie-affiliated demonstrators triumphantly believed that their construction of "reality" was being broadcast.

Two *East Village Other* reporters, writing dispatches in the heat of the convention turmoil, indicated the strength of their conviction that their truths were being broadcast to the nation. Allan Katzman affirmed, "The people of Chicago have never been more aware of the police state they live in. They see the brutality, the disorder and chaos caused by the police."[29] Dennis Frawley claimed, "The events of the past week in Chicago have created a bizarre situation in America. Never has it been so evident that this country's political system depended on force for its survival. Never has it been so apparent that only a handful of protesters could bring to bear so clearly the crisis of consciousness across millions of TV screens live and in living color."[30]

Unfortunately, as recent media theory has argued, meanings do not inhere in texts but are variously constructed by viewers based on their socially determined needs. That Katzman, Frawley, and, undoubtedly, most movement participants read the Chicago broadcasts as a clear unmasking of hegemonic coercion and brutality does not mean that all other television viewers shared that reading. Indeed, many read the chaos of Chicago as a matter of not enough force. Rather than viewing the police as the agents of brutality, disorder, and chaos, many TV viewers saw the protesters as the guilty party.

In an article for *TV Guide* columnist Richard Doan read selectively from the Walker Report, which had been commissioned by the presidentially appointed National Commission on the Causes and Prevention of Violence. The report determined that the police were primarily to blame and had, in effect, created a "police riot."[31] Doan, however, focused his concerns elsewhere. He quoted from the report about the Yippie strategy of playing to the cameras: "What 'the whole world was watching' after all, was not a confrontation but the picture of a confrontation, to some extent directed by a generation that has grown up with television and learned to use it."[32] Thus the report, in Doan's interpretation, denied the "reality" of the demonstrators. For participants like Katzman and Frawley it was crucial to read the coverage of the chaos as unmediated. If there was a "movement script," then that script, unlike the traditional ones used by the networks, told the truth. Conservative forces, on the other hand, needed to counter this reading strategy with one that denied the possibility that televisual images could broadcast unmediated reality. It was an unusual position for hegemonic elites to argue. Typically the construction of representations of "reality" are more firmly under the control of those elites. When that is the case, hegemonically constructed "reality" serves as common sense. Or, as Walter Cronkite put it at the end of each broadcast, "That's the way it is." In this instance a subordinated group appeared to have wrestled away that control for a few politically significant moments. Thus, the subordinate could argue that its representations were real, but the dominant needed to assert that such representations were ideologically constructed and reflected the political interests of a particular group.

As the *Connections* writer noted, the network reporters quickly attempted to reassert the old script. The Doan article exhibited that process in action. After quoting the Walker Report, Doan quoted CBS correspondent Eric Sevareid to bolster the argument that the Yippies had not achieved their ends by their media show: "Eric Sevareid, in a CBS 'Instant Special' analyzing the report, suggested the demonstrators may have defeated their own purposes. Widespread public support for the police, despite their often vicious clubbing of bystanders can be traced, Sevareid thought, to common revulsion against "screaming militants, foul-mouthed demonstrators, arsonists and looters.'" Sevareid's discourse indicated a scramble by one sector of (consensual/ideological) hegemonic power to realign with coercive/repressive formations. Sevareid's characterization of the demonstrators conformed exactly to that of Mayor Daley, his police force, and Republican presidential nominee Richard Nixon, who used that discourse to narrowly win the White House in 1968.[33] Sevareid's move revealed an anxious attempt to quickly paper over the rends and tears evident among segments of the power bloc.

For many in the youth movement this process of hegemonic reassertion was demoralizing. It seemed baffling that middle America chose not to read the movement's TV script according to its pre-ferred reading strategies. At an assembly of "revolutionary students" at Columbia University a month after the events at Chicago this issue became a flashpoint for debate. One participant, quoted in an *East Village Other* article, declared that the movement should have nothing to do with the dominant media.

> "People spend four hours a day in front of the box, but Chicago showed that the people were not moved by the press' bias for the kids."
> AMERICA LOVES MAYOR DALEY.
> The comrade said that polls and the press have found that Middle America loves Mayor Daley and the Yippie thing was a bust and Abbie Hoffman and Jerry Rubin are great manipulators of the media but remain freaks.[34]

Hoffman, in attendance at the assembly, weighed into the debate, brandishing a yo-yo. The article, describing Hoffman's electrifying effect on the gathering, quoted him at length:

> Never let 'em forget we're their children. . . . The heads they bash are their children's heads and they saw it on TV.
> So thousands of plastic people have told the pollsters (the Elec-tric Age's voting machine) that they love Mayor Daley because all those dirty jew bastard fuckin commies are bringing moral decay to America the Beautiful.
> But 15,000 kids got their heads bashed. And 30,000 parents watched. Yeah, my kid was a schmuck for going to Chicago, my kid doesn't understand that we've got to have law and order, and he shouldn't have provoked the cops, but Jesus, the cops didn't have to crack my kid's head, I mean, why hit him like that—and 30,000 par-ents got a bit revolutionized. (12)

Hoffman held onto the Yippie belief that any reaction to dissenting, provocative imagery was to the movement's advantage. Also glim-mering was the hope that maybe, just maybe, despite what the grown-ups said, some of the young demonstrators' meanings had broken through. Hoffman remained faithful to the power of images to resist the defining and controlling strategies of establishment forces.

The images and contested meanings about Chicago did indeed continue to cause enormous anxieties among various sectors of hegemonic power. Despite the after-the-fact reinterpretations by network correspondents and despite the widely publicized negative reactions by large numbers of television viewers, the politically disruptive and threatening connotations of the images of that event continued to reverberate. One place this anxiety played itself out was in entertainment television. Two of the Vast Wasteland's few programs to overtly acknowledge and deal with current issues of the day, *Rowan and Martin's Laugh-In* and *The Smothers Brothers Comedy Hour,* attempted to engage with the meanings of Chicago. The next chapter will examine how the Smothers struggled to bring the issue to their show. *Laugh-In,* a far less politically committed vaudeville/variety program that typically endured little of the censorship and network scrutiny suffered by the Smothers Brothers' show, found itself in this instance the victim of NBC's anxieties about disseminating any more discourse about Chicago.

Laugh-In producer George Schlatter had planned a series of jokes and gags about the "Battle of Chicago," Mayor Daley, and the excesses of his police force. One of the gags, described in a *TV Guide* behind-the-scenes cover story, involved Arte Johnson with his head bandaged and arm in a sling:

> "Oh, it was terrible," he moans, using a heavy *Mitteleuropa* accent. "People running and screaming. People shooting and hitting each other. I was caught in a violent mob."
> "I didn't know you were in Prague," says a bystander.
> "What Prague?" Johnson replies. "I was at the Democratic Convention in Chicago." [35]

According to the article, the network wanted no overt references to Chicago. Schlatter, apparently feeling strongly about the material, fought hard to keep it all in the script. In the end NBC censors deleted most of the Chicago material from the program. [36]

The network's squeamishness indicates that any representations of Chicago were still ideologically problematical. The meanings of the phenomenon had not been securely anchored within safe grounds. Chicago, as a discursive terrain, was still a site of struggle between those aligned with the youth movement and those aligned with establishment power. That the lines of ideological battle were so clearly imprinted on any circulated representations of Chicago suggested hegemonic fragility. Despite the networks' mea culpas over their coverage, the politically threatening possible meanings of the events in Cook County had not been defused. Even in an entertainment format, the networks could not countenance the disruptive potential of such material.

The disturbing nature of the Chicago coverage could not be countenanced by the mayor of Chicago, either. Daley had originally wanted to bar live television coverage of the convention entirely, using a strike by electrical workers as an excuse to make installation of equipment for live transmission impossible. A writer for the *Rat,* in a preconvention article, gleefully noted that this attempt at news management would backfire on the mayor and on his Democrats.

> The public already knows we are coming. The publicity about the demonstrations is considerable and growing. The Amphitheater and convention are going to be under military guard; the TV viewer will naturally wonder what they are guarding against. The media establishment is mad, some at this continuation of "credibility gap politics", some because they believe more will happen outside than inside the convention, some because they sympathize more with us than with Humphrey. By alienating the media in this way, the Democrats have helped us prove our argument about their manipulative nature.[37]

Clearly, Daley feared not only being unable to control the demonstrators but also being unable to control the televised images of whatever clashes occurred.

In the aftermath of the disturbances Daley demanded time from the networks to present the perspectives of his office and his police force. The networks demurred, but the independent big-city Metromedia chain, along with hundreds of other stations, did agree to air a documentary prepared by the mayor's office exonerating the Chicago forces of law and order. It didn't appear to be enough that Daley evidently had public opinion on his side. The mayor needed to replay and rework the imagery within the context of another television broadcast and, thus, assert and finally nail down the appropriate meanings and interpretations of those events.

Lawrence Lipton in the *Los Angeles Free Press* railed in characteristic outrage against Daley's action. Here was yet another attempt to steal from the movement whatever small, provisional, tactical, guerrilla victory the original coverage may have provided. Comparing the mayor to Hitler and calling the documentary an example of Nazi-like "Big Lie" propaganda, Lipton itemized every instance of the program's manipulation of material about those involved in dissent. The televised struggle to fix the meanings of Chicago did not stop with the Daley documentary, however. The ACLU and the Yippies also got airtime on many television stations for their documentary rebuttal to the mayor's broadcast. Thus, the struggle continued.

This flurry of attempts to define the proper meanings of the Chicago disturbances in the aftermath of their live broadcasts illustrates just how much was at stake here. The fact that the youthful demonstrators did not appear to have public opinion on their side did not appreciably defuse this television spectacle of its social and political threat. Power bloc forces found themselves compelled to labor out in the open (without the cover of taken-for-granted common sense) in order to impose their meanings. By forcing power to thus reveal itself, the Yippies succeeded with their tactic of media manipulation.

Talkin' 'Bout My G-G-Generation

Although the broadcasting of the "battle of Chicago" proved to be the youth movement's most widely circulated attempt at seizing control of the televisual apparatus, there were numerous smaller skirmishes over video meanings in nonfictional formats. The television talk show represented one such site of struggle. Talk shows seemed to be one venue where the unmediated voices of those in the movement might be heard. If those discourses encountered resistance, repression, and outright censorship by typically conservative hosts and program producers, that was fine. Such clashes, like Chicago, would continue unmasking power relations for all television viewers to grapple with.[38]

An early example of the destabilizing and disruptive potential of talk shows for youth rebels was a 1966 episode of the David Susskind talk show, *Open End,* which had invited various members of the East Village hippie scene. Susskind and his production staff quickly lost control of the situation as acolytes of Andy Warhol insisted on filming the crew filming the hippies. Cigarettes and marijuana joints suddenly appeared, passing from hand to hand. Susskind got incomprehensible answers to his rational questions. The *East Village Other* described how far Susskind's disciplining script had been subverted by the carnival-like atmosphere created by his guests: "Susskind is getting rattled. The roving cameramen, the disorderly group, the smell of pot, the occasional clicks, shrieks and catcalls from Barbara are apparently so much more than he expected. 'Could you control your little tinkle bell?' he asks Susanna [described as barefoot with flowers in her hair and a bell around her neck]."[39] "Control"—over guests, their actions, and their discourse—was precisely what Susskind could no longer wield. Numerous producers of television talk shows would face this same dilemma. They would find their talk show strategies unable to normalize and rationalize countercultural or youth politico participants. The genre's strategies for containment were ill equipped to handle the guerrilla tactics of these guests.

The *East Village Other* discussed this conception of talk shows as a battleground appropriate for guerrilla warfare in an article from May 1968 entitled, "Alan Burke Show Taken Over By Guerrillas." The talk show had invited a costume designer for the San Francisco Mime Troupe to exhibit costumes and to bring along other participants. The author of the *EVO* piece went along, anticipating that the group would engage in some form of spontaneous and improvised activity. The station, for its part, hired uniformed police to stand guard inside the studio. A number of Columbia University students, veterans of the recent police bust resulting from the student occupations of five campus buildings, turned up and were kicked off the show for disruptive behavior. The disruptions continued when the Mime Troupe costumer joined Burke on stage wearing a costume consisting of a dove nailed to a military helmet. The man refused to answer Burke's preformulated questions, grabbing the script from the host and waving it to the camera. Burke attempted to order the man off the stage:

> . . . we started shouting to Carl not to leave. Carl touched Burke on his knee and Burke cringed, shocked to be touched by a human hand. Then the others came on in their even weirder costumes, and began flinging fruit to the audience, which was enjoying this sudden freedom. Burke gave up trying to throw Carl out when Charlie Feinman called out from the back, "There's another costume," and came into the camera-area wearing his normal clothes.
> "What's the costume?" Burke asked, confused.
> "The costume of a human being—which you can't recognize," Charlie said.

Burke ordered Charlie off the set, but Charlie kept rapping at him.
I jumped out of my seat and started yelling in Burke's face, "Why are
you throwing him out, can't you talk to him, isn't this supposed to
be an audience participation show?"

Burke just stared at me in disbelief, shaken, drained.

"Television has to be free," I said to him.

"Nothing is free," he said.

I told him the air was free, and TV belonged to all of us, not to him,
or to the owners of the station or the networks. He signalled to the
cops to come get us.[40]

The writer and the other disrupters tried to "free" television (like
their Yippie-inspired comrades in Chicago) from hegemonic scripts.
By refusing to operate within prescribed bounds of behavior, the disrupters hoped to wrestle control away from established power, speak
in their own voices, and have their discourse disseminated in unmediated form.

The stumbling block to all this was film and videotape. How could
one achieve spontaneity and improvisation in a canned television
format? Ultimate mechanisms of control and power still rested in
the hands of establishment interests. Because of this dilemma, many
youth movement activists asserted the political necessity of *liveness* if
television was to be used as a site of struggle. The *EVO* writer explained that the demise of television as a predominantly live medium
had resulted in "a terribly controlled medium, perhaps the one most
under the thumb of the Establishment" (p. 19). If the later Chicago
broadcasts were perceived as a victory for the movement, it was
largely because of the liveness of the coverage. Hegemonic scripts
were more difficult to impose on material that hadn't been carefully edited beforehand with appropriate commentary to assure that
viewers constructed preferred readings. Liveness indicated unpre-
dictability, a certain freedom for dissidents to evade those containing
mechanisms.

Such an opportunity presented itself on June 25, 1968. A contin-
gent of movement people stormed into the studio of New York City's
public television station TV WNDT-TV during a live talk show about
the underground press. Yelling questions like "Why is the Establishment media always lying?" and "Why can't we change the form of
the show?" and "Why can't we say FUCK on the air?" the disrupters

took over the show until the station managers called the police.[41] For Allan Katzman, one of the show's invited guests, the liveness of the program was the key to its political significance: "What was happening in Paris, in Vietnam, in Berlin, in Tokyo, in practically every major city in the world was happening at that exact moment on the third eye of living-room consciousness: REBELLION" (p. 4). Later in the summer the televising of Chicago would serve the same function on a much vaster scale. Activists assumed that live television, used tactically, could become a site of revolutionary activity. It provided a means to "bring the war home," forcing a larger TV-watching public to confront and deal with a young population in revolt.

Liveness also ensured the dissemination of "reality." Jeff Shero, another invited panelist from the *Rat,* wrote in his paper that "the truth emerged—a chaotic spontaneous TV is more stimulating than the well prepared canned variety." The way Shero conceptualized this spontaneous live reality requires some interrogation, however. In describing the exhilaration of that assault on the airways, Shero put it this way:

> The underground like a tidal wave of sperm rushing into a nunnery impregnates the show. Bedlam. The show is no longer a show, real human tensions flash across the screen. Real anger. REal [*sic*] sweat from the moderator. Incoherence. The chaos of the virile ghetto crashed into the programmed calmly classified discussion in abract [*sic*] of issues. The first underground assault on the airwaves—the viewing audience gets spontaneity. People are tested before their eyes and the old formulas don't work. . . .
>
> The scalpel pairs away the facade and bares the man beneath.[42]

For Shero, political action was beneficial rape, the reality on display was virile masculinity. The phallocentric quality of Shero's metaphors forms an ideological link to the sexism in the manifesto circulated by the Diggers discussed in chapter 2, which proclaimed the FREE MAN who evades the attempts by the dominant media to capture him. The "reality" of youth dissent was thus one of manly manhood. In their discourses of televisual reality, the various movement spokes*men* discussed throughout this chapter valued representations of aggressiveness, assertiveness, and physical, as well as verbal, strength and threat—a whole range of attributes typically associated with machismo. Women became the structured absence within this discourse and "feminine" attributes became the Other against which the male-oriented movement defined itself. Shero saw the dominant order (which needed to be raped and forced to accept the values of rebellious youth) as essentially feminine in a desexed way. Thus the misogyny and sexism so rampant within movement circles popped up here in the very definitions taken for granted about what an "authentic" representation of youth rebellion looked like. Because female participants in youth rebellion and activism occupied so few leadership positions (and seldom appeared in active ways in television coverage) and because women had few opportunities to write articles in underground papers, this sexist discourse circulated as comfortably in movement circles as it did within the despised "establishment."

This problematic struggle for "truth" and "authenticity" operated not only within the macho discourse of movement activists. A small number of local and syndicated hosts of talk shows also encountered difficulties in their attempts to let dissident young people speak in their own voices. In the Alan Burke and WNDT-TV cases, unfettered, spontaneous eruptions of youth movement discourse resulted in police intervention. As Chicago showed, the repressive force wielded by the powers that be represented a crucial component of the larger set of meanings broadcast. Talk show hosts who exhibited too obvious sympathy for movement political positions found themselves the recipients of an alternative form of repressive force: censorship and cancellation.[43]

Les Crane was one such personality. His late-night program, produced in Los Angeles and syndicated to eleven major markets, garnered a certain amount of youth movement support, at least within the pages of the *Los Angeles Free Press*. Regular columnist Elliot Mintz praised Crane's show but acknowledged some ambivalence within underground circles about the show's merely capitalizing on youth style and politics. Mintz made his case for taking Crane seriously: "His program is a McCluanized [*sic*] diary of the great revolution of the senses currently taking place in our country. He provides the vehicle for turned-on people to rap about their trips without nasty provocation or unwarranted put-downs. He masterfully creates a mood and a magic which is so necessary for a healthy and often times, inspiring dialogue."[44] Other talk shows, such as *The Alan Burke Show* or *The Joe Pyne Show* also invited countercultural guests and young politicos, but their "shock talk" formats were more conducive to reinforcing moral panics about crazed youth than to providing a forum for dialogue.

In September 1968, on the heels of the events in Chicago, *The Les Crane Show* was canceled. Despite good ratings and unchallenged popularity, another *Freep* article pointed out, the show's sponsors were not eager to continue supporting Crane. Television and radio stations were facing license renewal and, as writer Paul Eberle pointed out, were "not eager to offend the federal administration by permitting discussion of a broad range of ideas on the air waves."[45] Eberle noted that talk shows with more conservative hosts faced no such difficulties with their sponsors, nor were they threatened with cancellation.

Another local Los Angeles show called *Tempo II,* hosted by Stan Bohrman, suffered a fate similar to Crane's. The show was also quite popular with audiences, and according to an interview with Bohrman in the *Freep,* the station wanted him to be opinionated and controversial. "Until they found out what I was saying—and I was saying things in favor of the black people, the students, the Mexican-Americans, the disenfranchised, and I was saying things that were not necessarily the establishment point of view."[46] The station manager took particular umbrage at Bohrman's on-air support for Eldridge Cleaver of the Black Panther Party. The station instructed Bohrman to refrain from discussing the Panthers, to book no more black militants, and to screen on-air calls referring to Panther-related themes. Bohrman balked at this heavy-handed censorship, refused to comply, and was yanked off the air at about the same time as Les Crane.[47]

Censorship did not only affect talk shows openly sympathetic to dissident political positions. *The Merv Griffin Show* experienced one of the most bizarre instances of censorship in television history. Abbie Hoffman, out on appeal for his recent conviction in the Chicago Eight Conspiracy trial, appeared as a guest on Good Friday, 1970. Wearing a fringed jacket, Hoffman walked onto Griffin's stage joining the other guests. After sitting down and engaging in banter, Hoffman remarked that the lights were rather hot and asked if he could remove his jacket. Under the jacket Hoffman revealed that he was wearing a shirt made out of an American flag. Hoffman had already been arrested for wearing a shirt made out of that material. Rather than call the police and have Hoffman forcibly removed, as had been the fate of other disruptive youth movement guests, or snip out that entire segment of the program, CBS adopted a different approach. When aired, the episode carried a prologue message from Robert D. Wood, president of the network. Wood explained to viewers that because of the serious legal problems presented by Hoffman's shirt, the network had decided to mask out the offending garment by electronic means.

Renfreu Neff, one of the *East Village Other*'s few female contributors, wrote gleefully about the entire incident. She and a party of other East Village freaks had gone to the taping, then gathered at Abbie and Anita Hoffman's apartment the next day to watch the program on the couple's color TV. Describing the network's coercive move, she exulted:

> And finally, Ladies and Gentlemen, Abbie Hoffman! Everything's cool, just like they taped it, only better, until he takes off that jacket, and . . . BLUE.
>
> The screen goes BLUE, this insane Day-Glo blue. I tell you, there has never been a BLUE like that one, and the next day when you read in the *Times* that the screen went *black,* you understand why revolutionaries, heads and freaks own colour-tubes. Black-out, your ass, that screen went the wildest blue you ever saw, and it was a head-fucker, all right. . . .
>
> This fucking BLUE SCREEN moving in and out of it all, intercutting the action, bi-secting the image, lingering for minutes on screen as the Voice, Abbie Hoffman's voice, speaks of the fear that keeps the system alive, the revolution, the basis of its protest. Signalling through the flames. His humerous [*sic*] remarks come across as black and outrageous as what is happening on that screen. The visual content transports us into area that is totally surreal, without an image his words take on an ominous clarity, a profound and frightening significance as they are broadcast out of the BLUE.[48]

For Neff the blotting out of Hoffman's image merely heightened the urgency of his words, and CBS had undercut its policing function by making the attempted coercion so obvious. Neff could take a perverse pleasure from the bizarre blue dot because it signified in concrete terms the power struggle going on between revolutionary youth and the power elite, just like the live broadcasts of the Chicago disorders and the skirmish on WNDT-TV. Youth rebellion must have been terribly threatening to those in power; how else to explain all these attempts at suppression of its televisual representation?

For Hoffman censorship actually served the cause of an oppositional movement. In his 1968 book, *Revolution for the Hell of It,* he used the example of the heavily censored Saigon newspapers. Portions of the paper would contain blank areas denoting censored articles. Hoffman believed that those blank spaces contained a great deal of information. He then described his tactics for television appearances: "I go on television and make a point of swearing. I know the little fuckers don't get through, but the image of me blabbing away with the enthusiasm and excitement of a future world better than this while being sliced up by the puritanical, sterile culture of the Establishment is information worth conveying."[49]

A number of commentators picked up on the selective nature of television's censorship of flag-as-apparel imagery. Meridee Merzer, who wrote a television column for Philadelphia's underground paper, *Distant Drummer,* noted that Roy Rogers could be shown wearing a shirt that looked like the flag and suffer no repercussions. As Merzer noted, however, a flag shirt meant something different when worn by Hoffman, who was "nasty and dirty and a Yippie-Hippie-dope-smoking Commie."[50] A writer in the *East Village Other* noted that just before the Griffin show aired, a General Motors commercial ran featuring a man dressed up in an Uncle Sam outfit.[51] The Hoffman censorship controversy ended up broadcasting useful information to help bolster youth movement positions about the forces arrayed against it. Thus CBS's blue dot served a function not entirely unlike the service performed by Mayor Daley's men in blue.

The Hoffman censorship flap led to protests, including the picketing of CBS's New York headquarters and the issuing of demands by an *EVO*-affiliated group.[52] The demands indicate how seriously some movement youth viewed television as a terrain of ideological struggle. The list of demands included the suggestion that Robert D. Wood come on prime time and debate the issues surrounding the controversy with movement people who would bring in Marshall McLuhan as moderator. The group also demanded that CBS make four of its big city stations available during non-prime-time hours for movement use in electronic linkups so that young people could talk among themselves over the airwaves. A fifth demand declared:

The AIRWAYS are supposed to be FREE PUBLIC DOMAIN. The people are supposed to be the government. *We are lots of people now.* We weill, [*sic*] therefore, petition the F.C.C. and we demand to be taken seriosly [*sic*] that in the upcoming reviews of the licenses of MAJOR networks, at least one of the major networks be denied renewal and that their license be given to our nation for a new non-profit system. We have the advertisers because we are the majority of the buyers, we have the know-how, and we have the financing.[53]

The (not-so-radical) assertion of the airwaves as a public resource received frequent attention in the pages of the underground press. The statement merely reiterated the central premise of the Communications Act of 1934, which the FCC was mandated to oversee. However, when words like *public* and *people* were used as signifiers to connote a social group in revolt against dominant forces that effectively controlled those airways, the statement assumed its radical character. As children of the "television generation" the drafters of this list of demands realized the crucial importance of being able to articulate their positions in their own way through the medium that so shaped their development. Surprisingly, they did not seem to question the commercial basis of the medium, putting themselves forth not only as "the public" and "the people" but also as the best consumers.[54] Nevertheless, they did circulate a vision of television as a medium that truly would be the possession of those who had been weaned on it.

Abbie Hoffman had said, "I fight through the jungle of TV."[55] This chapter has examined the various ways Hoffman, his fellow Yippies, and others associated with the youth rebellion struggled to represent themselves through that medium. The jungle of TV was not a hospitable terrain, but those who fought did have certain tools to work with. The extent to which they succeeded is certainly debatable. It seems clear, however, that significant numbers of the activated TV generation saw this particular arena of hegemonic power as an important place to wage one facet of an (ideological) guerrilla campaign.

Smothering Dissent

 *The Smothers Brothers Comedy Hour* and the Crisis of Authority in Entertainment Television

On Sunday, October 27, 1968, *The Smothers Brothers Comedy Hour* opened with the following teaser: A collage of newspaper headlines about Mexican students rioting appeared on-screen. Cut to Murray Roman, one of the show's writer-comics, dressed as a Mexican police official proclaiming, "The reason that the students of Mexico City are rioting this weekend is because of outside agitators." This was followed by another series of headlines about the spring uprisings in Prague. Roman, dressed as a Soviet general, stated, "The reason that the students of Prague are rioting this weekend is because of outside agitators." Headlines about the May uprisings in Paris and demonstrations in Japan followed. Roman appeared in appropriate French and then Japanese military costume blaming outside agitators. The final shot of headlines referred to the uprisings at Columbia University. Cut to Roman, as a New York cop, affirming, "The reason the students at the universities are rioting this weekend is because of outside agitators." Suddenly we cut to Tom and Dick Smothers who smiled broadly and, in unison, proclaimed, "Hi! We're the outside agitators!"[1]

The hosts of cbs's highly rated weekend variety show as instigators of youthful revolution? Two clean-cut tv comedians aligned with student rioting? The sketch was an absurd joke; however, there had to be some kernel of truth for the sketch to have any meaning and to be at all funny. The Smothers Brothers did attempt to align themselves with the youth movement. Unlike any other prime-time network entertainment show, the Smothers Brothers tried to carve out a space for countercultural, antiwar, antiestablishment discourse. Unlike any other product of American network television, the Smothers Brothers' show managed to attract a youth audience—that elusive sixteen-to-twenty-four-year-old cohort that had abandoned the medium to such a large extent. But more important, the Smothers were able to attract a particular segment of that youth audience. The show proved uniquely successful in grabbing the attention, grudging respect, and support from elements of the politicized, rebellious youth movement whose concerns the show was attempting to articulate. Significant numbers of this insurgent population watched the show, providing it with its crowning achievement. This success also paved the way for the program's censorship and summary cancellation by its parent network, CBS.

As we saw in chapter 2, by the mid to late sixties all three networks were aware of and troubled by the fact that the younger generation, which had been weaned on television, was staying away from the medium in droves. In particular, (CBS) worried about its image as the network of the geriatric set. Strategically placed opposite NBC's top-rated *Bonanza*, *The Smothers Brothers Comedy Hour* was CBS's major attempt to lure young people. However, the show's success, rather than providing the network with a feather in its corporate cap, led to an all-out generational battle—a crisis of authority. The Smothers seemed intent on luring not just any cohort of young people but rather the politically and socially disaffected edge of the baby boom. In their attempts to gain legitimacy with this leading edge of the era's radical, protesting campus revolutionaries and countercultural dropouts, the Smothers began incorporating more and more oppositional politics into their variety show. The entertainers' attempts to assert their political allegiances on prime-time television—when some of those positions were highly explosive—resulted in a popular-cultural playing out of social, political, and generational warfare. For CBS a prime-time series that appeared to support the perspectives and politics of an insurgent youth threatening to shred the entire fabric of the American social order could be nothing if not threatening. As we saw with the televising of the Chicago Democratic Convention riots, a movement script and a movement definition of reality jeopardized hegemonic control over the network's construction of reality. Like the Chicago riots, *The Smothers Brothers Comedy Hour* served as a flashpoint where the discourses of the young and the control mechanisms of the elders clashed, often brutally.

Hippies with Haircuts

When the Smothers first joined CBS's Sunday lineup on February 5, 1967, there was little inkling that the show would eventually become a site of such contestation. The show enjoyed surprising success, even next to the perennially top-rated family western, *Bonanza*. Initially it seemed that the Smothers, with their short hair, neat suits, traditional folk music, and whimsical banter over who mom liked best, would be able to bridge the growing generation gap and uphold consensual values. Popular press accounts played up this angle, calling them "hippies with haircuts."[2] Tom Smothers, whose intelligence and articulateness belied his slow-witted persona, told a *Time* magazine reporter in June 1967: "'We're so college-looking and clean-cut. . . . The American Legion likes us and so does the left wing.'" The reporter went on to note, "And so does every wing of the younger generation."[3] Here, it seemed, were two performers who identified with a growing generation of disaffected young people but who would offend nobody.

We can see the show's attempts to encompass the American Legion and the youthful left wing in the show's first season. In the opening credit sequence the resident dancers, dressed in marching band costumes, paraded around with trumpets, bass drums, and cymbals while other dancers marched by with placards and sandwich boards bearing the names of that week's guest stars. The John Philip Sousa atmosphere evoked a very traditional sense of small-town celebration, placing the Smothers within a nostalgic, Frank Capra-esque version of Americana. If subsequent sketches dealt with "pungent social commentary," the credit sequence assured viewers that the show was still patriotic and all-American.[4]

Sketches from the first season revealed an ideological balancing act as the show struggled for generational consensus. In an attempt to cater to the youthful portion of their audience the Smothers invited the rock group Buffalo Springfield onto their February 26, 1967, show. The group sang its anthem of political and generational division and fear, "For What It's Worth." Lead singer Stephen Stills began the song's famous opening lines: "There's something happening here / What it is ain't exactly clear / There's a man with a gun over there / Telling me I've got to beware."[5] Suddenly there was a cut to Tom dressed up in wild-west gear pulling a six-shooter. A cut back to Stills showed him breaking into a grin. In another verse Stills observed: "A thousand people in the street / Singing songs and carrying signs / Mostly saying 'Hooray for our side.'" The sequence cut to a shot of Dick holding a sign with that slogan painted on it. The audience broke into laughter.

The sequence's comedic cutaways succeeded in defusing the song's anguished message. Stills's comments about police power weighing down on the rebellious young and the generational gulf created by the war in Vietnam were obliterated by the manner in which the lyrics were illustrated. For those already familiar and aligned with Stills's sentiments the meanings of the song were still available despite the comic intrusions. For audience members who did not know the song and its political implications, the cutaways may have made the material politically meaningless. In their generational balancing act the Smothers seemed to lean away from the youthful segment of their audience in order not to frighten the elders.

Another sketch on the theme of protest revealed a similar kind of balancing. After a bit of banter between Tom and Dick, Tom turned to guest star Carol Burnett, saying he protested his brother's treatment of him. While giggling and flubbing her lines, Carol responded: "You never accomplish anything with anger and violence, you have to be well organized and have self control, a formal protest is very effective, it shows respect for the law and the willingness to work things out peacefully."[6] The three then launched into a song called "We Protest Here" to the tune of "Allouette." On the one hand, the number appeared to support protest activity with lyrics such as the chorus — "We protest here / Get it off your chest here / We suggest here / That you protest, too" — and the final stanza — "Picket signs and protest songs / That's the way we'll win the fight / Cause we believe two civil wrongs / Do not make a civil right." On the other hand, the number also ridiculed protests and sit-ins, with Carol explaining that she'd conducted a "freeze-in" at the supermarket to protest the price of ice-cream. With the show's dancers in the background marching about with signs reading "Go Home," "Keep," "Clean," "Peace," and "Love," Tom, Dick, and Carol got their own signs. The entire cast conducted a musical sit-in on the stage, and the trio turned their signs around. Dick's read, "Up with mom"; Tom's read, "Down with Dickie"; Carol's read, "Mash me." These carefully nonpoliticized protest signs dissipated the lyrics proclaiming support for civil rights protests.

Other sketches, although open to various interpretations, leaned more in the direction of dissident, protesting groups, such as a segment built around Phil Ochs's song, "Draft Dodger Rag." The November 19, 1967, episode featured guest star George Segal, who joined Tom and Dick to sing the song. Dick introduced the number by saying, "We're going to sing a contemporary song about a great effort that some of the young men in our country are making." Tom chimed in, "Yes, it's a song about a problem and how, with good old American ingenuity, some people attempt to solve it." They then launched into the song, whose first verse and chorus went as follows:

> I'm just a typical American boy from a typical American town,
> I believe in God and Senator Dodd and keeping old Castro down.
> And when it came my time to serve I knew better dead than red,
> But when I got to my old draft board, buddy, this is what I said:
> Sarge, I'm only eighteen, I got a ruptured spleen and I always carry
>   a purse,
> I got eyes like a bat and my feet are flat, my asthma's getting worse.
> O, think of my career, my sweetheart dear, my poor old invalid
>   aunt,
> Besides I ain't no fool, I'm a-going to school, and I work in a
>   defense plant.[7]

For those who knew the song was Ochs's handiwork and knew that he was a well-known antiwar folksinger, the song could be read as a tongue-in-cheek support for draft resistance by any means available. However, the song allowed for a different interpretation, less sympathetic to those who evaded the draft. Just as the show's "We Protest Here" number could be read as mocking and ridiculing protesters and their methods, so too "Draft Dodger Rag" could be read as an indictment against those young men who shirked their military duty. Context was crucial. Phil Ochs's singing the song to young people protesting Selective Service at an antiwar rally opened the lyrics to their preferred meaning. However, in the context of a prime-time variety show with a still fairly diverse audience, the song's preferred meaning may not have been so evident. Perhaps aware of this, the Smothers ended the song with the proclamation, "Make love, not war!"[8]

Although the segment was open to various interpretations regarding draft evasion, CBS's Program Practices division, which would soon become the bane of the Smothers Brothers' existence, requested a copy of the lyric sheet. A CBS memo about this episode focused particularly on the "Draft Dodger Rag" number. The memo noted that the "introduction . . . seemed complimentary to draft dodgers." (The network's censors apparently were not worried about the song itself.) The memo also mentioned that the number resulted in four letters objecting to the material.[9] Despite the concern, the network allowed the episode to be rerun in the summer, apparently with no cuts.

Despite this mildly political material, little distinguished the first season of *The Smothers Brothers Comedy Hour* from other television variety shows. Guests included Jim Nabors, who sang "The Impossible Dream," Jack Benny and George Burns, Eddie Albert and Eva Gabor, Bette Davis, Jimmy Durante, and Lana Turner—guests more suited to CBS's traditional audience than to the younger set. Reinforcing the inoffensive, middle-of-the-road quality of much of the first season, Dick Smothers frequently appeared in solo numbers. Seated in an often bucolically designed stage setting and wearing a cardigan sweater, Dick would croon ballads that suggested the singer had more in common with Perry Como or Andy Williams than with Phil Ochs or Pete Seeger. Shots of the studio audience revealed many middle-aged, conservatively dressed people. The younger members of the audience were clean-cut and neatly attired.

The show's political stance, if it could be said to have one at this point, was decidedly liberal pluralist. Take the opening dialogue between Tom and Dick on the show's second episode, on February 12, 1967: The brothers were doing a rendition of "MacNamara's Ragtime Band." As was his habit, Tom broke into the song having called for more "pungent social commentary" at the beginning of the dialogue. He claimed that MacNamara's band was discriminatory because it was all Irish. The duo then changed the lyrics to include non-Irish names—all races and ethnic groups would now play in "MacNamara's Integrated Band." The pungent commentary turned into an unselfconscious celebration of American diversity and social tolerance.

At this point *The Smothers Brothers Comedy Hour* was a prime example of what Todd Gitlin has described as "hegemonic ideology . . .

Hippies with haircuts. Clean-cut Tom and Dick in the
first season of their show. *(Courtesy of the Smothers
Brothers)*

domesticating opposition, absorbing it into forms compatible with
the core ideological structure."[10] Network television, a cultural institution that typically functions to celebrate ideological consensus, had
apparently found a mechanism to absorb portions of the discourse
of a growing insurgency movement through comedy and song. If
clean-cut singer-comedians could sing about draft dodging, integration, and the value of protesting, then perhaps these issues were not
so threatening after all.

Wading into the Big Muddy

The first indication that the Smothers and their show might not continue serving establishment interests and upholding liberal pluralist

ideology came with the inauguration of the show's second season and the episode's primary guest star, folksinger Pete Seeger.[11] Seeger had already achieved legendary status among the folk-music community. An avowed leftist with connections to the Communist Party, he had been blacklisted from appearing on television since the 1950s. The folksinger's return to television on the Smothers Brothers' September 10, 1967, second-season premiere was supposed to culminate with a rendition of "Waist Deep in the Big Muddy." The song's narrative involved a World War II military officer who attempted to force his men to ford a raging river. The men turned back as the waters rose higher and higher. They watched as their commander forged on, only to drown in the muddy currents. The song ended with the following lyrics: "Now every time I read the papers / That old feelin' comes on / We're waist deep in the Big Muddy / And the big fool says to push on."[12]

The CBS brass decided to censor the song, considering the final stanza an unacceptable jibe at President Johnson and his Vietnam policy. The move caused a public uproar. Popular-press accounts were generally sympathetic to the Smothers and Seeger and critical of the network's actions. An internal memo from Program Practices head W. H. Tankersley to a fellow CBS staffer reveals how CBS attempted to justify the action to its own personnel:

> Admittedly, our decisions concerning material of this nature will not always seem entirely consistent. Basically, however, our touchstone should be that we accept material which is obviously designed for the primary purpose of entertaining rather than to advance a point of view on a controversial subject. . . . Nevertheless, value judgments will have to be made from time to time, and we cannot open the door to all material simply on the basis that its principal function is to provide entertainment. I do not think that we could accept Dr. Timothy O'Leary [*sic*] singing a song extolling the merits of LSD and marijuana, nor can we ever ignore taste considerations such as that present in Pete Seeger's "Big Muddy," in which there is metaphorical reference to the President as a fool.[13]

The network censor attempted to map out the limits of hegemonic elasticity. As Gitlin has noted, hegemonic systems are absorptive.[14] However, as the brothers were to discover, there were limits to that elasticity. In September of 1967 CBS management set the boundary of discursive diversity by rejecting entertainment that served a dissident political position. The network attempted to take refuge in constructing a notion of entertainment as something essentially removed from the real world of political and social relations. However, as Tankersley's memo concluded: "I believe it is safe to say that the SMOTHERS BROTHERS program is a testing ground from which some refinements of policy are bound to emerge."

A refinement of policy did indeed emerge. Because of public pressure the network permitted the Smothers to invite Seeger back to the program later in the season to perform his controversial song. Correspondence reveals something of the ideological shift CBS underwent in order to encompass politically charged discourse within the network's modified definition of entertainment. Responding to an advertiser's complaint about the show, Tankersley wrote:

> The Smothers Brothers like to poke fun at "the establishment," and we have the daily task of deciding just where they may be abusing the privilege. Generally speaking we have tried to avoid imposing restraints too quickly (despite their protestations to the press), and guidelines are gradually evolving. Their material expresses to a great extent the concerns of a large segment of today's youth, and to suppress it entirely could be said to contravene the postulate that television should mirror life around us. In fact it is almost impossible to present contemporary popular songs which do not contain some comment directly or indirectly on issues of public importance: war, peace, civil rights, patriotism, conformity, and the like.[15]

In this case the network appeared to understand that to maintain legitimacy it needed to cater, to some extent, to views that were not held by the social and political elites with whom culture industry forces were aligned. Another letter from Tankersley's office to a viewer specifically protesting Seeger's reappearance further illustrates how the network attempted to negotiate the ideological conundrum:

> With reference to the appearance of Pete Seeger, we do not believe it is our proper function to exclude an otherwise talented and qualified performer from programs broadcast over our facilities merely because of his expression or advocacy of opinions in the political or governmental arena. . . .
>
> We have come to recognize the fact that protest songs and satiri-

cal skits constitute a sizable proportion of today's entertainment fare, caused undoubtedly by the intense concern the younger generation has for the moral and social issues of the day. To try to analyze and catalog the various attitudes and expressions contained in them, and to allow some and disallow others in an attempt to achieve some sort of balance, would in our view be a futile effort and ethically questionable. Thus we permitted, for example, the song "Open Letter to a Teenage Son," which many viewers found "hawkish," just as many others have objected to the Pete Seeger song which presented an allegorical criticism of the Vietnam war.[16]

In this letter to the viewer, who apparently had no connection to the industry, the network hid its policing function and appealed to pluralist ideals. The CBS network presented itself as ideologically neutral and willing to air conflicting sides of a controversial issue.

The network's change of direction may have been affected, to some extent, by events that occurred between Seeger's initial censored appearance and his second performance in February of 1968. The Tet Offensive, a massive and deadly North Vietnamese assault on American and South Vietnamese forces in January, shocked the nation. This, along with growing anti-Johnson sentiment in the Democratic Party, led many, including some at the highest levels of the Johnson administration, to begin questioning the president's war policy. Network anchorman Walter Cronkite's famous post-Tet estimation that the war was "hopelessly stalemated" suggested that Johnson was, indeed, mired in the Big Muddy. Saying so in an entertainment program may have seemed less controversial in February 1968 than it had in September 1967.[17]

The clear winners in this particular battle with CBS were the Smothers and Seeger. We can see how they succeeded in pushing the parameters of acceptable political discourse within a network-defined "entertainment" format by comparing the "Big Muddy" segment censored by CBS with the later version aired February 25, 1968. In Seeger's first visit to the show he and Tom chatted onstage about the meaning of folk songs. As Seeger began strumming the melody of "Big Muddy," Tom said, "You going to do that song now? You were telling us that story about . . ." Seeger interrupted, "I tell too many stories. I'll just let the song stand on its own two feet. You know, a song can mean a thousand different things to different people. What

Tom and Dick
welcome Pete
Seeger back to
their show.

"We're waist deep in
the Big Muddy and
the big fool says to
push on." *(Both
images courtesy of the
Smothers Brothers)*

does a song mean—well whatever it means to you. But I'm not going to tell you what it means to me—I might destroy your illusions."[18]

Seeger's comments seemed an attempt to defuse the politically charged nature of the song. In keeping with the show's tactics of allowing for various interpretations of controversial material, Seeger's introduction encouraged listeners to read the song variously as an indictment of Johnson's Vietnam policy or merely as a story about the Second World War or in any other way they chose. The song did not necessarily have to be seen as an antiwar parable.

No such equivocation was evident in Seeger's second visit. Sitting alone in a rocking chair on a bare stage strumming a banjo, Seeger went through a medley of war songs from American history, many of them carrying obvious antiwar sentiments. At one point Seeger commented that the wars from which these songs arose were all contentious. He then stood up, replaced the banjo with a guitar, and launched into a dramatic rendition of "Big Muddy." Within that context the preferred meaning of the song was undeniable. The victory of Seeger and the Smothers over the network came not only from getting the song broadcast but in broadcasting a politically uncompromised version. The liberal pluralist ideals the network put forth for public and intraindustry consumption were no longer shared by the Smothers. The consensual fiction that all views and interpretations were equal, that one side could and should be balanced against another (thus defusing and neutralizing oppositional positions) became less and less evident in the show's material. The Smothers Brothers were taking a position, as they had to if they were to gain legitimacy with an increasingly vocal and politicized youth movement from which they wished to draw their audience.

Hi(gh)! And Glad of It: Sharing a Little Tea with Goldie

The Smothers Brothers' attempts to align themselves with dissident youth and to appeal to their tastes and lifestyles was particularly evident with the character Goldie O'Keefe, who began appearing regularly by the show's second season. The creation of comedienne Leigh French, Goldie was the ultimate "hippie chick," as well as a Gracie Allen figure harkening to the show's vaudeville/variety format. Playing on both these feminine icons, she bore an infantalized demeanor with her wide eyes; constant giggle; beatific smile; long, girlish braids; and outrageously astute airheadedness. However, unlike the hippie chicks we encountered in chapter 2, French's Goldie often exploded and made ridiculous these taken-for-granted sexist assumptions about femininity. Along with that, her comedy revolved around television's taboo subject when it came to depictions of countercultural activity: she affirmed and celebrated mind-altering substances.

As we saw in chapter 2, television representations of hippies were frequently sympathetic to counterculture critiques of mainstream, acquisitive, materialist, rationalist American life. Network television often upheld perceived hippie values of love, simplicity, communalism, and spiritual search as social attributes that had been lost and needed to be embraced again for American society to renew itself. However, embedded in all hippie values, ideals, and activities were LSD, marijuana, and other psychotropic drugs. This presented a problem for television because illegal drug use could not be condoned, much less advocated. To uphold hippie values but to condemn the use of psychedelics was a contradictory stance that network television assumed over and over. In showcasing Goldie O'Keefe the Smothers Brothers found creative ways to broadcast support for the counterculture—drug use and all.

In one of Goldie's first appearances on the show Tom pulled her out of the audience where she sat next to a conservatively dressed middle-aged man. The man (who may or may not have been an actor) offered the opinion that the hippies seemed to live in a world of their own but that they never bothered him.[19] Tom brought Goldie onstage, where they discussed the flowers and bag of fertilizer Goldie had given him. Tom explained, "I shared it with my friends and we all grew a lot." Tom then thanked her for coming down from San Francisco. Goldie giggled and responded, "Oh, I never come down." She proceeded to give Tom a set of love beads made out of seeds that she compared to oregano.

Goldie O'Keefe became a regular on the show, appearing in a continuing segment called "Share a Little Tea with Goldie," a parody of afternoon TV advice shows for housewives. Goldie would open the sketch with salutations such as "Hi! And glad of it" or "Hi—isn't it? It sure is!"[20] In one sketch she mentioned that she had previously given advice on how to get rid of "unsightly roaches." She went on to thank viewers who had sent her theirs. She then demonstrated to the "ladies" in her viewing audience how to make whole wheat bread. Kneading the dough, Goldie began declaring in rapturous tones, "The more you knead it, the higher it rises. The higher it rises, the lighter you feel. Ohhh—I feel good already! Ladies, ladies, ladies, get it on this way. My bread is getting high. And I'm beginning to rise!"[21] In another sketch she pondered ladies' faces. "Which are directly connected to our heads. And we all know how important our heads are. And if you don't, I'm sure all the heads do."[22]

Goldie and her drug-oriented humor created potential censorship problems for the show and for the network, yet much of the material managed to make it on air.[23] A memo to CBS head censor Tankersley (written shortly before the network threw the Smothers off the air) catalogued many of the "disagreements" between the network and the Smothers over material, specifically what had been deleted and what had been altered. Listed here and there were examples of Goldie O'Keefe material, including "some half-dozen pot references" that were deleted from the June 11, 1967, episode. Nevertheless, much of Goldie's humor evaded the censor's scissors.[24] Another memo to Tankersley emphasized the fact that much of Goldie's material made it to the air. Written shortly after CBS had canceled the show, the memo responded to Tankersley's request for a rundown of marijuana references from the 1968/69 season. The itemized list included many examples from Goldie O'Keefe, including the following item: "Show 0217, for air January 26: The 'Tea With Goldie' spot included the line 'A lot of you ladies have written in asking when I'm on. . . . Ladies, I'm on as often as possible and I highly recommend it.' This was broadcast. The line 'You know anything with tea and pot in its name is going to give you a groovy sound' was scripted but omitted from the tape."[25]

How can we explain the relatively easy time Goldie's material had with CBS censors, who became progressively more and more vigilant and scissor-happy with the show's scripts and review tapes?[26] One answer is the discursive advantage the show's young writers had over the fifty-something Tankersley and his staff. Terms such as *roach, head, tea,* and, for that matter, *Goldie* and *Kief* all had drug-oriented meanings within countercultural circles. The show's facility with current drug slang may have assisted in legitimizing its material with young people and mystifying its meanings to the older generation. Tankersley and company may have realized that many of these terms were

Goldie O'Keefe: Prodrug and antiwar. *(Courtesy of the Smothers Brothers)*

drug code words but seemed incapable of preventing all the "roaches" from sneaking through. The slang and punning became means to evade the network's policing. Young "heads" could take pleasure from the broadcasting of celebratory references to drugs, supposedly taboo on network television.

The censors may also have been less concerned with Goldie's drug humor because the code language, in sheltering the uninitiated from its actual meanings, probably resulted in fewer complaints. The show's more overtly political material could not be coded in this manner. For it to have an appropriate impact on viewers, meanings had to be generally unambiguous. Goldie's playful ambiguity and appeal to "lifestyle" issues rather than "politics" may have given her comedy more room to operate.

Goldie's gender construction also worked as a site for potentially subversive play. As we saw in chapter 2, television representations of female hippies tried to "domesticate" manifestations of youth rebellion and render them less threatening. Goldie took normalized notions of domesticity (through the parody of housewife shows in "Share a Little Tea") and the various markers of femininity and stretched them into hyperbolic excess, thus deconstructing and denaturalizing them both. By taking the most innocuous and culturally safest genre of "ladies'" programming and turning it into a celebration of "dangerous" drugs, Goldie opened up to question not only the menace of pot and LSD but also assumptions of what it meant to be a "lady."

In her costuming and performance Goldie also foregrounded patriarchal constructions of feminine childishness so taken for granted in most televisual representations. Her braids, her wide eyes, her giggling were so exaggerated as to call attention to themselves. They could be read as signs pointing, parodically, to precisely the manufactured ways female hippie characters tended to be portrayed in many popular cultural representations.

As *The Smothers Brothers Comedy Hour* moved into its second and truncated third seasons, the Smothers attempted to slip through more unambiguous and politically charged material. The show's sketches became more overtly confrontational, almost inviting censorship from the network. The struggles between the brothers and the network became more pitched between the fall of 1968 and the spring of 1969, tracking with and mirroring upheavals reverberating throughout the American political terrain.

In the late sixties the vision of the United States as a consensual society in which a variety of voices had equal status and the opportunity to flourish in a marketplace of ideas began to unravel. Insurgent voices threatened various segments of hegemonic order, no longer accepting the ground rules laid down by those in power. Simultaneously, elites within those positions found themselves no longer ideologically unified, as oppositional movements challenged their assumptions. Entertainment television, whose ideological function was the perpetual reaffirmation of dominant ideas and ideals, began having a difficult time performing its mission.

The insurgency of many African Americans, for example, began departing from Martin Luther King Jr.'s assimilationist discourse, which, although certainly threatening many naturalized ideas about race, did not menace core American values. The ascendant black-power position proved far more frightening in its rejection of equality with whites based on white definitions of social behavior and success.[27] Segments of the antiwar movement had also shifted to a far more confrontational position as orderly picket lines and marches on Washington did not appear to be halting the war. The March on the Pentagon in October 1967 marked a turning point from the "politics of protest" to the "politics of confrontation." Thousands of mostly young protesters swarmed onto the grounds of the Pentagon to "confront the warmakers" and "obstruct the war machine."[28] Protests on campuses were also becoming far more militant, bringing down occasionally violent force onto student heads. A protest against recruiters for napalm-producing Dow Chemicals at the University of Wisconsin-Madison in October 1967 resulted in the teargassing and clubbing by city police of scores of students.[29] The tactically and politically militant directions into which these insurgent movements were heading struck at the heart of the dominant social and political order, questioning its legitimacy, revealing as myth many previously held tenets of what America was all about.

Perhaps nothing revealed the revolutionary possibilities residing with these mostly youth-oriented insurgent movements better than the series of crises the United States lurched through in the year 1968.[30] Beginning with the Tet Offensive at the beginning of the year and the public's growing realization that the president and the nation's military had lied about the progress of the war and prospects for military victory, one section of the dominant social and political order after another began to be called into doubt. The assassinations of Martin Luther King Jr. and Democratic presidential hopeful Robert Kennedy shattered hopes for many that any potential progressive leaders would live long enough to promote change peacefully through approved channels. The pent-up rage King's murder unleashed in the nation's ghettos led to riots, burnings, and countless casualties, causing concern that America's black population perched on the edge of outright insurrection. The police clubs and blackjacks that battered the heads of protesting Columbia University students led to questions about whether higher education in the United States could function at all anymore. How could colleges and universities continue reproducing the social order through production of suitably educated personnel when educational assembly lines appeared to be grinding to a halt all over the country? The televised agonies of the profoundly divided Democratic Party in Chicago called into question whether the political process could continue to function. National Guard troops with barbed wire stretched across their vehicles mediated between the disintegrating party and militant young demonstrators who seemed far more unified and purposeful than those who were supposed to be their representatives in political office.

Thus 1968 epitomized a crisis of authority.[31] A whole range of social institutions seemed to be coming undone, no longer able to legitimate themselves through dominant ideology and resorting to coercion to maintain power. As we saw in chapter 3, television was intricately bound up with the unmasking of power at the Chicago Democratic Convention as the Yippies and their allies used the medium to reveal the brutal power that hid behind American liberal democracy. The crisis of hegemonic legitimacy wreaked havoc through the universities, the ghettos, the military complex, and the political process. This crisis also played out within the popular-culture industry. The turmoil on Chicago's Michigan Avenue in August reoccurred metaphorically on *The Smothers Brothers Comedy Hour* in September.

Tom and Dick Smothers, Propagandists

The Smothers Brothers' third-season premiere, aired September 29, 1968, put on display all the anguish, rage and righteousness felt by the youthful militants who had felt the coercive power of unmasked authority in Chicago, at Columbia, and wherever police batons cracked heads. The Smothers attempted to illustrate in their opening segment the transformation that these events had wrought. The brothers appeared standing behind a podium looking noticeably different from their clean-cut, short-haired, burgundy-suited previous selves. They now both wore longer hair, moustaches, and mod nehru jackets.[32] After Tom banged a gavel, Dick announced, "The first order of business will be to vote on the subject of the physical appearance of Tom and Dick Smothers." Tom asked, "All those in favor of the Smothers Brothers *having* moustaches say 'aye.'" Some in the studio audience gave a small, unenthusiastic "aye." Tom then asked, "All those in favor of the Smothers not having moustaches say 'no.'" This elicited a huge

The new, "mod" Smothers Brothers: nehru jackets, longer hair, confrontational politics. *(Courtesy of the Smothers Brothers)*

response from audience members, who shouted, "No!" In consternation Tom gaveled the podium and announced, "In the true American democratic, conventional, spirit, the 'ayes' have it. The moustaches stay!" The camera panned the audience as members began booing, jumping up and down, waving arms, giving the thumbs down, and launching into "We Shall Overcome." Tom gaveled away, shouting

"Drown them out, bring in the band!" The audience continued to boo as the familiar marching band credit sequence commenced. As the show's dancers went through their routine, there were cuts back to Tom and Dick at the podium and shots of the audience booing.[33]

The opening is significant not only in its clear reference to the attempted suppression of dissent in Chicago but also in its refusal to uphold traditional rituals. The old-fashioned Americana opening could no longer be played out unselfreflexively. Just as the various shocks of 1968 had disrupted the operations of the social and political order, so too the Smothers disrupted the operations of their show to indicate their awareness that things were not right. If television viewers thought they could escape the political chaos reverberating throughout the nation by tuning into an entertainment show, the Smothers seemed to be saying that the chaos and political breakdown represented by Chicago reverberated here as well.

The politically confrontational stance continued with the brothers' opening duet:

> The war in Vietnam keeps on a-raging
> Blacks and whites still haven't worked it out
> Pollution, guns and poverty surround us
> No wonder everybody's dropping out
> But we're still here We're still here
> We face the same old problems But we're here
> The weekly grind is stretching out before us
> The bleeping censors lurking in the wings
> CBS would like to give us notice
> And some of you don't like the things we say
> But we're still here We're still here
> You may not think we're funny But we're here

The brothers metaphorically gave the finger to CBS and to critics and viewers who complained that the comics were no longer funny. The song seemed to target viewers like Paul McCalib in St. Cloud, Minnesota, who wrote to *TV Guide*: "*The Smothers Brothers Comedy Hour* was once fresh, original and true satire because it was impartial in choice of targets. By the end of the season the brothers seemed to have been converted to hippyism, the so-called new politics and similar 'causes.' Having lost objectivity, they, their cast and guests have become propagandists—and propagandists are rarely funny; they take themselves too seriously and consign all who disagree, even slightly, to limbo."[34] Their song appeared to say that if they were perceived as propagandists for youth politics, then so be it; however, the final stanza included an attempted appeal to the pluralist positions they once upheld:

> Both of us have grown a manly moustache
> Red blazers that we always wore are gone
> Our clean cut all-American look is changing
> But underneath we're still old Dick and Tom
> But we're still here We're still here
> You may not recognize us But we're still here

The half-hearted attempt to reassure older or more conservative viewers and fans that the old Smothers—the ones who could appeal equally to the New Left and the American Legion—could still be found under the mod clothing and unequivocal political positions was unconvincing. The Smothers in this third-season premiere took every opportunity to emphasize where their political allegiances lay. And like the young demonstrators in Mayor Daley's Chicago, they too had to pay for attempting to unmask unjust authority.

The brothers paid dearly for a song by guest star Harry Belafonte. Although the entire episode was rife with allusions to Chicago, next to the opening sketch, none was so pointed as Belafonte's number "Don't Stop the Carnival." Some lyrics to the calypso piece went as follows:

> Oh Lord, I feel so low About the toddlin' town
> Of old Chicago
> Humphrey, Muskie, McGovern and McCarthy
> Split the party Now nobody be happy
> Tell all the population
> We're havin' a confrontation
> Let it be known freedom's gone
> And the country's not our own
> Lord, don't stop the carnival
> Carnival's American bacchanal.[35]

Later in the number Belafonte sang about a sly mongoose: "Dogs know your name / Sly mongoose / Dogs know your name / Mongoose puts on his wooden gloves / Go out hunting for flock of doves /

Harry Belafonte's censored "Don't Stop the Carnival" number.
(Courtesy of the Smothers Brothers)

Hunting is what the mongoose loves." Belafonte and the Smothers
wanted to use footage from the Chicago convention and demonstrations to illustrate the song, and CBS initially agreed, with two provi-
sos: the footage could not show close-ups that might identify anyone,
and the footage could contain no violence.[36] The second demand was
rather ludicrous given that the police beatings that occurred both on
the streets and on the convention floor defined much of what was
politically significant about Chicago. The network's concern about
allowing the Smothers use of the material is telling. News footage
and photos of the event had been widely disseminated. It was not as if
viewers were unfamiliar with the material. Even CBS had carried ex-
tensive, live coverage. Its news reporter Dan Rather had been uncere-
moniously clubbed by police inside the convention hall, and anchorman Walter Cronkite, on the air, referred to the officers as thugs.[37]
The news division encountered a barrage of complaints regarding its
coverage, charging bias toward the demonstrators. Clearly, representations of Chicago carried politically charged meanings—meanings
that network executives feared could not be contained. Even within a
news context, where strategies of journalistic distance and objectivity

should dampen politically explosive material, the imagery from Chicago could not be controlled. As we saw in the last chapter, the networks, Mayor Daley, the Yippies, and other participants in the youth movement all battled over definitions of that politically contentious broadcast footage. That CBS considered this material explosive and threatening seems clear because the network believed it had to police the further dissemination of that imagery by allowing the Smothers to use footage only in ways that would have effectively defanged the material.

The "Carnival" number went through different run-throughs as network representatives and the Smothers negotiated allowable footage. Somehow they found material with no violence, but the network objected to recognizable shots of Mayor Daley that appeared just after Belafonte sang about the sly mongoose. Ultimately, CBS summarily censored the whole sketch, but the Smothers refused to insert new material to fill the five-minute gap. The network in turn sold the time to the Republican Party, which ran an advertisement for the Nixon/Agnew presidential ticket in the last five minutes of the Smothers Brothers' Sunday-night time slot.

A Doily for Your Mind: Smothering the Smothers

On October 13, 1968, the Smothers Brothers' opening teaser tracked down a line of men in suits (all played by the show's writers, including the still-unknown Steve Martin).[38] Each in turn looked down at the show's script, laughed uproariously at what he read, then tore out those pages and handed the rest of the script to the next in line, who did the same thing. The script, with one page left, got down to the last man on line who read it without laughing. He then turned to Tom and Dick, handed them the page saying, "Nothing funny in this. Here you are boys, we're through censoring your show."

Although the Smothers and their supporters recognized only political repressiveness as the network's motivation, CBS faced a clear economic dilemma that shouldn't be ignored. Some advertisers protested the show's politically sensitive material. However, by the third season much of the advertising on the show clearly targeted a youth market. Volkswagen became a participating sponsor, an astute marketing strategy given that inexpensive VW Beetles and microbuses had become synonymous with youth culture.[39] And Volkswagen's famous advertising campaigns of the 1960s sat quite comfortably with nonconformist, countercultural values.[40]

More troubling to the network was protest from affiliates. The head of a group of stations in Michigan and Nebraska wrote CBS's head of affiliate relations, complaining about how "sick" the show was, "especially from its political orientation and religious standpoint."[41] The letter strongly suggested CBS not pick up the show for renewal and warned that if the network was "unable to temper the show, there is a serious question as to whether we will be able to clear it next year, especially in prime time." The writer suggested that if the show should be on the air at all, it would do best in late-night slots with such "kook" programs as the *Alan Burke Show,* the *Les Crane Show* and the *Joe Pyne Show.* As we saw in the last chapter, such "kook" talk shows, especially the *Les Crane Show,* allowed some in the youth movement to feel they had found a bit of space to speak in their own voices. The midwestern affiliate clearly did not think that prime time was the place for antiestablishment youth discourse. Another affiliate in Topeka, Kansas, protested to the network as well. The station's general manager even took to the airwaves in an editorial denouncing the show's "filth," proclaiming that "we've had enough."[42] Even if it had wanted to, the network could not ignore such sentiments.

The show's ratings also elicited concern. The Smothers started the season as the seventh-most popular program, with a thirty-seven percent share of the audience. Archrival *Bonanza* stood right behind in eighth place.[43] By the end of the year the show had dipped slightly to twelfth place.[44] By March 1969 the Smothers sank further down to twenty-fourth place, whereas *Bonanza* staged a robust recovery, grabbing third place on the Nielsen totem pole.[45]

If the ratings had begun to fall off, it may have been because the Smothers no longer gave more than the appearance of wanting a pluralistic audience. They were going after young people, experimenting with ways to bring them into the brothers' tiny and ever-under-attack semiliberated zone of prime time. The Beatles, for instance, appeared a number of times in taped segments. Tom introduced their rendition of "Revolution" with this thought: "If you watched our show last week, you saw the Beatles sing 'Hey Jude.' And if you also watched the show the week before, you didn't see Harry Belafonte sing 'Please Don't Stop the Carnival.' Which has nothing to do with the fact that the Beatles will now sing 'Revolution.' Or does it?"[46] Jefferson Airplane appeared with lead singer Grace Slick in bizarre blackface and gloved fist, clenched in a black-power salute, as she sang the group's paean to dissident youth, "Crown of Creation." The Doors came on and did a decidedly strange number called "Wild Child." If these were all attempts to appeal to the cultural side of the movement, the show also included material with which insurgent young people could identify in other ways. In the opening sketch on December 15, 1968, Tom fiddled with a helmet, gas mask, and leather gloves as he complained to Dick about what a drag it was that eighteen thousand people had to go through with this. "A group of certain people make you do this," he added as he put the helmet on. Dick asked him what he was doing. With helmet and gas mask in place, Tom replied, "I'm getting ready to go to college."

In their clearest overture to insurgent and countercultural youth the Smothers tried to depart entirely from their show's conventional TV variety setup. The show experimented with a number of concert-in-the-round programs that broke the proscenium-arch performance environment, bringing the audience into the scene. This kind of performance space suggested the folk music/coffee house roots of the Smothers and the nonhierarchical, participatory ideals of that entertainment form. Spectators could be seen in every shot and from every camera angle, and they were almost uniformly young and "hip" looking. This set design provided the Smothers with a tangible way to point out to television viewers exactly who they thought their audience really was and exactly who they wanted to address.

The choice of guests reinforced the countercultural milieu. Concert-in-the-round performers were almost exclusively associated with youth culture. Hippie folksinger Donovan, who appeared on two such programs, performed one of his hit songs while sitting cross-legged on a furry mat. At the end of the number audience members tossed flowers at him. Folk trio Peter, Paul, and Mary appeared in another concert-in-the-round show, leading the entire cast and audience in a finale of "Day Is Done." Performers mingled with spectators, and members of the audience moved toward the stage, giving the impression of a big love-in.[47]

The appearance of another folksinger in a concert-in-the-round episode led to one of the Smothers Brothers' final showdowns with CBS censors before the network removed the show from the air

Joan Baez's censored appearance in a "concert in the round" episode.
(Courtesy of the Smothers Brothers)

entirely. Joan Baez had been closely associated with both the civil
rights and antiwar movements. When she appeared on the Smothers
Brothers' show, her husband, antidraft organizer David Harris, faced
a lengthy prison sentence. She dedicated a song to him and explained
why he was going to jail: "He refused to have anything to do with
the draft or Selective Service or whatever you want to call it. Militarism in general. If you do that and you do it up front, overground,
then you're going to get busted. Especially if you organize—which
he did."[48] CBS not only censored the Baez segment but pulled the
entire episode from its March 9, 1969, scheduled airdate. The network relented, to a degree, broadcasting the show a few weeks later;
however, the censors snipped out Baez's explanation of why her husband was going to prison. According to one account of the affair,
"Tommy was sure viewers would figure Harris was guilty of grand

larceny or worse."[49] The network rationalized its actions, according to a *Saturday Review* article, by arguing that Baez's "remarks on the Smothers Brothers show were 'editorial,' and not suitable for entertainment programs."[50]

Despite these attempts to break out from the variety show format, *The Smothers Brothers Comedy Hour*, for the most part, remained stylistically quite traditional. In this area the show provides a useful contrast to another "youth-oriented" variety series that began climbing the Nielsen totem pole just as the Smothers Brothers were sliding down. *Rowan and Martin's Laugh-In*, which premiered on NBC in 1968, was indebted to the Smothers Brothers' show in the latter's opening up of prime time to politically and socially oriented humor but also diverged from the *Comedy Hour*, proving much more adept at playing an ideological and generational balancing act. Dan Rowan purportedly observed that whereas the Smothers Brothers used comedy as a platform for politics, his variety series used politics as a platform for comedy.

Hosting *Laugh-In* were two aging, tuxedoed, Las Vegas–style lounge performers whom no one could mistake for youth movement fellow travelers. However, although Dan Rowan and Dick Martin may have seemed the picture of establishment middle-agism, what surrounded them on *Laugh-In* partook far more of the counterculture than the Smothers Brothers show ever did, even with their concert-in-the-round episodes. *Laugh-In* abounded in hallucinogenic flashes, zooms, breathtakingly quick cuts, and a barrage of psychedelic colors, along with volleys of one-liners that frequently mined the same anti-establishment terrain as the Smothers Brothers' show. Take, for example, these comic observations from a recurring *Laugh-In* sketch, "The Party," in which Dan and Dick invited viewers into a go-go style dance party to view hip young things gyrating among the cast regulars while the camera flashed and zoomed among participants. Judy Carne, the Cockney-accented "sock-it-to-me girl" stopped dancing long enough to observe: "All the kids at my school really admire the astronauts. Imagine staying that high for that long." After more dancing and frenetic editing, Arte Johnson appeared as an Indian guru in white nehru jacket with a hand up in a peace sign. He intoned wisely: "What with the ankle, the hip, the elbow, and the wrist—boo to those who speak evilly of the joint." More hallucinogenic editing and camera swoops, and we cut to Dave Madden: "I sure hope

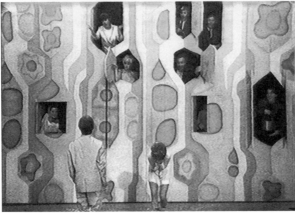

Laugh-In hosts Dan Rowan and Dick Martin:
middle-aged men in tuxedoes surrounded by
psychedelia; *Laugh-In*'s counterculture-inspired set
design: the Day-Glo joke wall.

our new president ends the war in Vietnam so that we can bring
our 500,000 advisors back home—to reload." [51] This was precisely the
kind of material that CBS had an increasingly difficult time counte-
nancing from the Smothers Brothers; however, NBC tended to let its
top-rated variety show get away with these kinds of jokes, objecting more to sexually daring material. Also, the blackout, rapid-fire
manner of the delivery tended to blunt the political implications of
much of this humor. By the time the viewer got the message behind
the joke, two or three other nonpolitical jokes or blackouts had al-

ready whizzed by. The Smothers Brothers' slower-paced approach to political comedy allowed far fewer distractions than did *Laugh-In*.

The Smothers were less daring in their visual style and more insistent of their political content. But they also continued to feature middle-of-the-road entertainers more likely to appeal to the older set. The Smothers used performers like Kate Smith and Burl Ives strategically, not so much to bring in a pluralistic audience as to legitimize the discourses of the young. Kate Smith, who guest-starred in the same episode as the Jefferson Airplane, appeared in a sketch about the Bill of Rights. Unlike *Laugh-In*'s the humor didn't whiz by before audiences could get the message. Smith and Pat Paulsen played a married couple sitting in their living room with Smith doing a crossword puzzle. In the segment Smith asked Paulsen for a series of seven-letter words:

> *Smith:* A seven letter word that means United States.
> *Paulsen:* America.
> *Smith:* A seven letter word that means difference of opinion.
> *Paulsen:* Dissent.
> *Smith:* One who loves his country.
> *Paulsen:* Patriot.
> *Smith:* Objection made to official of the government.
> *Paulsen:* Protest.
> *Smith:* Word that means all those things.
> *Paulsen:* Freedom.[52]

Unlike the "We Protest Here" sketch almost two years before, this piece contained no ambivalence or gentle mocking of dissenting behavior. The message was clear, and Kate Smith's participation seemed to sanction that activity. The sketch was as much an example of "editorialization" as opposed to "entertainment" as the Baez segment (neither had a comic punchline). Kate Smith was not publicly aligned with an insurgent protest movement, however, which made the political sentiments she spoke seem less threatening. Nobody could question the patriotism of Kate Smith.

Burl Ives had a left-wing/folk-singer background similar to Seeger's but, unlike Seeger, seemed to have rehabilitated himself in popular television. He was known to many as the snowman narrator of the Christmas favorite *Rudolf the Red-Nosed Reindeer* and, by the late 1960s, was a familiar fixture on variety shows. On the Smothers

Brothers' show Ives was used in a manner similar to Kate Smith in a long sketch that reworked Thornton Wilder's *Our Town*. Ives appeared as a man returning to his old hometown, relieved to see that the rioting and mayhem of the big cities had not troubled his community. Everything was still the same. However, a series of blackouts revealed something different. In one a barber railed against "those commy pinky, long-haired peace-niks." In another a woman asked her druggist for codeine, diet pills, pep pills, and tranquilizers. The latter she needed to deal with jury duty. She wanted to see the accused get what he deserved. When the druggist asked what the accused was up for, she replied, "Drugs." After a series of vignettes about small town hypocrisy and narrow-mindedness, Ives launched into a version of Bob Dylan's "The Times They Are A-Changin'." As if to emphasize the song's message, the lyrics were printed on the bottom of the screen:

> Come mothers and fathers throughout the land
> And don't criticize what you can't understand
> Your sons and your daughters are beyond your command
> Your old road is rapidly agin'
> Please get out of the new one if you can't lend a hand
> For the times they are a-changin'.[53]

This particular segment came to the attention of underground press readers through a rave notice from Harlan Ellison, science fiction writer and resident television critic for the *Los Angeles Free Press*. Ellison praised the "unsettling" quality of the piece. He then described the segment for his readers and went on to declare that it was their "unholy chore" to support the Smothers:

> Dig, this is somewhere near where it's at, I think. . . .
>
> So, inexorably, they will kill a show like *The Smothers Brothers Comedy Hour*. They have to. It threatens them [the entrenched forces who rule the mass media] too much. Courage and honesty such as Smothers II show us each week must be protected. And if a couple of hundred dingdongs can get something like *Star Trek* renewed, it would seem to behoove all of us who *care*, to start writing letters to CBS to counteract the potency of those assassin diatribes from Mashed Potato Falls, Wyoming.[54]

Ellison affirmed that "the hip folk are watching the show religiously (or anti-religiously, depending on where your Valhalla is located)."[55] Ellison's review also pointed out that the very fact that the show was "somewhere near where it's at" threatened network forces terribly. After all, CBS could not really tolerate the dissemination of counter-cultural sentiments that were attracting socially and politically uncontrollable "hip folk." Something had to give.

Inevitably, the network took action against the show. On April 3, 1969, Robert D. Wood, president of the network, informed Tom Smothers by wire that because he had not sent in an acceptable broadcast tape in time for preview by the Program Practices Department and affiliated stations, the contract between the brothers and the network was officially terminated.[56]

A Matter of Taste

If CBS's previous censorious behavior encouraged an interpretation of the network as coercive authority, then the cancellation merely strengthened that perception. The action generated an enormous amount of media publicity, much of it condemning the network, from an editorial in the *New York Times* to a cover story in the popular magazine *Look*. The CBS network struggled hard to deny the coerciveness of its operation and to reassert a naturalized position of cultural leadership. If the network's battle with the Smothers unmasked the ideologically repressive workings of the dominant order, then the network needed to deny that ideological struggle was going on at all. Its argument was that it all came down to taste.

The network's public campaign to explain and justify its censorship and cancellation of the Smothers Brothers revolved around notions of good and bad taste.[57] Robert Wood articulated the network's position this way:

> The central issue involved in the cancellation of this program was very simple: whether a broadcast organization has a responsibility to the public with respect to questions of taste and, if so, whether they are entitled to establish reasonable procedures in order to exercise that responsibility. . . .

On the one hand, we have an obligation to the ideals and purposes of creative art, and we try to do everything we can to expand creative freedom and encourage artistic expression. On the other, we have an obligation to the audience—and to its sense of decency, propriety and morality. The alternative would be to eliminate all standards of taste, and let the viewers fend for themselves—remove all impediments to what could be seen in the living room by any person at any time of any sensibility.[58]

The network disguised its coercion by posing as the guardian of a consensual, commonsensical notion of "decency, propriety and morality." Standards of taste were self-evident and agreed to by all, not subject to the need for definition. By appealing to "taste," the network attempted to depoliticize the struggle over discourse it would allow and discourse it rejected.

Richard Jencks, president of the CBS Broadcast Group, also raised the banner of taste in a speech before affiliates shortly after the Smothers Brothers' show was canceled:

Television, to be sure, must cope with changing standards of taste. We must do everything we can to expand creative freedom and encourage artistic expression. Above all, we must reach out to the young, and attempt to understand and reflect their tastes—as much for our good as theirs. . . .

To achieve the objective of expanding creative freedom, we rely on a spirit of understanding and active cooperation in dealing with our artists. *We* must be as interested as *they* in exploring legitimate cultural frontiers. *They* must be as interested as *we* in avoiding unnecessary offense to the pious, the immature and the innocent (emphasis in original).[59]

The discursive give-and-take Jencks advocated was somewhat restrictive. The network would determine what was legitimate and where the boundary of the cultural frontier lay. Political material was fine as long as it did not offend anyone—as long as it did not call into question power relations and the naturalized social order. Because that was precisely what the insurgent movements of the 1960s attempted to do, CBS could not allow a show "somewhere near where it's at" to continue broadcasting.

Just as the network attempted to render its ideological construc-

tion of taste as plain common sense, so too did it attempt to naturalize and deproblematize its dichotomization of news programming
and entertainment programming. Appended to *Look* magazine's very
sympathetic article on the stifling of the Smothers Brothers show was
a letter from Robert Wood giving the network's side of the controversy. The Wood letter contrasted what was appropriate in news television with what was appropriate in entertainment. Dissident and
antiestablishment views, such as those expressed in coverage of the
Chicago Democratic Convention, were fine in news. "On the other
hand, the Smothers Brothers took the position that we must abrogate
the standards that we apply to all *entertainment* programs and make a
special exception of them" (emphasis in original).[60] Dissident political
discourse, presumably, could be contained by the strategies of news
management, although the controversy surrounding the coverage of
Chicago rendered that position somewhat problematic. Whether or
not the network believed it could contain such discourse within its
news division, it clearly did not want it "infecting" entertainment.

In a rare special editorial *TV Guide* proudly took up the network's
banner:

> To many good, sensible citizens of this Nation, the Smothers Bro-
> thers have been crossing these lines [of sacrilege and affront] too
> often. . . .
>
> The issue is taste. And responsibility. And honesty. And perspec-
> tive. And a proper respect for the views of others. . . .
>
> The issue is: Shall a network be required to provide time for a Joan
> Baez to pay tribute to her draft-evading husband while hundreds of
> thousands of viewers in the households of men fighting and dying in
> Vietnam look on in shocked resentment?
>
> We can only agree unreservedly with a network policy that is de-
> termined not to insult the general mores of the country.[61]

The magazine used the same rhetorical strategy as the network it so
proudly supported. The editorial appealed overtly to consensual positions: "good, sensible citizens" who were justifiably outraged by the
deviant opinions of the Smothers. The magazine appealed to "general mores" that, like standards of taste, were understood by all—
except the Smothers and the insurgent youth they represented. Yet,
with such insistent emphasis on general mores, taste, and the consensual system from which they arose, both *TV Guide* and the net-

work threatened to expose that system as an ideological construct. Both attempted to find shelter in consensus even as the system that constructed and legitimized it was being undermined.

The editorial, again echoing the network, tried to defuse the political nature of the censorship controversy through an appeal to taste. The question, therefore, was not Baez's political speech. It was bad taste for her to pay tribute to her draft-evading husband, not because she expressed a political position but because she offended the audience's sense of "decency, propriety and morality." Wrapped up with standards of taste was the unquestioned assumption that television viewers naturally supported American involvement in Vietnam. That particular ideological position, however expressed, was unlikely to be deemed in bad taste.

The Smothers Brothers and the Underground Press

Most of the print press sympathized with the Smothers Brothers, arguing that the cancellation of their show infringed First Amendment free-speech rights. Meanings circulating by those writing in the underground press were more complicated, befitting the movement's oppositional relationship to the dominant social order. The fact that the underground press paid as much attention to the show as it did (the series received more ink in the undergrounds than any other television series) signals that the Smothers achieved some success in their bid to align themselves with youth dissent.

The *Los Angeles Free Press* covered the show in Harlan Ellison's column and in news articles on the Smothers Brothers' Seeger and Baez censorship woes. Chicago's *Seed* also began paying attention as censorship and cancellation threats loomed: "Middle America has been sending nasty letters to CBS about the Smothers Brothers Show. Whether you see the show as an agent of radicalization or just laugh a lot, it might help to send a letter of support."[62] Ellison's column also urged *Freep* readers to write the network to counteract the "moral indignation and raw-throated outrage from the neatsy-clean and ticky-tacky types out there in the Great American Heartland. The scuttle-fish."[63]

It should come as no surprise that the underground press began taking an active interest in the Smothers as soon as the show became the target of repressive institutional practices. The show gained legitimacy as an expression of oppositional, antiestablishment politics by the amount of metaphorical billy clubbing the Smothers endured. Movement organs could embrace the Smothers because they saw the state power that menaced insurgent youth mirrored in the duo's situation. Thus Allan Katzman in New York's *East Village Other* described Tom and Dick as "the men who took the 'New Left' teachings and made it [*sic*] entertainable."[64]

The *Freep* campaign to support the Smothers went into full gear in the aftermath of the show's cancellation. The paper launched a letter-writing drive to try to force the network to reinstate the show. The "letters to the editor" section featured an open letter to CBS from a reader, giving some clue about how the show's fans constructed the controversy:

> Relatively speaking, Easter nights [*sic*] Smothers Brothers Comedy Hour was groovy entertainment—back on November 10, that is, when everybody first dug it. Thanks a lot, Big Brother, for suppressing the regularly scheduled show, substituting a re-run, and thereby protecting your precious Easter Sunday sensibilities from those nasty, sacriligeous "sermonette" satires. . . .
>
> One other thing, oh Great Fraternal Protector. Rather than the standard "thank you for your comments" form letter, how about a straight-from-the-gut, tell-it-like-it-is, written reply to all those Free Press readers who have taken the time to mail in "Censorship Sucks" ads to your local Program Practices Department.[65]

The ad the letter writer referred to ran in the paper's notorious classified section. It read: "CENSORSHIP SUCKS. Black-out Columbia Bullshit System, Sundays 9 p.m. Viva Tom and Dick & their right to speak. If you agree, cut-out this ad & mail to Program Practices Dept., 7800 Beverly Blvd L.A. 90036."[66]

A few weeks later the *Freep* used its classified pages again to run a half-page petition in support of the Smothers:

PETITION OF THE PEOPLE WHO ARE THE TRUE OWNERS OF THE AIR-WAVES WHICH ARE ONLY LICENSED BY THE FEDERAL GOVERNMENT TO: COLUMBIA BROADCASTING SYSTEM (CBS)
WHEREAS the SMOTHERS BROTHERS SHOW was one of the few entertaining shows on CBS;

WHEREAS THE SMOTHERS BROTHERS SHOW's ratings were always high;

WHEREAS the SMOTHERS BROTHERS SHOW, even though liquidated, won a top television award;

WHEREAS censorship of this show is against the ideals of American Democracy;

WE do humbly request, implore, petition, require and demand that you restore the SMOTHERS BROTHERS SHOW to the airwaves, without imposing new restrictions.

AND IF our petition meets with no response, we do promise to engage in a consumer boycott of all products of any sponsor appearing now in the SMOTHERS BROTHERS airtime.[67]

Printed along the side of the petition was: "IT's NOT JUST THE SMOTHERS BROTHERS. IT's FREEDOM." The ad asked those interested in distributing the petition to contact the *Free Press.*

Much of the ire and wrath evident in underground press articles was directed at CBS as unjust authority attempting to exert its domination on a public resource. A column in the *East Village Other* characterized CBS and its action this way: "The precise control device of television was being pushed and too much information was getting to the people. CBS's action against the popular Smothers Brothers Show was unprecedented and has established a repressive trend by the power structure to stomp out all alternative information. The Smothers presentations were certainly not radical but CBS still felt them a threat to honky culture."[68]

The piece also mentioned *TV Guide*'s "alarming" editorial, suggesting the columnists recognized the magazine's ideological alliance with the network. The article implied that although not radical, there was something effectively subversive about the Smothers show, something that needed to be repressed. Alice Embree, writing for New York's other major underground paper, the *Rat,* also took pains to point out that the Smothers were not radical, but that wasn't the point—at issue was the network and its actions: "The question is not whether CBS made a mistake, but why CBS is permitted to exist. The question is one the movement must resolve (having never mounted a successful media campaign)." Embree then appealed to her media-savvy television cogenerationists: "When is the generation that grew up closer to the tube than to Mother's Milk going to be able to objectify Media enough to say, "Stop! Stop using your homogenizer to taking [*sic*] our history from us and deforming it!'"[69]

Although movement organs exhibited clear support for the Smothers, they also expressed a certain amount of ambivalence. Distrust for all dominant institutions was so great that anyone involved with them, even in the underdog position of the Smothers, inevitably raised some doubts. Alice Embree, in her interview with Tom Smothers, expressed inital concern about his neatly groomed appearance. She observed that he seemed "the type who would have gone through all the Proper Channels." But when he indicated that he knew all about the recent controversy between Berkeley's two major underground papers, the *Barb* and the *Tribe,* Embree eased up a little. Although the article supported Tom Smothers and the show, Embree apparently felt a need to put forth another view: "Most radicals [and the *Rat* was a radical/sDS-oriented rather than hippie-oriented paper] would argue that the show was a perfect co-optive device, diverting youth energy away from anything destructive, giving kids a sense of representation."[70]

The *Freep*'s ever wrathful columnist Lawrence Lipton worked this theme far more forcefully. Adopting an apocalyptic vision of impending revolution that allowed for no mediation between "us" and "them," Lipton had nothing but contempt for the Smothers and their ilk. "Mort Sahl and the Smothers Brothers are weeping and wailing, not because they were dropped out by the Top Rats of the television Rats Nest, but because they are not being invited back again in/on acceptable sell-out terms."[71]

Another *Free Press* article, written before the cancellation, detailing the Joan Baez controversy, also chided the Smothers. The article pointed out that by collaborating in any way with the network's censorship system, the Smothers acted as accomplices to the stifling of free expression over the airwaves. Imagining the comics possessed more power than they did, the article observed that "since c.b.s. has already indicated that it wants the Smothers back next year, they are obviously in a position to bargain for their own artistic manumission. Otherwise, why should it matter if there is no Smothers Brothers Show next season?"[72]

These harsher views indicate the confrontational stances the insurgent movements adopted in the later part of the decade. The appeal to use "proper channels" for the address of grievances had long since proven ineffective. Working within the system would not bring the war to an end, would not bring economic and social justice to African Americans, would not change the established order of power relations. Many in the movement saw the Smothers Brothers incident as another marker of that very fact. The Smothers were unable to negotiate proper channels to bring even sanitized antiestablishment youth perspectives to television. Those who condemned the Smothers for even trying were responding from their own rage and despair. The desire for fundamental change was too deep and the pitfalls to achieving it too numerous. The absorptive powers of the dominant order raised legitimate fears among members of a movement that saw bits and pieces of itself constantly co-opted. For these commentators *The Smothers Brothers Comedy Hour,* regardless of the censorship it faced, proved to be just another example of popular culture's ability to absorb and defuse any form of political opposition.

Although plenty of criticisms about the Smothers Brothers being co-opted appeared in the underground press, they never formed the majority perspective among undergroundlings. The brothers were able to use evidence of the coercive power imposed on them as their ultimate validation. Thus, the shadow of the censor's scissors—the imprint of hegemonic force—served as an enabling device for the brothers. By displaying the markings of political repression evident on their youth-oriented material, they gained legitimacy from a disaffected social segment that was disinclined to view anything coming from the boob tube as politically subversive. Had the Smothers not encountered such heavy-handed censorship, they might never have achieved such staunch, albeit conflicted, movement support.

The measure of support and affirmation the Smothers received in youth-movement circles may have given Tom Smothers added ammunition to launch his own public campaign proclaiming his show a martyred example of successful youth programming in the Vast Wasteland. A few days after CBS terminated its contract with the Smothers, Tom put out a press release aligning his show and all it represented unambiguously with the youth movement. He pointed out that the cancellation involved far more than a quarrel between CBS and himself; rather it went to the heart of an ever-widening generation gap. He asserted: "Television, which reflects the social climate of the older generation but which could serve a tremendously important role in creating and maintaining a dialogue *between* the generations, has simply turned its back on this challenge. It has dedicated itself instead to the perpetuation of institutions which to very many young people seem increasingly irrelevant."[73] He criticized television for allowing one generation, the older one, to take over the airwaves. Young people would inevitably turn away from this medium, leaving important issues unaddressed, either seriously or humorously.

Tom took his campaign to Washington, D.C., where he met with sympathetic Democratic liberals and the FCC's house radical Nicholas Johnson. The meeting, according to William Kloman's article in *Esquire,* led to agreement "that the airwaves did, in fact, belong to all the people, and that the young people of the country were not getting adequate representation in network programming."[74] Tom and Dick also took an opportunity to speak before the American Society of Newspaper Editors. The *Los Angeles Free Press* excerpted portions of the speech and *Look*'s cover article described at some length the entire affair.

The speech expanded on themes in Tom's press release. Describing the gulf that separated the generations, Tom observed, "TV is on the verge of becoming an internal house organ for one generation, just as the underground press, underground radio, and rock music have become an internal house organ for the other."[75] Tom called for television to be an arena for dialogue between the generations but observed that because "the channels of general communication are always controlled by the older generation, it often seems easier to simply shut off the question . . . rather than engage with the questioner in that search for an answer" (ellipsis in original).

The *Look* article (penned by First Amendment champion Nat Hentoff) described a despondent Tom Smothers brooding in his hotel room after the speech. " 'Those people tonight just turned off. And CBS, where is that fear they have coming from? How are we so dangerous?' He paused. 'Nobody bothers hawks like Bob Hope.' "[76] Of course Bob Hope's viewpoints weren't at odds with those in positions of power.

Tom Smothers's discourse of the televisual generation gap achieved wide circulation both in the mainstream and underground press. As Alice Embree noted in the *Rat:* "The liberal press has made Tom Smother's [*sic*] case for him over and over."[77] Tom rehearsed that case particularly cogently in *Senior Scholastic,* a magazine aimed at high school students:

As we received more and more complaints from older people, I realized I should have suggested making it a program "for kids only."

It's the kids who know what's happening. They're not frightened by controversy or so self-important that they've lost their sense of humor. We could have had a real free-wheeling program. As it was, we just tried to tell a little truth.

We made mistakes, but we were trying to give young people a voice. We were trying to reflect the nonviolent, antiwar attitude.[78]

Tom Smothers wanted television to be a terrain of dialogue between generations. However, as cultural studies theorists have pointed out, television as popular culture is a terrain of struggle. Stuart Hall has noted that "popular culture is one of the sites where this struggle for and against a culture of the powerful is engaged. It is also the stake to be won or lost *in* that struggle. It is the arena of consent and resistance."[79] Tom Smothers envisioned a popular culture without this fundamental element of contestation, resistance, and consent. The comic was certainly cognizant of the fact that powerful elite forces controlled the medium, yet he still held on to the dream of an essentially consensual, liberal pluralist system of give and take in which those in positions of power would allow discourses that fundamentally threatened that power some room to flourish. The show's more radical supporters in the underground press saw the situation with more political sophistication. Nevertheless, Tom Smothers's vision of a truly democratic, diverse, and open system of broadcasting—considering the private, capitalist, sell-audiences-to-advertisers nature of American television—was in fact quite revolutionary.

The Smothers Brothers Comedy Hour was enormously significant in the cultural context of the late 1960s because it showed that popular culture could function not only as a potentially progressive force.[80] Popular culture could have radical implications at certain historical moments when every institution and facet of the social order suddenly become possible grounds for the unmasking and overthrowing of delegitimized power. The textual operations of the show, the public controversy that swirled around it, the repressive strategies of the network, the outraged responses of the show's supporters all came together to create a crisis of authority in entertainment television. It mattered because this crisis was woven into the shredding fabric of a much larger crisis reverberating throughout American society. *The*

Smothers Brothers Comedy Hour developed into a crisis of authority at the very moment that crises of authority threatened other institutions of social, political, and cultural power. The turmoil and controversy surrounding the show were symptomatic of the fissures and cleavages menacing the social order both internally and externally. The show, in its contested production and conflicted reception, revealed that more was at stake on Sunday nights at 9:00 than whether two folksinger/comedians would be allowed to entertain the households of America with material of questionable taste. At stake was a new political and social common sense. The question posed by the Smothers Brothers' ill-fated show was what kinds of negotiations and struggles would be necessary to bring this new common sense into the living rooms of a desperately torn nation.

As we will see in the next chapter, television producer Aaron Spelling and his bosses at ABC thought they might have an answer. Taking up the ideological balancing act that the Smothers Brothers had abandoned, Spelling would try to bridge the generational chasm with a hippie police squad. As we will see, *The Mod Squad* visited many of the same issues that proved so explosive for *The Smothers Brothers Comedy Hour*, but it did so in ways that prime time was ready for.

Negotiating the Mod

How *The Mod Squad* Played
the Ideological Balancing Act
in Prime Time

The Mod Squad, Aaron Spelling's ABC series, premiered in 1968, the same time the Smothers Brothers were locked in combat with their CBS bosses. As it turned out, the Spelling production, rather than the Smothers Brothers' controversial variety show, served as the proto-type for a wave of "socially relevant" television programming that would follow it in the years ahead.[1] The premise and structure of the show reveal the successful ideological balancing act the program performed in its attempts to both garner a young audience to maintain the mature, adult viewers that formed the medium's core constituency. This latter was the audience that the Smothers Brothers apparently lost when they abandoned their attempts to play the balancing game. Because television entertainment had traditionally endeavored to reach less-differentiated national audiences (even during its turn to "relevant," youth-oriented programming), the medium's attempt to represent the discourses of politically and socially oppositional movements can provide clues to the larger social circulation of the popular meanings about those movements. *The Mod Squad* reveals another instance of how the process of incorporation functioned. However, as we have seen, this process was by no means smooth, safe, nonconflict-ual, or necessarily disempowering for oppositional social and political movements.

From the outset *The Mod Squad* attempted to work through the moral panic about rebellious, antiauthoritarian, wild-in-the-streets youth. At the core of this panic was the question of how to encourage the young to obey and respect institutions such as law and order, the family, education, the judiciary, and the military, whose strictures so many of the young rejected wholesale. Stuart Hall et al. have described a moral panic as "one of the principal surface manifestations of the [hegemonic] crisis . . . [and] one of the key ideological forms in which a historical crisis is 'experienced and fought out.'"[2] In its move to engage overtly with the crises of the day, entertainment television, through shows like *The Mod Squad,* found itself struggling with these very explosive ideological issues. Just as those issues had proven dangerous for *The Smothers Brothers Comedy Hour,* so they would for this program. The outcome for the Spelling production would, however, be very different.

Producing The Mod Squad

Producer Spelling bought the idea for *The Mod Squad* from a former LAPD cop who told him about an undercover narcotics squad composed of young police officers. Spelling played with the premise and decided to make the young officers juveniles who'd been in trouble with the law. They had the choice either to go to jail or to be part of an undercover unit. "The show, very simply, was about three hippie cops," said Spelling. The youth squad's purpose was "to infiltrate the counterculture and do something about the adult criminals who were always trying to take advantage of the young."[3] The three "hippies" who made up the secret and unarmed squad were Linc Hayes, an angry ghetto black male (Clarence Williams III); Julie Barnes, a blonde, white "hippie chick" (Peggy Lipton); and Pete Cochran, a white, alienated rich kid, disowned by his Beverly Hills family (Michael Cole).

On the surface the show's structuring principle offered a simplistic solution to the moral panic about dissident youth: encourage the young to join the system they believed was oppressing them by showing how that system really worked in their best interests and for their sincerely held beliefs. In its ideological balancing act the show could appeal to television's broad audience: the under-thirty viewers could identify with the young protagonists, who were never entirely comfortable with their law-enforcement status, and the older generation could take comfort from the law-and-order format of the show.

Linc Hayes, Pete Cochran, and Julie Barnes: one black, one white, one blonde. *(Author's collection)*

Audience testing data produced for the proposed series before its network debut indicated a certain amount of tension between young and more elderly test audiences. One arena of divergence proved to be the proposed title of the series. Spelling, in his fluffy autobiography, claimed that he came up with the title "The Mod Squad" but had to fight for it. Executives at ABC disliked it, believing it too "radical" and likely to alienate viewers. Their proposal: "The Young Detectives." Spelling exclaimed to ABC's president, "I can't do a show that's supposed to be hip and cutting edge and call it that." He then threatened to walk away from the project.[4]

Testing data revealed that teenage viewers were more apt to tune in to a series called "The Mod Squad" and more likely to bypass one called "The Young Detectives." For older viewers it was the opposite. Many were completely uninterested in watching a series called "The Mod Squad." Although the younger ones liked that title, after having viewed a test episode, many believed that it was not altogether appropriate because, in their estimation, Linc, Pete, and Julie were not really all that "mod."[5] In the end Spelling's title won, largely because both the producer and his network realized they needed to lure a new cohort of younger viewers rather than merely maintain the older ones. The scuffle over something as seemingly insignificant as a television series title became yet one more site for enacting the generation gap and showcasing how material that might prove even marginally of interest to the young consequently became unappealing to the elders. It also showed the sensitivity of young viewers to questions of representation. Spelling may have thought that his young protagonists were "hip" and "cutting edge," but his teen test audiences knew better. Nevertheless, this audience appeared to approve of the show, according to the report, because it was timely, showed young people being given responsibility, and, perhaps most important — especially in view of what other cop shows such as *Dragnet* and *Adam-12* were doing — this proposed cop series showed "positive aspects of their generation."

Another test screening conducted shortly before the series premiered indicated that the audience appeared to understand the show's ideological purpose in attempting to defuse the moral panic about youth out of control. This audience liked the way the show "dealt with the present social problems" and, most significant, liked the fact that the show "helped bridge the gap between the younger generation and the police."[6] This was the heart of the series' ideological work to reconfigure consensus. Although it appeared to work with a test audience, the premise ran into a great deal more contestation as the series went public.

Initial public response was enormously negative. In May 1968 the *New York Times* carried an ad for the as-yet-untelevised series: "The police don't understand the now generation and the now generation doesn't dig the fuzz. The solution: find some swinging young people who live the beat scene [*sic*]. Get them to work for the cops."[7] The network received an avalanche of mail condemning the proposed show solely on its advertised premise. According to Spelling, "We were stuck with that stigma of the kids being undercover dragnets, kids finking on kids. We got letters before we went on the air saying, 'You dirty cop finks!' "[8] Michael Cole, the actor Spelling wanted for the lead role, refused to read for the part. After the show went into production—Cole having reconsidered—the three young stars apparently precipitated a confrontation with Spelling about the representation of young people in the early scripts. According to *TV Guide,* "At a showdown confrontation one night at La Scala, the kids 'let it all hang out' and Spelling did the improbable thing. He jumped the Generation Gap. At the studio the next morning he actually *threw away* four 'hack-type' scripts he had paid $4500 a piece for and three storylines at $850 each. 'We have a chance to explode [*sic*] stories of today,' he announced. 'We're going to take that chance.' "[9]

This lionizing portrait of Spelling illustrates a recurring theme in the television relevancy period: the adult white male establishment figure had to indicate by some concrete action that he shared and supported the positions and politics of rebellious youth.[10] The article suggests that for Spelling Production's balancing act to be successful, the show would have to weight itself more toward the concerns and desires of the antiestablishment young rather than toward the law-and-order elders.

The controversy that surrounded *The Mod Squad* in its early incarnation reveals the woeful failure of attempts to cobble together some kind of new consensus in which disaffected young people and law enforcement officials could exist in ideological harmony. This effort at incorporation merely unmasked and made slightly ridiculous the entire process. The show's initial fumble illustrates the delicate and perilous procedure of hegemonic attempts at containment and incorporation. As Stuart Hall has suggested, we need to examine the "double movement" of containment *and* resistance at work in the terrain of the popular.[11] Both forces were clearly at work in *The Mod Squad* at the level of text and reception.

Resistance forced the producers to retool the show. According to *TV Guide,* "The initial brouhaha about kids finking on kids made the producers hypersensitive on the subject. Subsequent scripts have been routinely furbished with lines like, 'I do not fink on a soul brother.' Youth crime, in fact, has been avoided. Most of the heavies have been adults with power." [12] In chapter 2, we saw the same strategy used by the hippie-oriented shows. The self-consciousness of the producers in attempting to portray the young as heroes or victims and adults as villains reveals one of the principal tactics of negotiation operating in these texts. However, textual negotiations that arise out of the need to revitalize traditional genres by including innovative and—in this case—politically "relevant" materials can also cause a certain amount of narrative tension.[13] In *The Mod Squad* the tension, which could never be resolved, revolved around the social impossibility in 1968 of a union between disaffected young people and the institution of law and order. The show, therefore, achieved a high degree of (ideological) relevancy both in the tortuous ways it tried to force that union as a way to resolve the moral panic about out-of-control youth and in the ways viewers—especially younger ones—made varied meanings of it. The show was, thus, a site for the working out of insoluble social and generational conflicts.

The Underground Press Responds

Along with *The Smothers Brothers Comedy Hour, The Mod Squad* was one of the few examples of entertainment television to receive significant attention in the underground press. Unlike the Smothers Brothers' show, however, Spelling's program generated a much more conflicted response: anger, rage, and disgust, along with a limited amount of grudging support. Shortly after the show went on the air the *Chicago Seed* ran an outraged call to arms against the programme from a Yippie-oriented group calling itself the "6th Street Surrealists." The group deconstructed the show's ideological intent as wholly in line with the Nixon administration's law-and-order campaign. " 'Mod Squad' justifies the existence of the narc, holds him up as a shining example in its [the media's] perverted view of the universe, and on a weekly basis defines our community. But just as we would cut the throat of 'Mod Squad,' confronting dead fantasy with fantastic reality [*sic*]." [14] Here again members of the hip community agonized about how the dominant media was appropriating, stealing, and deforming the movement's sense of itself. The "perversity" of the media manifested itself in the ways it chose to represent the youth movement. Other underground press articles and letters also pointed out the absurdity of hip kids turning into police informers and narcs—and remaining heroes. The preposterous nature of the premise merely revealed the mechanisms of incorporation. One letter writer to the *Los Angeles Free Press* indicated his awareness of this attempt at hegemonic processing. He took the show's premise and inverted it in order to show its ideologically suspect intent:

> The Fall TV season ushers in some exciting new programs. Mod Squad (Tues. 7:30, ch 7) is a series based on three BP (beautiful people) who give up their dissolute life and become police informers. Their crazy threads and "natural" [*sic*] get them into "A thousand places we can't get into," says their employer.
>
> I think that programs such as these are a constructive force for MD (meaningful dialogue). I suggest that, along the same lines, we could get even more MD by having a TV series about three young police officers who get straightened out by an understanding ACLU attorney, Adam Earth. . . .
>
> The three youthful officers are privy to inner circles and master planning of law enforcement gangs and are able to get the goods on the murder and beating of unprominent citizens. The name for this TV show would obviously be "Pig Gig."[15]

The 6th Street Surrealists had other ideas about how to counter the menace of *The Mod Squad*. Their article listed seven different means to "END THIS SHIT." Appropriating playfully—or perhaps not so playfully—tactics of political boycotts and civil disobedience, the authors encouraged readers to inundate the sponsors and network with letters of protest. Readers were advised to adopt the identities of outraged elderly people or form fictitious "Citizen Decency" groups and complain about the prevalence of sex, long hair, and slang language on the show. "Behave super-straight, and liberal-straight in the mail and like a normal crazy motherfucker in personal confrontation," the group advised. "They'll think it's a whole cross-section of the population." They also encouraged the picketing of producers' and executives' homes, the storming of network offices, the replacement of the offending program "with a Marijuana Hour hosted by local freaks." Finally, with tongue lodged in cheek, the group proclaimed: "If all else fails, we would never advocate disruption of the transmission.

Transmitting equipment is very expensive. We would not even advocate tearing into executive offices every week as the show is being broadcast and screaming obscenities, taking off your clothes and demanding it be removed from the air immediately. We would never advocate that."

Although many of these protest tactics were not meant to be taken seriously, the tone of the 6th Street Surrealists piece reverberates with palpable anger. Clearly the authors and the *Seed* believed *The Mod Squad* was politically dangerous. It could not be summarily dismissed, ignored, or laughed off. By engaging with the show at all, these responses indicated that the meanings circulated by this example of televisual fare needed to be countered, subverted, attacked. The 6th Street Surrealists' manifesto may have been an attempt to resolve and work through in hyperbolic fantasy the movement's desire to gain control over mass mediated representations of itself and eradicate the offensive ones.

If, as *TV Guide* suggested, *The Mod Squad* was modified in order to throw its sympathies more to the disaffected young, then later commentary in the pages of the underground press suggests a softening of positions against the show by movement critics. Meridee Merzer, who wrote a regular "Television" column for Philadelphia's *Distant Drummer,* gave qualified support for the show in an October 1969 piece:

> Their [*The Mod Squad*'s] characterizations are about as favorable towards youth as American TV has yet presented: Julie, the lovely daughter of a prostitute; Linc, the handsome black guy with the Afro; Pete, the white guy with the neatly shaggy hair. They're your typical hip, socially-concerned, all-American undercover cops.
>
> Although it's not realistic, "The Mod Squad" does a good propaganda job for youth. The audience sees that the squad are basically good and kind people, despite their "Funny" clothes and "outlandish" ideals and moral standards.[16]

Merzer's argument suggested that, rather than containing and defanging youth rebellion, the show offered up a more palatable version of that rebellion for television audiences. Merzer's argument implied that this "propaganda job" would be worked on nonmovement viewers who needed to be convinced that freaky-looking kids with outlandish ideals were in fact good people. If the show could achieve that objective in some manner, then, it wasn't justifying the Nixonian law-and-order regime as the 6th Street Surrealists argued but rather was serving the more subversive antiauthoritarian values and ideals of the youth movement.

The Mod Squad achieved a reputation for dealing sympathetically with the issues and perspectives of concern to the nation's rebellious young but did so in a manner that did not seem calculated to unduly ruffle establishment feathers as the Smothers Brothers had done. The show quickly shot up into the Nielsen's top-ten programs.

The Mod Squad Joins the Underground

We can see how the show played the ideological balancing act by examining an episode first broadcast December 31, 1968, dealing with the bombing and subsequent trashing of an underground newspaper called the *Guru*.[17] Pete, Julie, and Linc, avid readers of the paper, informed their captain that the hip community considered police attempts to safeguard the paper's premises from attack to be inadequate. Captain Greer suggested that the Squad get jobs on the paper and, thus, supply it with some police protection. In a pointed close-up Pete looked uncomfortable, then answered, "We don't like the idea of having to spy on an underground newspaper." Greer jumped up angrily and confronted Pete. "What do I have to do to win your trust? Wear beads? I read the *Guru*." I like the newspaper. I think it has a healthy attitude. It says something. Do I surprise you?" A cut to Linc showed him beaming and looking very pleased: "Constantly."

Greer adopted a position that would become increasingly common in youth-oriented relevant dramas: the white, male establishment figure showing how he had "jumped the generation gap" and allied himself with the young rebels. Of course, Greer's dialogue was suitably vague about the *Guru*'s healthy attitude or about just what the paper was actually saying about anything. The rest of the episode did nothing to render more concrete the political stance or issues of concern to the paper and its youthful readers.

If the paper itself was deemed healthy and worthy, the narrative tended to undercut that position in the way it portrayed the *Guru*'s editor, Rick. We see him as overbearing, tyrannical, violent, and cold. To make his apparent villainy more extreme, the narrative revealed

The Mod Squad and Captain Greer in Julie's
hippie-style apartment.

that he was responsible for the bombing. Cajoling one of his writers, a black youth, into helping him trash the office after the bombing, Rick and his ambivalent coconspirator made it look like outside vandalism from reactionary thugs. According to Rick, the publicity from both these incidents would help them get their message out to a larger public. What really clinched Rick's villainy, however, was not so much his political methods but his insensitive treatment of his rather plain, adoring girlfriend, Daphne, another writer for the paper. Constructed as the victim, Daphne was seen spying on Rick as he appeared to be seducing the lovely, willowy Julie Barnes in his apartment. The scene focused on the masochistic pain of the pathetic Daphne.

In due course Julie found herself figured as victim—of Rick's scheme to get her to admit that she, along with Pete and Linc, were connected with the police department. His seduction of her was merely a ploy to trap her into admitting that connection—which she blithely did. However, before he could blow their cover by writing a *Guru* exposé about them, Rick got mysteriously murdered. The episode then turned into a traditional "whodunit," with Daphne along with the other writer who had helped Rick destroy the office as the likely culprits.

In the end neither of these suspects was the guilty party. Both were portrayed as idealists, racked with guilt and shame at Rick's

The faces of female victimization: Daphne, the
political radical as lovesick wimp. Julie, the weeping,
incompetent undercover cop, confronted by Rick.

power-grabbing machinations. In an already familiar plot twist, the
final (true) villain—Rick, through his murder, having turned into
another victim—was Daphne's brother. A wealthy property owner in
the *Guru*'s neighborhood, he, like other landlords, worried about the
drop in property values in the area, which was turning into a haven
for longhaired radicals. When the brother was first introduced, he
was physically accosting his sister over her continual association with
Rick and his freaky friends. Later, on his yacht (named "Daphne"),
he ordered the Squad off his property. He didn't want their kind in
his vicinity. Linc made a comment "linking" this bigoted response
to young people with similar bigotry directed at black people. So

The true image of villainy. Daphne's short-haired,
business-suited brother. Pete intervenes as Daphne is
accosted.

the ultimate villain of the piece was a clean-cut, moneyed, property
owner whose irrational hatred of nonconformist youth led him to
murder. Intolerance and bigotry superseded political megalomania
and romantic insensitivity as the markers of evil. In this narrative balancing act a crusading, idealistic underground paper serving a community of protesting longhairs was counterposed with its unscrupu-
lous "radical youth" editor. An establishment more concerned with
property values and law and order was counterposed with a police
captain who valued the paper threatening those property values and
his youthful undercover squad whose job was to protect the paper.
The radical left-wing villain was counterposed with the "straight"
right-wing villain.

The only element of the narrative that didn't get balanced in some
manner was the representation of the female victims. Reflecting
patriarchal discourse of the period, the narrative saw no need for
examination or self-consciousness about gender construction. *The
Mod Squad* was particularly troubling in its characterization of Julie
Barnes. As the quintessential "hippie chick," she was all blondness,
light, sweetness, emotion, and fragility. The show's opening credit
sequence cemented those attributes in a sequence featuring the squad
running down a dark, wet, menacing underpass apparently pursued
by some unseen force. Pete and Linc positioned themselves on either

Julie, the physically weak cop, needing to be
propped up by her male comrades. Freeze-frame
from the end of the series' opening credit sequence.

side of their female associate, propping her up by the arms as she appeared unable to negotiate the run under her own speed. Thus, from
the outset, Julie was generally helpless physically, needing her male
colleagues to rescue and support her.

The show's episodes did little to undercut this representation. Julie
frequently portrayed a damsel in distress needing to be freed by Pete
and Linc. Her only resources were her insights into human nature
and her ability to intuit other people's psychological motivations and
states of mind. In "The Guru" Julie instinctively knew that Daphne
was desperately in love with Rick. She encouraged Pete to go out
with the young woman when it became clear that Rick was going to
make a move on Julie. With Pete together with Daphne, the hand-
some Mod Squadder found himself conveniently in place to rescue
the young woman when her straight, bigoted brother began to assault her. Julie's insights into human emotions also helped convince
her associates that Daphne could not have killed Rick despite her confession after a botched suicide attempt. Although her intuition led to
the fingering of the brother, her male comrades had to actually conduct the vigorous chase through the marina to finally nab the culprit.
Julie remained standing decorously in the background while Pete and
Linc leaped over boats, barriers, and ran down piers.

If Julie Barnes was a cop with limited law-enforcement skills,

Daphne was a youth radical with limited politics. Whereas Rick and the other male writer spouted dialogue that in general and vague terms articulated their politics, Daphne had no political dialogue at all. She existed to fulfill the role of martyr and masochist—to Rick, who betrayed her love and called her ugly, and to her brother, who beat her up for fraternizing with hippies and freaks. In the show's coda the Squad met up with her again on her brother's yacht. We learn that she had sold the boat to get together financing so that she and the other writer could start up the paper again. However, her dialogue didn't focus on the future of her underground paper but on her concern about whether she was ugly or not. She turned to Pete to ask if he thought she was pretty. "You're beautiful. Do you have to be pretty, too?" This overriding concern with physical appearance was not questioned by the narrative, which naturalized feminine narcissism over feminine political activism. The narrative requires that we accept on faith that Daphne was a committed radical writer. What we see is a weak, emotionally lovesick victim whose actions and reactions have nothing to do with politics but rather with interpersonal relationships—the traditional feminine sphere.

The episode drew a number of comments from the pages of the "real" underground press. Not surprisingly, none commented on the representation of gender. The *Free Press* made special note of the episode in part because the *Guru* seemed a thinly disguised fictional version of the *Freep*. And like the *Guru,* the *Freep* had recently been bombed. Lawrence Lipton, in his typically outraged fashion, gave the episode one of his "Fur-Lined Shit-Pot Awards for 1969." He elaborated: "To LEIGH CHAPMAN, TV script-writer who wrote the scurrilous, libellous, dishonest script called "The Guru" for the vomitous Mod Squad series on Channel 7, aired Dec 31, 1968: about an underground newspaper editor who bombed his own paper, somewhere around Fairfax Ave, dig? [The *Freep* was located in the youth ghetto Fairfax District] just for the publicity! The shit-pot reserved for you is inscribed with the honored name of one of your great forebears in the art of the BIG LIE: Paul Joseph Goebbels."[18]

Lipton was being hyperbolic as usual, but his reference to propaganda is interesting. As we have already seen, Meridee Merzer found the series unrealistic but thought it generally positive propaganda for the youth movement. For Lipton the show was dangerously fraudulent propaganda. Another *Free Press* writer, Paul Eberle, tried to be a little bit more evenhanded in his assessment of the episode. He also argued that the show bordered on the libelous because of the obvious connections between the *Guru* and his paper. However, he read the episode in comparison to other televisual representations of radicals, contrasting *The Mod Squad* to a recent episode of *Adam-12,* a production of Jack Webb, who was known for his right-wing politics. He described a scene in which the cop-buddy protagonists chased an erratically driving suspect and pulled her over. "As the kindly officer admonishes her, she delivers a harsh diatribe about police malpractice, with all the clichés of radicalism. But it is made clear that this is a hysterical, unbalanced person. The message? Radicals are full of shit. Right?"[19] Eberle wrote that he expected no better from *The Mod Squad* episode. However, he discovered that the writer and director had obviously done some minimal research on their subject matter. "There were all the superficial trappings of the Free Press— the long-haired youths, the dilapidated building, the decor, the garb. But the characters and the rhetoric had little or no resemblance to the scene in which I have worked and lived for the past two years, nor to the people with whom I work for most of my waking hours" (p. 5). As was so frequently the case with mass-media representations of "real" events or phenomena, viewers were struck by the dissonance between their own experiences and the televised depiction of them. Todd Gitlin, in *The Whole World Is Watching,* discussed the struggles between SDS and its representation in news reporting. Within the realm of fictional, entertainment television, similar struggles and ambivalences prevailed. Eberle, although clearly seeing the fictitiousness behind the facade of authentic visual detail, still found something redeeming about the episode: "Taken as a whole, the play was not unkind to us. The underground press people were portrayed as sincere, dedicated idealists, and the villain—the man who turns out to be the murderer—is an uptight, businessman-landlord with super-short hair, and a fanatical hatred for 'hippies'" (p. 5). In his negotiated reading Eberle picked up the not-too-subtle textual mechanisms for throwing sympathy toward the young. This strategy of narrative construction, in which the concerns and preoccupations of antiestablishment youth were handled in ways that attempted to validate their positions, became to some extent the hallmark of the "relevant" cycle of entertainment programming that followed on the heels of *The Mod Squad.*

Pete, Linc, and Julie Feel a Draft

The show's canny balancing act proved particularly useful in an episode that aired April 8, 1969, about a radical pacifist draft resister whose father just happened to be a brigadier general in Vietnam. The show appeared during an important transitional period for the Selective Service System. By 1969 the draft faced some fundamental challenges to its operations. Lawrence M. Baskir and William A. Strauss have argued in *Chance and Circumstance,* an analysis of Selective Service and its evaders during the Vietnam War, that by this time sss was becoming increasingly discredited in the eyes of a public demanding a restructuring of the system.[20] A 1969 poll revealed that 75 percent of high school sophomores considered the draft and Vietnam among the problems that most worried young men.[21] Increasing numbers of them were considering active resistance to draft laws. A 1968 Lou Harris poll suggested that between 20 and 30 percent of college students would seriously consider refusing induction. A year later 253 student body presidents (presumably all male) informed the White House that they would all refuse induction. "Throughout the course of the war, more than a half million draft-age men did exactly that" (p. 68). Avoiding, evading, or resisting the draft was, in general, not a contentious issue among baby boomers. Demonstrable antiwar politics were not a necessary prerequisite for young men who wanted to evade military service. Male New Left politicos, as well as their apolitical cogenerationists, all wanted to avoid being drafted into combat. Among adults, however, the situation was far more conflicted. On the one hand, they criticized the draft system; on the other hand, they elevated the "draft dodger" to the status of popular folk devil. According to Baskir and Strauss, "With the war calling into question so much of America's self-esteem, and with so many young men resisting the war, the nation needed assurance that patriotism still had meaning. Draft resistance and deserters thus became the folk villains of the times" (p. 10). *The Mod Squad* needed to navigate carefully through this contentious terrain of sentiment about the draft.

The episode opened outside a federal building where the trial of Arly Blau, draft resister, was concluding. Out front antiwar activists and counterdemonstrators congregated, along with the Mod Squad. Julie stood off some distance from Linc and Pete as the latter two engaged in some explanatory dialogue. Julie, we learn, knew Arly in high school. Pete informs us: "She digs the stand he's taking." Later in Greer's office, after Arly had suffered injury in what appeared to be a politically motivated attempted murder, the Squad tried to persuade Greer to allow them to provide to Arly with protection.

> *Greer:* Why are you guys pushing so hard? What is it—you like
>   Arly's politics?
> *Pete:* We just think a kid should be able to speak his mind without
>   getting killed for it!
> *Greer:* Well, I think so, too, Pete.[22]

In both these instances the dialogue neatly skated around whether the Squad actually supported Arly's draft resistance stance or whether they just supported his right to freely choose to take a stance. Because Arly was portrayed as a total pacifist, Julie could "dig" the fact that he was being consistent in his pacifism without this necessarily indicating that she also "dug" draft resistance per se. Likewise, Pete may or may not have liked Arly's politics. All he admitted to in the discussion with Captain Greer was a politically uncontentious support for the First Amendment. The dialogue scenes were constructed in an open enough way to allow differently situated viewers to negotiate a comfortable reading. Youthful antidraft viewers would find it fairly easy to read these opening sequences as support for draft resistance. More conservative adult viewers could find the dialogue equivocal enough to not challenge their positions too much.

The ideological balancing act continued in a scene between Arly and his father, the brigadier general. The episode neither ridiculed the military man, as *The Monkees* had done in their 1967 spoof, nor demonized him. In the script he was described as "a distinguished man" with rumpled look and stubbled cheek—clearly a father anguished by his son's political principles and impending imprisonment. The sequence further insisted on the great familial love that underlay the father-son generation gap by having Arly run to his father and hug him when the brigadier general first entered Arly's flat. With the Mod Squad in the other room the general began to beg his son to go and register for the draft:

> *General Blau:* Please—this business will haunt you for the rest of
>   your life!

Arly:	No! Oh, Dad, be fair! Have I ever asked you to give up the Army? Have I ever said, "Get out of Vietnam because I don't think it's right?"
General Blau:	You can't compare—
Arly:	Yes! Yes I can compare! I don't agree with what you're doing but it's your thing and I respect it. Well, this is my thing and I'm asking you to respect it!
General Blau:	I can't respect it. [Deeply] What do you think I've been doing for two years? I've been sending boys out to *die!* Boys who could have been my son, too. Should I stop respecting *them?* Should I say they died for *nothing?*
Arly:	Yes—if it's true—!

The dialogue here very cleverly negotiated a minefield of Vietnam War politics. Arly appeared in a sympathetic light not necessarily because of his antiwar stance but because of his mobilization of liberal pluralist discourse. He chastised his father not so much because of his participation in an unjust war but because of his unwillingness to sanction a diversity of views about the war. Arly did not criticize his father for participating in the military or for being in Vietnam: "It's your thing and I respect it." This kind of "do your own thing" dialogue blunted the antiwar position put forth at the end of the sequence when Arly, ambivalently, suggested that the boys dying in Vietnam were dying for nothing. The general appeared principled in his stance, but because of his rigidity—his inability to respect Arly's standpoint—the sequence judged him more harshly. The general was the ideologically intolerant one, unable to accept pluralism. The general's position was made even more questionable when, immediately after Arly suggested the general's boys might be dying for nothing, he reacted by slapping his son. Arly immediately apologized, but that wasn't enough for the military man. He demanded that Arly stand up to him and hit back—fight for what he believed in. Arly, the total pacifist, of course, refused.

The sequence put on display two entirely different "structures of feeling" played out, as Raymond Williams would have expected, generationally. On offer were two visions of masculinity, two visions of what it means to be a man who stands up for what he believes in, two visions of how one negotiates the views of others, two visions of war as the arena of masculine activity. The brilliance of *The Mod Squad* in this episode lay in its ability to gravitate toward the younger generation's structure of feeling without thoroughly discrediting the worldview of the elders. Arly was our hero, but his father, the brigadier general, was not correspondingly constructed as villain.

The episode ended up sidestepping thorny questions about Vietnam and the moral dilemma of service in an unpopular war by focusing instead on the issue of absolute pacifism. Once Arly has been shipped off to prison, we see him refusing to fight in any context. Hostile fellow prisoners took his food away from him and contemptuously called him "flower child." His black bunkmate tried to slip him some of his own food and got beaten for his action. Arly not only refused to fight back, but he also refused to identify the culprits. Mod Squadders Pete and Linc ended up going undercover as prison inmates to protect Arly from his attempted assassin, who had managed to infiltrate the prison. During another fight sequence Pete saved the passive Arly from the other prisoners and wound up with a broken leg. Later in their cell Linc said to Arly, "Well, you made it, Arly. They're shipping you out in one piece and you never compromised once." After a beat he continued, "I gotta respect it. I mean, when you say you don't fight, *you don't fight.* . . . Pete gets clobbered but you don't lift a finger. That's principle, man." Arly pointed out that he didn't ask for their help. Linc acknowledged that but countered that there were times one had to fight or one wouldn't survive.

> *Arly:* Justifiable violence, right, man?
> *Linc:* Maybe.
> *Arly:* But where do you draw the line? You hit someone today—
>   you bomb someone tomorrow—is there really any difference?
>   People are dying in Vietnam right now because we just accept
>   violence as a part of life.

A subtle critique of Arly's pacifism managed to enter in these sequences. In the all-male environment of a prison, not to mention the inherently action-and-violence milieu of a police genre series like *The Mod Squad,* male passivity such as Arly Blau's could not help but raise anxieties in the narrative. A male character who refuses to raise his fists, especially when his buddies are threatened, leads to questions about the character's masculine identity. *Mod Squad* episodes almost inevitably relied on some sort of climactic fight scene with Linc and

Pete using their macho prowess to overcome the bad guys—physical force being all the more necessary given that the Squad did not have recourse to guns. Arly's refusal of any form of violence would tend to question some very essential aspects of a television series that was, on the whole, attempting to construct him as hero.

This anxiety resolved itself in a very forceful way in the episode's final fight scene. Prisoners again set on Arly, demanding that he shape up and stop embarrassing his father. Arly found himself cornered as hostile prisoners converged on him. Linc jumped to Arly's rescue, punching and hitting the menacing pro-war inmates. The Mod Squadder ended up overcome by prisoners, pinned down and about to be pummeled. At that moment Arly suddenly screamed and launched himself into violent action, punching and hitting. Just as the prison warden, along with Arly's father, the brigadier general, entered the room, we discover Arly, in a fit of crazed violence, on top of a guard, choking the man. Linc, yelling that Arly was killing him, forced the former pacifist off his victim. The scene ended with Arly yelling out to all, "Is this what you wanted! *Is this what you all wanted!*" [23] From an extreme of pacifism to an extreme of violence the episode seemed to have no other way to consider the questions of militarism and conscientious objection.

This episode, along with one about a militant black priest, compelled Harlan Ellison, TV critic for the *Los Angeles Free Press,* to revise his initial condemnation of the *The Mod Squad.* The savvy producer of the series, Harve Bennett, invited Ellison to a special screening of the two episodes. The invitation was clearly an attempt by Bennett to reach out to movement young people via the underground press. He must have believed that the ideological balancing game undertaken in the series favored the politics and perspectives of antiwar young people enough for him to invite the attention of the underground press's principle television commentator. Bennett's invitation bore fruit. Ellison praised the episodes and lauded the series: "Neither show copped-out. The three undercover kids who work for the Laws were used eminently well in context; the acting was, in the main, superlative; the scripts were authentic and honest; and the series has developed into one of the heavier items in mainstream programming." [24] Ellison urged his readers to watch the show.

Harve Bennett showed himself an astute judge of the best means to reach the desired audience for his series. His negotiations with ABC network brass also indicate how political positions associated with dissenting groups could make it onto prime-time television screens. Discussing the draft resistance episode, Bennett told *TV Guide,* "I thought we were in trouble, but if you can do a show where a draft resister is the sympathetic character, you have done something worth doing."[25]

It may be instructive to compare the treatment of draft resistance in the "Arly Blau" episode with the treatment of the same theme in *The Smothers Brothers Comedy Hour,* both having been, respectively, broadcast and censored at about the same time. When Joan Baez wanted to dedicate a song to her draft-resisting and prison-bound husband, she was censored by CBS. *TV Guide* castigated her and the Smothers for offending the mores of the nation. The network claimed such speech was inappropriate for entertainment television. Yet over at ABC a fictionalized draft resister proved to be no offense to the mores of the nation and could actually be portrayed as a positive character, resulting in no outraged editorials from *TV Guide.* How do we account for the remarkable discrepancy in responses to these evocations of the draft resister?

One reason for the difference in reaction may have to do with a contrast between the range of popular meanings available for actual public figures compared to fictional characters. Fictional figures can be manipulated in creative ways in order to negotiate and massage the differing political stances of a diverse television audience. Actual public figures such as Joan Baez and draft-resistance leader David Harris cannot have the meanings that circulate around them so pointedly manipulated. As an activist, Harris and his actions had demonstrable effects in the political arena, especially in encouraging young men to resist the draft and in organizing others to resist. When Baez evoked Harris's political activities in the context of an "entertainment" program, the boundaries between "fiction" and "actuality" disintegrated, and unmediated political activism invaded the tube. Arly Blau may have been a figure very similar to David Harris, but Arly Blau, as a fictional construct, was unable to rally actual, in-the-real-world draft opponents to his cause. Arly Blau could stand for and speak much the same discourse as Joan Baez or David Harris but without threatening to incite anyone. On the one hand, Arly's discourse was "safer" because it was bound by a world of fiction. Yet on the other hand, Arly as a counter to the "draft-dodger-as-folk-devil" image could massage a more attractive representation of draft resisters that may have been more difficult for public figures like Harris.

The Mod Squad Investigates the My Lai Massacre

In November of 1969 journalist Seymour Hersh began publishing reports about a horrifying massacre of Vietnamese civilians—babies, children, women, and elderly men—in the hamlet of My Lai. Conducted as "open season" against "slant-eyed gooks," the young American troops of Charlie Company under the command of 2d Lt. William L. Calley Jr. managed to kill approximately five hundred unarmed villagers. The massacre occurred in March 1968, and although the army conducted a perfunctory investigation, the incident might never have come to public attention, much less to military prosecution, were it not for Hersh's investigative reporting. Hersh's story suddenly put My Lai and attendant questions of whether American troops in Vietnam were engaging in war crimes onto front pages and newsmagazine covers.

In large part American public opinion (at least that which was constructed by pollsters) remained unmoved and unbelieving. "Most Americans," notes historian William O'Neill, "reacted like good Germans to the news."[26] According to polls taken within a month of the avalanche of news reports, a majority of Americans refused to believe the massacre had, in fact, occurred. Others wondered why the incident attracted so much attention, and only a very few admitted that the revelations had changed their opinions about the war. A fair amount of hostility was directed at the news media and television for expending so much attention on the incident.[27] Like "Good Germans," many Americans were uncomfortable and unwilling to entertain the idea that their soldiers were murderers and war criminals.

Almost exactly a year after Hersh's reports first began appearing in American newspapers, *The Mod Squad* broadcast an episode that would not have assuaged the sentiments of this apparent majority of the American public. "A Far Away Place So Near," which aired November 17, 1970, is a remarkable example of televisual popular culture trying to engage in a serious, complex, and critical way with the experience of American troops in Vietnam while the United States was still waging war. A thinly veiled account of the My Lai massacre, the episode also explored soldier psychology and white racism toward the Vietnamese and other people of color. That such material found its way onto an entertainment television series at this period is all the more notable given that the Hollywood film industry largely avoided dealing with Vietnam narratives until the late 1970s, when the war was long since lost and the wounds inflicted on the national psyche, although not healed, were at least starting to scab over.[28] During the war years Hollywood produced only one feature, the unapologetically promilitary John Wayne effort *The Green Berets* (1968), that was set in Vietnam and engaged forthrightly with American involvement. In general, the commercial film industry was skittish about dealing head-on with the war in Southeast Asia. Meditations on the war and critiques of it tended to be displaced into the past, usually in the genre of the western. Michael Klein has noted that Arthur Penn's *Little Big Man* (1970) could be viewed as an allegorical statement about the My Lai massacre in its depiction of U.S. cavalry massacres of Indian villages.[29]

Network television, on the other hand, emerged as the primary medium whereby Americans confronted the war. In general, of course, television viewers encountered stories about Vietnam on the evening news and on network news documentaries. Nevertheless, the familiarity of seeing Vietnam stories in this one arena of broadcasting may have meant that stories about the war in entertainment television might not have been quite as unsettling as they appeared to be for the motion picture industry. Although episodic television did not abound with Vietnam stories, dramas like *The Mod Squad* provided a venue for viewers to negotiate meanings about the war that the motion picture industry would not countenance for almost a decade.

Although the episode's larger purpose was to explore the murderous behavior of American troops in Vietnam, it also had to abide by the codes and conventions of the cop show. The narrative thus revolved around the mysterious disappearance of Linc's friend Hank, a returning Vietnam veteran who did not get off the plane with his other returning buddies. Standing around the tarmac at the airfield, the vets became noticeably uneasy when Linc asked them where Hank was. Finally they informed him that Hank had been killed by a sniper's bullet. Linc, suspicious of this explanation and of the vets' behavior, decided to begin an investigation.[30] Built on to this "whodunit" frame were the much larger and more important issues with which the episode was really concerned. To engage those issues the episode needed to tread carefully. Producer Harve Bennett, in a *TV Guide* article, indicates his savvy use of the ideological balancing act in order to appease potentially nervous ABC censors:

> To even try this on an action-adventure show . . . was insane, insane! When I called Dorothy Brown of Program Standards and Practices I thought she'd simply say, "You are out of your mind" or "Go jump out the window." I said, "Dorothy, I would like to do this show for one reason only and this will be the theme of the show—that a country which is capable of admitting there's a possibility that we killed innocent civilians and is capable of putting it in print and talking about it cannot be a bad place in which to live." She gave me some ground rules, such as soft-pedalling the fact that children were killed, and we took it from there.[31]

Here again we see an appeal to liberal pluralist sentiments. Even mass murder and war crimes could be excused and brought within the discourse of Americanism so long as they could be freely talked about. The My Lai massacre, in its public circulation as media event (and here as fictionalized event), served not as a horrifying indictment of an American racist, out-of-control, and imperialistic war policy but rather as a comforting assurance that American liberal democracy and freedom of speech worked. America was okay because a television series like *The Mod Squad* could broadcast a show like this. Bennett's preferred reading of the episode attempted to discourage interpretations that might lead to a national sense of self-loathing, criticism, shame, or disgust. Whatever the narrative itself might have been suggesting, the fact that such material could be aired was, for Bennett, good news for America.

The narrative itself did have to skate carefully around its painful subject matter, but it is to the credit of scriptwriter Theodore Apstein and producer Bennett that the episode ended up pulling relatively few punches. The episode's fictional "Charlie Company" comprised five characters: Hank, the only African American; Mike Sierra, a Chicano prospective law student; Dawson, a Caucasian pill popper, married to a Vietnamese woman; Arnie, a semi–white trash southerner; and Bob, a neutrally figured white guy who appeared to be the group's leader. The composition of the actual Charlie Company was quite different from this in its racial and educational makeup.

African Americans made up half of the company with a few Latinos, including Company Commander Medina. Very few had even a year of college education. Whites, such as second in command, Lieutenant Calley, formed a minority in Charlie Company.[32] The episode clearly whitened the unit, giving us Vietnam veterans who were much more the picture of racial and class diversity than was actually the case. As a politically liberal series with a certain amount of race consciousness, it would have been ideologically tricky and potentially troublesome to emphasize the actual composition of the troops at My Lai. In this instance, by reconstituting the racial makeup, the episode attempted to negotiate meanings about My Lai that would discourage viewers from potentially constructing racist interpretations about black American troops and their behavior in combat.

The episode did a sensitive job suggesting the post-traumatic stress disorders all the vets suffered, with the notable exception of Bob. Dawson couldn't stand getting close to his Vietnamese wife, not even wanting to look at her. Later in the episode we see her with a bruised face, suggesting the brutality American troops were inflicting on Vietnamese people but also the way in which the brutalization *of* American troops in combat could lead to domestic abuse once they were stateside.

Mike, the budding law student, had grown so disillusioned by the war experience that he refused to consider pursuing the law. In dialogue with Linc he heatedly explained:

Mike Sierra: People need lawyers like they need soldiers. To knock
                  other people's heads together. . . .
Linc: Well, seems a shame if you got the G.I. Bill.
Mike Sierra: Listen, I don't want nothing out of the war—like what
                  was I doing there in the first place?

Arnie had his traumatic flashback to the war while he was with Julie. The female Mod Squadder had decided to use her feminine charms to try to get some information out of the southern good ol' boy. Using a camera as a prop, she appealed to the shutterbug Arnie by playing the helpless female, unable to understand how her camera was supposed to work. Later, talking about the war with her, he said that nobody could imagine what it was like. He began recounting an "in country" story that would have been familiar to many viewers because it frequently circulated as an explanation for American behavior toward the Vietnamese population. Arnie told about a soldier coming up to a young boy and offering him some candy. When the soldier got up close, the boy suddenly pulled a gun from his basket and fired. Arnie then picked up Julie's camera, saying, "I wish . . . I wish this was the only kind of shooting there was." As he pointed the camera at her there was a sudden cut to an image of an elderly Vietnamese man on the ground looking up. Hysterical, Arnie cried out, "I can't get it out of my mind! . . . Why did he do it!"

These three vets were clearly racked with guilt and revulsion over something they had seen or done in Vietnam. The first to break the code of collective silence that Bob had commanded was Mike Sierra. Linc discovered that Mike had been with Hank when Hank got hit. Suddenly, out of the blue Mike insisted that he didn't pull the trigger, that he had told the others that his gun was jammed. "I made up my mind I wasn't going to fire. And I didn't!" Hank hadn't wanted to fire either but did. Mike insisted he didn't think Hank had hit anything. Then the entire story poured out of Mike.

> *Mike:* Look, you got to understand the whole thing. The five of us, we got cut off and it was getting dark . . . we were tired, thirsty . . . and we came on this small place . . . not even a village . . . just a few houses and a field. . . . Out of the blue this old man came running at Dawson. Dawson was stoned. He thought the guy was V.C. . . . He opened fire.
>
> *Linc:* Was the old man V.C.?
>
> *Mike:* (Shakes his head) He was just an old man. (Moment) Mistakes like that happen in a war! What can you do? But then—all these *other* people came rushing out of their houses. . . . I don't know what they were screaming, but Bob said, "The old man was a big shot or something. We'll hang for this, we'll hang for killing him!" (Beat) So the decision was made to cover up. We opened fire on the others . . . we kept firing—and firing . . . till there were no witnesses. (Beat) I don't even know how many we killed.
>
> *Linc:* (A beat; after the horror sinks in) We? I thought your gun was jammed.
>
> *Mike:* I was there! I could have tried to stop it—! But I was afraid to, man—so was Hank.

Linc: Why?

Mike: Because if we tried, maybe one of our buddies would have let
    us have it, too!

Linc: Which one?

Mike: Any one of 'em, man! We were all strung out. Everybody was
    scared, crazy scared.

This account, although notably horrifying for a prime-time entertainment show, ended up soft-pedaling more than just the killing
of children that the ABC censor worried about. In this account the
massacre was in no way premeditated. Thirst, weariness, and drugs,
although not excusing the actions, can be read as mitigating circumstances that at least help explain the killing.

Seymour Hersh's reporting about the My Lai story provided few
such mediating tactics to soften the impact. The actual My Lai massacre occurred early in the morning as a planned attack. The ostensible mission was to engage and destroy a Viet Cong battalion supposedly hiding out in the area. Whether Commander Medina or Second
Lieutenant Calley actually expected to find any Viet Cong remained,
for Hersh, a very debatable question. Many of the troops thought
that the point of the mission was to revenge the killing of a company soldier, whose funeral had taken place the evening before the
My Lai action. During the mission the members of Charlie Company systematically shot, bayoneted, and hand-grenaded the entire
village, ignoring the shrieks and cries of villagers shouting, "No V.C."
According to some observers, many of the soldiers appeared to be en-
joying themselves. *The Mod Squad*'s My Lai presented a troubling, but
not quite so horrifying, narrative of troops *reacting* to the actions of a
villager after having stumbled, dazed and lost, into unfamiliar terri-
tory. The premeditated quality of the actual My Lai action may have
been just too difficult to bring into the moral universe of prime-time
television.

The episode's boldest move came at the climax in a scene that,
without equivocation, laid out how white racism underpinned the
American war effort and how the dehumanizing of the Vietnamese
was of a piece with domestic racism against African Americans. Arnie
and Bob kidnapped Dawson and Linc before Linc was able to get the
tortured vet to the judge advocate's office to confirm what had actually happened to Hank and to the Vietnamese civilians. In an aban-

doned, dark warehouse Bob tried to compel Dawson to kill Linc because, according to Bob, Dawson was responsible for getting them into the mess they were all in. Linc then corrected Bob by saying that although Dawson killed the old man, Bob understood Vietnamese, knew that the villagers were saying "Don't shoot, we're civilians," but lied to his buddies about it so that he could open fire. Arnie, in shock and outrage, asked Bob if that was what the villagers were saying.

Bob: (Flashing) Who knows what they meant, Arnie. They were a bunch of gooks, so what difference does it make!
Arnie: What difference—!
Linc: See, Bob? It does make a difference to some people. To Arnie—to Hank—

Linc then revealed to Arnie that Bob had killed Hank.

Bob: Arnie, keep this in focus. Remember who you are—what you and I have gone through—creeps all around us.
Arnie: (Demanding) *Is it true!*
Bob: We're talking about half a dozen lousy gooks—
Arnie: Hank was no gook!
Bob: (Wildly) *Yes, he was!* (Quickly) He was going to turn us in. He was just a different kind of gook. (Indicates Linc) Like him! Like all of them.

As the truth started slowly to dawn on Arnie, he softly insisted that Hank had been their buddy. He started toward Bob to try and take his gun away from him. Linc warned Arnie, but Arnie shook his head and said, "No, he won't kill me. . . . I'm his kind. Right, Bob?" As he advanced toward his buddy, Arnie continued, "Come on, Bob, you got no excuses this time. You can't call me no funny names, can you— so gimme the gun." Bob fired anyway. Linc then wrestled him to the ground while the disoriented Dawson, apparently thinking he was back in a fire zone in Vietnam, started yelling wildly for a medic.

The episode located racist hatred within the individualized figure of the evil white male, who, unlike the other vets, had no ethnic or class markers of "difference." On the one hand, we can see Bob as yet another evil "establishment" type, like the hippie-hating property owner in "The Guru." All the other vets were either wracked with guilt and remorse or, in the case of the only black participant, Hank, were on the verge of heroically seeking justice. Only Bob showed no remorse and exhibited no concern for the value of human life. Figuring Bob as the only participant incapable of seeing the moral reprehensibility of the massacre does help to soften the indictment against American activities against the civilian population in Vietnam. Bob could be seen as merely a bad egg. However, on the other hand, to represent any Vietnam veteran in such a damning manner in 1970, while Americans were still fighting, killing, and dying in Southeast Asia, was a bold move in American popular culture. The psychotic Vietnam vet would become a staple of American popular imagination later in the 1970s and beyond but not in this early period. And Bob did not really appear as psychotic and thus easier to dismiss but rather as a very sane equal-opportunity racist. The depiction of his racism allows for a potentially radical reading strategy. From this reading position Bob can be viewed as the embodiment of American institutionalized racism oppressing and murdering black people on the home front while extending this hatred of the Other into a genocidal slaughter on the war front. The "niggers" at home and the "gooks" overseas are all "creeps" against which the besieged white American tries to construct a sense of identity: as Bob says to Arnie, "Remember who you are." This linkage of racisms was the episode's most powerful indictment of the war, in part because it refused to keep the hatred that led to My Lai more safely away on the other side of the globe. That hatred, the episode suggested, was right here at home.

With such a harsh indictment of American military action in Vietnam, Apstein and Bennet apparently felt the need to soften their portrayal of the armed forces in other aspects. The war and its soldiers may have been out of control and brutalized, but military justice still worked. We see the Squad working in harmony with the army's judge advocate, who seemed sincerely interested in investigating the case. When Pete succeeded in bringing Mike Sierra in to tell his story to the judge advocate, Sierra said to him, "I guess I'd rather get it from the Establishment than from my buddies." In Sierra's dialogue with Linc in the episode's coda, the narrative worked particularly hard to contain potentially explosive indictments opened up throughout the hour about the war, American racism, and the murderousness of American troops. Mike Sierra informed Linc that he's decided to apply for law school after all.

Linc: Thought you were pretty down on justice.

Sierra: So? I changed my mind.

Linc: Why?

Sierra: (Shrugs) Look, man. I didn't think they'd listen—the army, the papers—people. I didn't think they could take the truth about what happened to us out there. Well, they are listening. Maybe some of them even understand.

"Blackening" Linc Hayes

It is no accident that when *The Mod Squad* endeavored to grapple with issues around race and racism, the show put Linc at the center. Far more than either Pete Cochran or Julie Barnes, Linc Hayes, as the figure of the angry, young, black male, literally embodied the potential for political opposition and threat. To the extent that the show could claim any amount of "hipness" or "coolness," it rested largely with Clarence Williams III's portrayal of Linc. He quickly became the Mod Squadder most favored by youth viewers.[33]

Linc was also the only one of the three whose character history was grounded in a historically specific incident of political revolt. Linc's reason for joining the police unit resulted from his participation in the violent uprisings during the 1965 Watts riots in Los Angeles. Pete and Julie, on the other hand, rebelled against the establishment in much more vague ways. Julie messed up because her mother was a prostitute; Pete rebelled because of his family's Beverly Hills affluence. The show never made anything of the two white Mod Squadders' obvious divergent class formations. It appeared sufficient to construct their back story around generalized generational conflict and leave it at that. Linc's rebelliousness, however, was directly connected with the political and economic disenfranchisement of black Americans in the urban centers, along with the rise of black-power sentiment. As such, he could be a potentially frightening figure to large segments of white America. He had neither the suave, debonair sophistication of Bill Cosby in *I Spy* nor the tame and easy-to-integrate comic sweetness of Diahann Carroll's *Julia*.[34] These two could be (and were) dismissed as "white Negroes," reassuring white America that blacks could be just like them. Williams's angry ghetto youth seemed the (quite literal) dark underside of these upwardly

mobile inheritors of the American Dream. Sandwiching Linc between two fellow social outcasts, who just happened to be white,
may have helped to defuse some of the potential menace associated
with the figure for some audiences. On the other hand, for teenage
and youth audiences Linc's ghetto origins, marked by his perpetual
shades, Afro hairstyle, disinclination to smile, and penchant for physical confrontation and (always justified) violence, served to further
legitimate his character and, by extension, the show itself with these
viewers.

The series still needed to negotiate Linc's blackness, however.
Given the heightened consciousness over the politics of black representation during this period, Linc's "blackness" served as a site for a
certain amount of tension and debate at the level of the show's production.[35] Linc may have been visibly black, but to what extent was
he "written black"? Scriptwriter Allan Sloane weighed in on the dilemma in a November 1968 letter to *Mod Squad* coproducers Tony
Barrett and Harve Bennett:

> I have thought and thought, but I must say I do not dig your use—
> or the writer's use—of the spade cat. . . . He did not seem to come
> through to me as, for the quality I had expected—let's call it black-
> ness. I mean you could put someone in a natural nappy fright wig
> and call him Stokely—but in terms of involvement inside the story
> as black, that isn't all you need.
>
> I don't mean, of course, involving him in anything so obviously
> apposite as an undercover investigation of a Black Nationalist plot.
> But I have been thinking of a way in which to exploit (in the best and
> proper sense of the word) *black* that is real and speaks to the subject
> honestly.[36]

Sloane went on to detail a story pitch. A few years later Clarence
Williams III in a *TV Guide* article self-consciously titled "Clarence
Williams III on 'How I Feel Being Black and Playing a Cop and
Blah, Blah, Blah'" inveighed against white scriptwriters who were
incapable of understanding the experience of black people in Watts.[37]
In the late 1960s, as African Americans began appearing on tele-
vision screens after being largely absent since the *Amos 'n' Andy* era,
debates abounded about how to depict blackness realistically. Both
Williams and Sloane suggested that Linc Hayes's blackness was a

Linc's "Black Power" signifiers: bushy Afro, dark
shades. *(Author's collection)*

figment of the white imagination, loaded down with the semiotic
markers of that category but with little else. Sloane's reference to
the show's use of Linc's Afro as insufficient to connote the character's black identity resonates with a section in the *TV Guide* profile of
Williams. For the magazine the growing prominence of Williams's
hairstyle was somehow significant to both the actor's and the character's identity: "[Williams] wears his hair in an Afro style, the way he
wore it, except in the Army, all his life. Last season management made
him cut it shorter than he likes. With the show on firmer footing
this year, the hair is bushier."[38] Williams's struggle with the network
here suggests a black-power victory over a honky establishment attempting to quash black political expressiveness. Williams's and Linc's
bushier hairdo linked him, in the white imagination at any rate, di-

rectly to black-power symbol Stokely Carmichael, the Black Panthers in general, and to political prisoner Angela Davis, whose big, wide, and round Afro became a veritable fetish object. Although this may have been enough to render Linc suitably, rebelliously, black for many whites, however, the question remained: how to render him black within the context of the narrative?

The draft resistance and My Lai episodes we have already examined provide some strategies used by the show to "blacken" Linc. It seems no coincidence that in discussion with pacifist Arly Blau, Linc would be the one to question his extreme nonviolence. Linc's argument that violence was sometimes justified in the interests of survival could be read as a subtle nod to black-power and its calls for self-defense against a law-enforcement system seen by many African Americans as bent on the destruction of black communities and the emasculinization of black males.[39] Hippie flower child Julie could unproblematically embrace nonviolence—that stance would merely bolster her femininity. However, in order to "write" Linc convincingly as a black ghetto male, the embrace of righteous violence had to be part of the package.

Scriptwriter Sloane's desire to see Linc's blackness "exploited" in the best and most proper manner was most likely realized in an episode entitled "Keep the Faith, Baby," written by Harve Bennett.[40] Guest star Sammy Davis Jr. appeared as a militant black priest trying to bring relevant ministering to the ghetto. An assistant to a white pastor in a middle-class white church, Davis's Father John Banks criticized his church and other religious institutions for their racist attitudes and for being out of step with the needs of people living in the ghettos. In the episode's opener Linc had come down to volunteer in one of Father John's inner-city initiatives for ghetto youths. Thus, from the beginning Linc aligned himself with Father John, with the ghetto, and against the racist white religious establishment. When Father John's life was threatened by a white murderer who had confessed his crime to the priest and now feared Father John might reveal the confession, Linc and the other Mod Squadders were called into service by Captain Greer to provide the embattled priest with police protection. Thereupon followed the almost ritualistic confrontation between the antiestablishment character suddenly disillusioned that his hip supporters turned out to be "fuzz."

> *Father John:* Have I been your *assignment* since that first day?
> *Linc:* No, man. That's not why.
> *Julie:* We've been around because we wanted to, Father.

Just as the squad proved themselves supporters of the underground paper the *Guru* and of draft resister Arly Blau before they agreed to do undercover police work in order to provide protection, here too police work came along only as a consequence of their, and especially Linc's, political allegiance to the militant black priest. Protecting Father John, which largely fell on Linc's shoulders, served as a means to put into narrative action his support for the priest's activities. In this and other episodes Linc was "being black" by protecting and advocating for other blacks. In "A Far Away Place So Near" Linc acted "black" by investigating the death of his black friend and by discovering the pervasive racism that led to both Hank's and the Vietnamese civilians' murders. In "Keep the Faith, Baby" Linc acted "black" by putting himself in harm's way so that he ended up being beat up by white thugs over and over again in order to save Father John. Linc was, thus, a "soul brother" because he could save his black brother from white assailants.

Conclusion: The Mod Squad *Formula*

The Mod Squad cracked the list of the twenty-five highest rated series in 1969 and 1970 at twenty-three. The next year, the "season of social relevance" discussed in the next chapter, it achieved its highest rating as the eleventh most popular show, according to A. C. Nielsen's figures.[41] Although these were good numbers, the series never did as well as the staunchly right-wing, J. Edgar Hoover–approved law-and-order series *The F.B.I.* Yet when all three networks, at the beginning of the new decade, were casting about for models to help them revamp their programming, *The Mod Squad* served as the prototype. As we will see, this show's balancing act of advocating the politics and perspectives of dissident young people and wrapping it all within the comforting confines of traditional institutions run by benevolent grown-ups would be reworked all over the dial in 1970 and 1971. Response to the formula was ambivalent, at best, among the politicized youths that we encountered in the pages of the underground press. However, enough young people appeared to be tuning in to assure network executives that this model would help them lure the young back to the tube and would do so in ways that did not carry too many political costs.

The Mod Squad succeeded in pushing the bounds of acceptable political discourse within American mainstream entertainment by doing what successful popular culture always does: keeping itself open to a range of interpretations, even as it prefers some over others. Whereas the Smothers Brothers tended to shut out perspectives that did not side with their increasingly politicized viewpoints, *The Mod Squad* advocated much the same structure of generational feeling yet suffered no censorship or network battles. The show may have been an example of how the culture industry can effectively incorporate bits and pieces of oppositional discourse and make it palatable. However, in making New Left, antiwar, countercultural, and even black-power perspectives palatable, the show may have assisted also in bringing those perspectives closer to "common sense."

Make It Relevant

How Youth Rebellion

Captured Prime Time

in 1970 and 1971

> For years we've known the buying power of our
> nation's adults, but this year we are witnessing a dra-
> matic phenomenon. The younger people have be-
> come a social and political force, challenging us to
> reexamine every facet of our society. For the first
> time they are organizing their energies and express-
> ing their awareness and concern by showing the older
> political pros how to conduct a real grassroots politi-
> cal campaign. The younger minds are being courted
> as never before. We know why we appeal to them—
> because we have the ability to be more unconven-
> tional than our competitors. And we are going to be-
> come even more unconventional as we become more
> meaningful.[1]

Thus spoke Elton Rule, president of ABC-TV, to a meeting of the
network's affiliates in April 1968. Two years later, at another affiliates' meeting, he proclaimed essentially the same message: the network needed to appeal to the nation's politically committed young
people. Quoted in *Variety,* Rule argued, "These young people are the
experimenters, the curious, the thrill seekers; [they] are also brighter,
better educated, more concerned, more vocal." He pointed out the
growing communication gap between the younger and older generations and declared, "The communications industry must serve these

young people."[2] Rule's rhetoric echoed that of Tom Smothers in the aftermath of his show's cancellation. Television, the great popular communicator, could, unlike any other current medium or technology, bridge the polarized generations, heal the rifts, and "bring us together."[3]

We have already seen how the Smothers Brothers' show did succeed in "serving" these politicized young people to some extent. In the last chapter we saw how *The Mod Squad* attempted to bridge the ideological divide between youth and elders by affirming antiwar and counterculture values without necessarily ruffling the feathers of more conservative viewers. In this chapter we examine how far Elton Rule's ABC (*The Mod Squad*'s network), as well as NBC and CBS, succeeded in their increasingly emphatic proclamations that they wanted to woo young audiences.

Beginning in 1967 and gaining urgency as the decade ended, executives at all three networks grew apprehensive that their top-rated shows were skewed to an increasingly elderly audience. Shows such as ABC's Lawrence Welk, CBS's Jackie Gleason, Red Skelton, and Ed Sullivan, along with tried-and-true westerns like *Gunsmoke* and NBC's *Bonanza* were all showing their age, both by their longevity on the broadcast schedule and by the viewers they attracted. These shows, although pulling in large bulk ratings numbers, did not entice the younger and increasingly more commercially attractive audiences who, according to Madison Avenue marketers, made up the segment of the population buying the most commodities.

Just what constituted this younger audience was never entirely clear. As we saw in chapter 2, the "youth" audience in network parlance and Nielsen breakdowns consisted of those between the ages of eighteen and forty-nine. This demographic segment managed to encompass both the cohort of disaffected youth and that of the "grown-ups," thus cobbling together the generation gap with its sharply divergent tastes, interests, viewpoints, and politics. Although broadcasters and advertisers tended to fall back on the eighteen-to-forty-nine demographic as the general age composition they wished to attract, they continually tried to refine and further limit the age range in attempts to figure out what audience they really wanted. Sometimes the twenty-five-to-fifty age range was the most attractive.[4] Other times eighteen-to-thirty-four-year-olds were the most appealing audience.[5] "Young adult" as a category proved unstable politically and socially, but, as television industry discourse revealed, it was equally unstable and volatile as a term with any useful meaning.

Les Brown, *Variety*'s astute editor for television and radio, pointed out the networks' dilemma in a December 31, 1969, article. He noted that advertisers were most interested in those eighteen to thirty-five, especially those at the younger end of that demographic. Network television, however, tended to generate audiences closer to the high end of the eighteen-to-forty-nine demographic. He observed that when the medium had tried to entice truly young adults, "the networks have sometimes looked as ridiculous as a matron in a miniskirt and love beads."[6] He also emphasized the fictitiousness of the eighteen-to-forty-nine category:

> To speak of an 18–49 viewership is to obscure the fact that 18–25 scarcely exists—for television. The new adults don't log many hours before the set. Radio is their medium and motion pictures their art form. In a mass sense, they're just not around for the Nielsen census. . . .
>
> The webs can't stand the thought of it, in view of the advertisers' demographic penchant, but television's most natural and dependable audience is still old people and young tots. . . .
>
> It isn't that American youth will not watch television, but rather that it doesn't watch very often. Although the population census may represent 18–25 as a large group, it's probably a small one before the set at any given hour. And with three networks and any number of independent stations trying with all their might to capture that single element of the audience, it necessarily is being splintered almost to negligible size.[7]

The networks faced an economic problem. The elderly and children were not "quality" consumers. As a commercial medium selling audiences to advertisers and making its profits on the amount of money those advertisers were willing to spend to reach those audiences, network television needed to show that it could deliver the audience that counted.[8] Increasingly advertisers warned networks that "old-skewed" shows would not continue commanding high spot prices if the audiences delivered didn't have high buying power.

This situation provided CBS, in particular, with a disturbing dilemma. William S. Paley's network had commanded top spot on the Nielsen totem pole for years largely on the strength of its countrified schedule of rural-oriented programming. *The Beverly Hillbillies, Mayberry RFD,* and other "hayseed shows" were consistent ratings winners, but as advertisers began to examine those audience numbers more closely, they discovered that many of the viewers were over fifty and lived in more rural areas.[9] A study comparing viewership in New York City to the total national audience revealed that most shows that rated highly with the national audience rated poorly with cosmopolitan residents of the Big Apple. These urbanites completely rejected CBS's "rube" lineup.[10]

Sensing that the CBS ratings colossus may have had feet of clay, the other two networks jumped into the breech, asserting they were the real ratings winners because they drew more young adults—more of the audience advertisers really wanted. Elton Rule proclaimed in the pages of *TV Guide* that over half of the television audience was under the age of thirty-four, completely contradicting Les Brown's assertion that the "new adult" audience was a myth.[11] Consequently, the network constructed a notion of "youth" that fitted its economic need to please advertisers. Youth was, therefore, anything the networks said it was. Robert Wood, president of CBS-TV, proclaimed that his network wanted to attract viewers who were part of the "now" generation. He had, of course, very successfully reached exactly that audience with *The Smothers Brothers Comedy Hour* and had found the youthful "now" viewers unpalatable in their politics and in their tastes. Wood's construction of youth was similar to Rule's. "Now generation" served as an elastic phrase meant to lure anyone who wanted to assume a place in that demographic category. As Rule went on to say in his analysis of the television audience, even those between thirty-five and forty-nine were "younger-*thinking.*"[12] Even middle-aged establishmentarians could be part of the now, with-it generation; they only needed to think themselves young.

The network executives' smoke-and-mirrors routines about their youth audiences did not stop nagging concerns about the ramifications of the "television generation" having abandoned the medium. Warning bells were ringing within industry circles, suggesting that the seemingly successful formula of escapist fare consisting of sitcoms, westerns, cop shows, variety shows, and the like were quickly alienating younger and highly educated viewers. According to *TV Guide* industry observer Richard Doan, the networks had mastered the ratings game and were loath to experiment in any way with different kinds of programming.[13] Paradoxically, the tried-and-true approaches for maximizing the total audience were driving away the more lucrative viewers the industry needed in order to maintain its economic growth in the future.

Donald McGannon, president of Westinghouse Broadcasting, came to a similar conclusion in a statement to the FCC. He argued that the medium no longer gave viewers enough compelling reasons to tune in, and the irritating quality of network fare was alienating various segments of society. "The programming has not kept abreast of the evolution of values and the social crises of the '60s and to that degree TV programming is not relevant to our times."[14]

Compounding anxieties that the medium was chasing away younger, educated viewers, television executives worried about the motion picture industry. By 1967 the film studios had quite deliberately and unambiguously decided to chase after the under-twenty-five audience, appealing with various degrees of success to its dissident, antiestablishment perspectives.[15] The networks, which relied heavily on Hollywood features to round out programming schedules, became increasingly nervous about the implications of films like *Easy Rider, Woodstock, The Strawberry Statement,* and their ilk coming available for broadcast showings in a number of years. These films were not family viewing material; they appealed to those in their teens and early twenties with countercultural values. As one industry executive admitted in what may have been a momentary fit of honesty, "And that bunch doesn't *even watch* TV!"[16]

Clearly, the nation's baby boomers had lost the TV habit. Had they done so because of their particular position within the age cycle? Had they done so because many of their members were politically, socially, and culturally disaffected from institutions that represented the dominant order? It was impossible to tell. This was, after all, the first generation to grow up with the medium. No precedents existed for charting what role television would play as its viewers went through their life cycles with the medium. In 1970 industry insiders were very worried that baby boomers, having largely abandoned the medium for films, radio and recordings, might never be wooed back to the set. Vice president for economics and research at CBS, Dr. David M. Blank, noted that television was the only medium that tended to be skewed to an older audience. Young people tended to prefer films because that medium took them away from the home, whereas the older segment of the population tended to watch TV precisely because it was in the home. Blank pointed out that "the program material in these media differ substantially in their appeal to different age groups and tend to reflect the interests of the dominant group of consumers."[17] Television's placement within a domestic space with family-oriented programming reinforced its irrelevance to the young. Blank suggested optimistically that, as they aged, today's raucous youth would switch back to television, "but, with the country subject to as much and as rapid social change as it is today, I think only the future can really tell" (p. 142). The dislocations and upheavals associated with the activities of the era's young rebels made confident long-term planning on behalf of dominant institutions terribly difficult. Not only did the television industry find itself incapable of satisfactorily determining who or what constituted the youth audience, but the industry also could not figure out how to factor that audience into its future decisions. However, as the biggest demographic bulge in the entire population, this market could not be ignored—even if it was apparently ignoring television. At the very moment the politicized youth of the sixties were questioning, critiquing, and rejecting the trappings of commodity capitalist American society, their generation's sheer numbers and spending power continued to make all of them irresistible to those very institutions.[18] Corporate America did not have the luxury of being able to ignore this unpredictable, hostile demographic. As the motion picture industry had so perilously and precariously ventured forth in "thinking young!" so too did the three networks.

Thinking young meant thinking "relevant." To woo back disaffected young viewers, the networks came to the conclusion that escapist, bucolic, vaudevillian fare, the very forms of programming that had proved so successful for so long, could no longer be counted on to deliver the quality audience. Entertainment shows would have to acknowledge and grapple with the social dislocations of the period. The question was how.

The Season of Relevance

In the fall 1970/71 network season, CBS, NBC, and ABC all touted their relevant, "with-it" programming. It was a season of transition for the broadcasters in many ways besides their attempt to remake the face of television so that fewer wrinkles showed.[19] It would be the final year cigarette advertising would be allowed on television, thus marking the end of the networks' relationship with a particularly lucrative group of advertisers. It was also the year the FCC promulgated its Prime Time Access Rule, chipping back to three hours the amount of programming the networks could feed to their affiliates in prime time. Much was riding on a successful new season.

Although ABC and CBS were the most obviously committed to youth-oriented new programs, CBS received particular attention because it was taking the most chances in remaking itself and its schedule to get rid of its "country cousin" image. The network offered a number of youth-oriented relevant dramas. One was a "Mod Squad goes to the bar" series called *Storefront Lawyers*. It featured a young attorney who quit his job at a prestige law firm to open up a nonprofit law clinic with two other idealistic young attorneys in a poor Los Angeles neighborhood, where they dispensed legal counsel to the underprivileged. *The Interns,* a "Mod Squad goes to the hospital" series, featured an array of idealistic young doctors under the tutelage of the fatherly Broderick Crawford. *Headmaster* relocated Andy Griffith from Mayberry to a private high school, where Griffith had to deal with the dilemmas of youthful drug taking and protest. The show clearly took inspiration from the critically acclaimed *Room 222,* which had joined ABC's lineup the previous year.

The network spent a great deal of effort ballyhooing these programs and their "tell it like it is" qualities. Throughout the summer the network ran promotional spots for the upcoming season, using unprecedented rock music scoring and various "mod" designs to go along with their theme, "We're putting it all together this fall on CBS." According to the network's vice president for advertising and design, " 'Putting it all together' is an expression of today. It's in the vocabulary of youth: it's part of the phraseology of the world of music."[20] Presumably this phrase could somehow lure the young to the network's new fall lineup, and the rock music would convince these recalcitrant nonviewers to return to the set.

Publicity for individual shows revealed a woeful misreading of dissident youth perspectives in relation to institutional power and strategies for social change. Publicity at CBS for *Storefront Lawyers* proclaimed that the young attorneys were "trying to change and make

society better within the rules." *The Interns* were involved in "changing the establishment from within." Their "fights with authority"
would be important elements of the series. A *Variety* correspondent
commenting on this hype noted dryly that these programs amounted
to "a kind of genteel anti-establishmentarianism."[21]

A two-page advertising spread in the industry journal spotlighted
Headmaster with copy noteworthy for its extreme self-consciousness:

> This is a funny way to look at educational problems.
> In case Andy Griffith and Jerry Van Dyke have you thinking that
> *Headmaster* is straight comedy, we'd better tell you that *Headmaster*
> takes up topics like sex education and student militancy.
> And takes them pretty seriously, too.
> But always with the understanding that most serious subjects today
> can also have a funny side.
> That's an unusual attitude these days.
> *Headmaster,* which premieres this fall, is an unusual series. . . .
> The students are teen-agers, amused, involved, and concerned with
> the
> same issues that now amuse, involve, and concern teen-agers all over
> America.
> Because it treats these issues with respect, we think *Headmaster*
> will be popular with the young.
> Because it treats them with good humor, we think it will be popular
> with everyone.[22]

The publicity appeared terribly uncertain about the subject matter.
Appeals to the binaries of seriousness and comedy, the young and
everyone else, respect and good humor indicate a network promotion
department that didn't seem to know what it wanted to say. Clearly
the network wanted to appeal to those involved and concerned (but
somehow also "amused") young people, while reassuring the grown-
ups that the show's subject matter would not alienate and offend their
values. If the young were "amused" (thus by implication also amusing)
then the issues that concerned them couldn't be terribly threatening
to establishment sensibilities.

Room 222 may have been more successful because the show took
seriously the dilemmas of drug use, racism, protest, pollution, and
the other myriad of social problems the kids of Walt Whitman High
grappled with. Situated in an inner-city neighborhood and filmed at

an actual Los Angeles high school, the show achieved a sense of television realism that Andy Griffith's elite private high school lacked. *Room 222* also consistently depicted the schoolteachers—including leading man Pete Dixon, the sensitive black history teacher, along with crusty principal Kaufman—going out of their way to support their confused but idealistic young charges.[23] Pulling a leaf or two from *The Mod Squad*'s manual of successful social relevance, *Room 222* showed how the educational institution was there to, in Elton Rule's words, "serve the young."

With these two youth-oriented successes already under its network belt, ABC entered the fray in 1970 with a new batch of relevant youth programs. Considering Rule's rhetoric about the network's unique abilities to serve the unconventional young, one would expect ABC to be in the thick of the relevancy phenomenon. The network's offerings included *Dial Hotline* (renamed *Matt Lincoln*), about a youth crisis hotline run by an idealistic but crusty psychiatrist and manned by a group of young, idealistic helpers. *The Young Lawyers* had a concept suspiciously similar to that of *Storefront Lawyers*. In this series the intrepid, do-good attorneys took cases for the subordinated classes in the Boston area. Also in ABC's lineup was yet another Aaron Spelling effort, *The Young Rebels*. This series, set during the American Revolutionary War, focused on the exploits of three young patriots as they struggled against the British. The program clearly wanted to draw thematic parallels between the rebelliousness of contemporary youth and that of the nation's first revolutionaries. Such a premise, however, could carry some political dangers. Network publicity touted the series as "a totally new television experience, providing not only an insight into Yankee initiative and early American patriotism, but of stirring relevance to today's society and its youth." Richard Doan, in his *TV Guide* column, asked pointedly: "will viewers think the drama is quietly encouraging today's student militants?"[24] He reported that the network was considering a title change. The title remained, as did questions about what the program actually advocated. *TV Guide* critic Cleveland Amory wryly noted, "This show goes all the way back to the Revolution to prove that the youth of yesterday were no different from the youth of today even if they were a little—well, older. Anyway, today they blow up a few things. So what? In those days they blew up the British. The youth, in other words, will not only set you free—they did set you free."[25] A viewer from Hopkins, Minnesota, wrote the magazine, asking if ABC wasn't afraid that "a program of this nature could warp the minds of the super-patriotic, freedom-loving Americans who know that there is no such thing as a long-haired patriot?"[26]

Had the show been effective drama and had it become popular, these questions might have generated a storm of controversy around questions of patriotism, revolution, violence as a means of social change, and the position of young people as agents of change. By 1970 the cutting edge of youth activism had taken a decidedly revolutionary turn. The Weathermen were engaged in their campaign of bombings, and campuses all over the country experienced a rash of incendiary destruction, usually targeting facilities connected to militaristic endeavors. However, *The Young Rebels* proved to be a cynical and misguided attempt to appeal to the perceived patriotic pieties of middle America while subtly advocating an essentialized notion of youth as a force for ameliorative change.[27]

Screening Relevance

Although this new crop of shows garnered the greatest amount of attention with their themes of social relevance and consciousness, they were not the only ones on the network schedule in 1970 and 1971 pushing antiestablishment youth issues. Prime time was awash with dramatic reenactments of campus upheavals, portrayals of drugged-out youngsters, and images of disaffected kids protesting and agitating against the status quo. The bulk of these stories appeared in law-and-order programs such as detective, lawyer, and cop shows but also on series that focused on the goings-on within "establishment" institutions such as the magazine industry, the motion picture business, or state government. And, as we saw in chapter 2, even a western like *Bonanza* tried to show its social conscience and awareness of current youth strife by displacing a countercultural, peace-oriented, longhaired community of outcasts into the Old West.

That law-and-order genres were often the vehicles for the exploration of these issues provides a telling case study of the process of cultural negotiation and incorporation of threatening, counterhegemonic positions. Tom Schatz, in his analysis of Hollywood genres, has noted that genres, in order to remain vibrant, must constantly examine and reexamine cultural conflicts and raise questions about insoluble contemporary concerns, even as they attempt to reinforce dominant values and close down conflict through narrative closure. According to Schatz, "the genre's fundamental impulse is to continually *renegotiate* the tenets of American ideology. And what is so fascinating and confounding about Hollywood genre films is their capacity to 'play it both ways,' to both criticize and reinforce the values, beliefs, and ideals of our culture within the same narrative context."[28] Genres can become ideologically unstable when, during periods of intense social upheavals, their narratives attempt to work through the dislocations and stresses of the era and its turmoils. In the late sixties and early seventies, generic attempts to "play it both ways" were proving difficult. As we saw with *The Mod Squad,* the show's attempt to affirm law enforcement while validating the value of youth dissent created a text that tended to unmask its ideological operation. Rather than provide a comforting closure, the program could not help but keep the rift open and unresolved. The textual strategies employed by television's various genres can give us some clues about the cultural handling of the threat posed by youthful disruption and challenges to received values, norms, and dominant institutions. They can indicate the way a process of ideological renegotiation evolves.

One narrative strategy to deal with the phenomenon of youth rebellion involved situating it within a familiar, reassuring context of American patriotism, as *The Young Rebels* attempted to do. Anxiety about the implications and threat of this social upheaval could be soothed if it didn't look so alien and strange. *The Young Rebels* proved a rather inept example of this strategy, but a number of other programs employed visual motifs of the Revolutionary War in attempts to make metaphorical sense of youth rebellion in sympathetic and supportive ways. The pilot episode for *The Young Lawyers* used its Boston setting to insist on this connection. An early scene depicted a protest-rocked college campus. There was a cut to a bunch of protest signs strewn around the base of a statue. A tilt up the statue revealed it to be Paul Revere. In a later scene a young black female lawyer hailed a cab and found herself harangued by the bigoted opinions of the driver. He complained that special quotas kept his son out of college and then started denouncing the demonstrations on the campuses. He informed his youthful passenger that one could not change things quickly. "This is no place for a revolution." There was a quick nondiegetic cut back to the statue of Paul Revere.[29]

We can read these "revolutionary" motifs a number of ways. On the one hand, revolution as a signifier carries little concrete meaning as a radical method for totally reconfiguring the distribution of power. The American Revolution, arguably, has been defused of its political meanings in popular narratives and representations that have tended to focus more on the construction of heroic exploits of illustrious individuals rather than on the examination of political and economic struggle. Therefore, the mobilization of American Revolution iconography in connection to sixties youth rebellion depoliticizes the more contemporary example of revolt and turns its representations into more empty signs. Campus revolution is, finally, no more a sign of radical social change than are the icons of the country's first revolution.

However, the insistent yoking of images so frequently used to represent American patriotism to images of radical youth who were so often referred to as "un-American," subversive, "pinko," or otherwise traitorous to their country carried a certain amount of potential political valorization. The discursive impulse behind this juxtaposition insisted on the emphatically American quality of protest and dissent and, equally, argued for its salutary social effects. By situating the phenomenon of youth revolt within popular conceptions of Yankee resistance to unjust authority, these representations functioned to persuade more outraged "middle-America" types that their children's rebelliousness was, in fact, all-American.

If appeals to liberal conceptions of patriotism and Americanism provided one strategy to incorporate manifestations of youth revolt, another strategy involved figuring the "establishment" as the problem. In numerous relevant dramas we see a "Great White Father" type attempting to convince a particular representative of youth revolt or disaffection that he and his institution could be trusted. In fact, the Great White Father figure aligned himself with youth, not with the dominant system of power the young opposed. The ideological impulse behind these narratives was to locate coercive hegemonic power elsewhere. "The System" was something vague and generally undefinable but something that all liberal interests, not just dissident youth, could oppose.

An October 3, 1970, episode of *Bracken's World,* "Jenny Who Bombs Buildings," provides a particularly illuminating example of this strategy.[30] Movie studio head, Bracken, and his top director, Kevin Grant, decided that they wanted to make a documentary on Jenny, a former pacifist from a wealthy family who had turned to urban terrorism in an attempt to "destroy the Establishment." The character was modeled on real-life Weatherwoman Diana Oughton, who had recently been blown to bits with a number of other Weathermen in an accidental explosion in their Greenwich Village bomb factory. Initially wary about the project, Jenny argued that in all other such documentaries "we come across like freaks." Bracken, with great concern and sincerity, insisted that he did not intend for that to happen here. He wanted to do this film to show what Jenny believed and why. He pointed out that a growing number of people shared her beliefs (which, of course, were left suitably vague) but questioned her methods—specifically bombing.

This program is particularly noteworthy because its narrative is constructed around the ideological attempt to negotiate what in 1970 was the most frightening and despised form of radical youth dissident —the violence-embracing urban terrorist. The Weathermen, with their rhetoric and practice of street fighting, destruction of property, aggressive cop-baiting, and now their campaign of strategic bomb-ing, pushed the envelope of youth rage at a perceived intransigent, racist, imperialistic political order ("Ameriκκκa" in Weather par-lance). Weather leaders like Bernardine Dohrn quickly found them-selves on the FBI's Ten Most Wanted list. In a year when, according to opinion polls, campus upheaval topped the list of national crises— ahead of the war, racism, or crime—the Weathermen represented the most loathed manifestation of that upheaval.[31]

The *Bracken's World* episode attempted to humanize this despised figure and argued that she warranted sympathetic attention. The nar-rative impulse revolved around Bracken and Grant's trying to show that their intentions were honorable, that they were not part of the establishment Jenny wanted destroyed. They were, in fact, really on her side. On the face of it such a narrative might seem politically radical. Even within the circles of student and youth radicalism, the Weathermen found few who were willing to align themselves with this brand of apocalyptic "Fight the People" revolutionism. Yet here was a mainstream, fairly successful prime time drama arguing for a compassionate hearing for the furthest extremes of New Left militancy.

The show employed a number of means to temper and defuse this apparent defense of Weather politics. One strategy involved casting. Jenny was played by Sally Field. At this point in her career Field still carried with her the persona she had developed in her roles as Gidget and the Flying Nun.[32] In her performance of Jenny, Field brought along all the squeaky-clean, wholesome, lovable qualities associated with those two familiar roles; thus, the episode managed to turn Jenny into a wholesome terrorist and to mitigate much of the threat posed by the sympathetic treatment of such a figure. On the other hand, viewers were left with a generally positive characterization of an advocate of property destruction in the furtherance of radical social change.

Although the episode did contain a number of scenes designed to let Jenny explain her beliefs, they tended to be hopelessly vague. In an interview scene with Bracken Jenny railed against war but never mentioned Vietnam; she discussed the killing of students but made no reference to Kent State. In fact, Bracken and Grant's attempts to understand Jenny revolved mostly around her personal history. Her bombing of buildings was turned into a psychological symptom— something in her wealthy background impelled her to this extreme activity. Rage at an ongoing unjust war or a racist, imperialistic social order were not explored as causative agents. The desire to bomb was a manifestation of personal pathology.

By the end of the show Jenny had decided to bomb another building, blowing up herself, her partner, and an innocent custodian. But rather than using this as a justification to demonize her, the narrative resolved with dialogue between Bracken and Grant heavily weighted with liberal guilt. If only they could have understood her better. At a screening of the film's footage studio executives told Bracken the film could not be sold—it was too ugly; Jenny was anti-American. Bracken insisted on releasing the film—he'd given his word to Jenny. The episode closed with Bracken's observation that only in America could a picture like this be made; Jenny had taken that fact for granted. The appeal to liberal pluralist notions of an American social order that could contain all manner of incendiary discourse certainly helped to make palatable the issues raised in the program. But the very fact that by 1970 American television entertainment needed to find strategies for accepting into mainstream popular discourse the positions of the most extreme of New Left activism indicates the power of that activism to force its way—as always in highly compromised fashion—into mainstream social circulation. The youthful revolutionary could not be turned into a "low Other" to be marginalized and dismissed as deviant. Even she, somehow, needed to be incorporated.[33]

The season premiere of *The Name of the Game,* a ninety-minute series about a magazine publishing empire, displayed another prime-time attempt to win back disaffected youth. The sensitively written episode penned by Steven Bochco involved magazine editor Steve Farrell (Robert Stack) and an article he had written about a group of middle-class teenage drug addicts and their experiences in an experimental group home where they tried to kick their habits through communal activities.[34] The conflict revolved around the teens' adamant desire to remain unnamed while a nosy congressional subcommittee on drug enforcement threatened Farrell with a subpoena for the identities of all the youths discussed in his article. The narrative focused particular attention on the relationship between Farrell and one of the group's most vocal members, Katie, an emotionally and psychologically fragile hippie chick. Farrell needed to prove to Katie that her confidence in him was well placed.

Although the young recovering addicts all received very sympathetic treatment in the episode, representatives of adult institutions tended to be depicted as intolerant, rigid, hypocritical, and pompous. The head of the congressional subcommittee was arrogant, officious, and completely unconcerned that his attempts to force Farrell's subjects into a public spotlight might be shattering to them. In another scene the teens presented themselves to a group of journalists covering the congressional hearings. One middle-aged male journalist opined that the youths were victims of their own self-indulgence. Katie, figured as heroine, retorted that he did not have an understanding bone in his body and that she pitied any kids he had. He countered that he had a well-adjusted daughter who didn't need drugs. Katie argued that drugs weren't the worst thing in the world—worse than war and men killing other men. She then approached the journalist and asked when he'd last hugged and loved his daughter. He looked confused and said Katie was not his daughter. She attempted to embrace him, but the journalist pushed her away. "I'm sorry. My daughter is not a junkie." Katie then explained to the gathering that he was just like men who picked her up hitchhiking. They were all very straight, carried briefcases, and all said they had daughters just like her. And they all wanted to check into motel rooms with her. As the journalist hastened away, the scene ended with Katie calling after him, "Is it so hard to love us?"

If these were the establishment forces arrayed against the young people, Farrell had to prove that he was not aligned with them. Like Bracken and Grant in "Jenny Who Bombs Buildings," he had to convince the teens that he shared their values of tolerance and understanding and that he accepted the legitimacy of their pain.

This kind of thematic construction, in which the dominant adult social and political order formed the problem, did not go by without comment in the mainstream press. Edith Efron, a politically conservative staff writer for *TV Guide,* put together a two-part series on shows like this episode of *The Name of the Game.* Efron noted that programs such as this one resulted from a call by the Nixon administration in April 1970 to encourage the networks to plan narratives in their dramatic series that focused attention on the horrors of the "drug culture." Producers were invited to a day-long conference at the White House, where they were plied with information and research on the shocking effects of drug abuse among the young.[35] The result was a flurry of narratives in the 1970/71 season dealing with drug themes.

Unfortunately, according to Efron, the message put out by the White House and the messages displayed in the network programming were quite different. Efron conducted a content analysis of twenty-four episodes dealing with drug issues and discovered that in almost every single one of them the reason for youthful drug taking could be laid at the feet of "the American social and political system":

> Remarkably, these "baddies"—usually parents—invariably represent the following groups or institutions: Business; industry; army; police; Congress; entrepreneurs; law, courts, and prison systems; middle class "squares," old and young.
>
> The "baddies'" sins are equally remarkable. Apart from the standard "lack of communication," and a few unexplained charges of "hypocrisy," they are: gratuitous malevolence, combined with the "pressuring" of young people toward cleanliness . . . obedience to the

law . . . scholastic excellence . . . individual responsibility . . . discipline . . . and career achievement.

These network plays create the impression that if anything is driving millions of young people to drugs it is neurotics who cling to the Protestant ethic, the Horatio Alger virtues, and the American legal system.[36]

In her next installment, the following week, Efron discussed with a group of television producers why the networks had adopted such an apparently antiestablishment stance. The producers laid the blame on the networks' desires to attract younger audiences. They argued that because these young people held antiestablishment politics, the networks needed to come up with "heavies" who were associated with dominant adult institutions. Efron noted dryly, "So, it would seem, the networks were pandering to the leftist young, who are the primary drug consumers in white middle-class society."[37]

Efron had uncovered the very workings of hegemonic strategies for rewinning consent. Her concern and outrage at the way the process manifested itself within this popular cultural sphere should alert us to the fact that the attempt to cobble together a new ideological consensus always ends up leaving certain social and political groups out in the cold. Efron's indignation at the sympathetic treatment of alienated, disaffected, drug-taking young people reveals how shocking it could be when a previously naturalized, taken-for-granted "common sense" was suddenly up for question. Efron and the conservatives for whom she spoke found themselves having to deal with the fact that pillars of their social reality—such as the Protestant work ethic; the justness of the legal system; and the unquestioning virtues of individual cleanliness, discipline, obedience, and responsibility— were being threatened. And the threat was not coming primarily from the dissident young (who wielded no political power and presumably could be ignored if necessary) but from a crucial ideological state apparatus whose function was the expression and continual reaffirmation of dominant norms and values. Suddenly, those norms and values appeared unstable and changeable.

What we also see here is one institution of the sociopolitical order —that of governance, the State, or political society—proving not to be in ideological harmony with another—that of civil society, in this case the culture industry. The Nixon administration, which articulated the positions of more right-wing, hard-line, law-and-order social groups, had assumed that its views on the menace of youthful drug taking would be taken up unproblematically and broadcast by the networks. As one of the producers quoted by Efron observed, "President Nixon got the very opposite of what he was looking for." And as Efron noted in her closing paragraph, "It is a most unfortunate result, because Mr. Nixon was unmistakably acting on the country's behalf. It is the country itself that has been hurt by this network misadventure."[38] This "misadventure" showed the inability of the presidency to impose its antiyouth common sense onto a deeply destabilized cultural and social terrain.

If the Nixon administration was likely to have been unhappy with the spate of drug-oriented network dramas, the White House would have been equally displeased with some other "relevancy" offerings of the 1970/71 network season. Along with programs that tended to point to dominant institutions as the social problem rather than to disaffected young people, other shows openly embraced and valorized youth activism and protest. They usually did so, however, through the familiar figure of a white male mediator.

Tin Soldiers and Nixon Coming: Renegotiating Kent State

One of the most remarkable attempts to validate the positions of protesting students came in a two-part episode of *The Bold Ones,* broadcast November 22 and 29, 1970, entitled "A Continual Roar of Musketry."[39] Ballyhooed in *TV Guide* with a "Close-Up" caption drawing viewers' attention to the broadcast, the show apparently received high ratings, especially for the second installment.[40] The program focused on Hayes Stowe (Hal Holbrook), a junior senator from an unnamed state noted for his abiding commitment to justice and fairness. In this two-parter Stowe was ordered to head a three-person commission investigating a campus tragedy. The tragedy was a thinly disguised fictionalization of the May 4, 1970, Kent State massacre.

In the wake of President Nixon's April 30 decision to invade the neutral Cambodia to track down supposed Viet Cong guerrilla bases, students at hundreds of universities and colleges around the country mounted huge, outraged protests. Angry students at the northern Ohio state university at Kent were no different. They paraded through the town, smashing windows and demanding an end to the war. On May 2 they incinerated the campus ROTC building. Monday, May 4, the governor, having declared a state of emergency, ordered the Ohio National Guard onto campus. In the midst of a nonviolent, if angry, student demonstration, the Guard, outfitted with bayoneted rifles, pistols, and shotguns, suddenly fired into a group of hundreds of unarmed protesters. When the barrage of gunfire was over, four young people lay dead, and nine others were injured, one permanently paralyzed.

In the aftermath of the massacre President Nixon proclaimed that "when dissent turns to violence, it invites tragedy." His "blame the victims" comment obscured the fact that the violence came from the Guard, not the protesting students. Nevertheless, public opinion seemed to be on the White House's side. According to *Newsweek,* 60 percent of Americans condoned the shooting. Novelist James Michener discovered in his study of the tragedy that a large number of Kent State students "had been told by their parents that it might have been a good thing if they had been shot."[41] In the midst of this fear and loathing, rock supergroup Crosby, Stills, Nash, and Young hastily recorded an anguished warning to their cogenerationists: "We're finally on our own / This summer I hear the drumming / Four dead in O-Hi-O." In the days immediately after May 4 more than half of American campuses were rocked with protest. Fifty-one schools shut down for the rest of the year; 536 closed down for some amount of time. Sixty percent of the American student population—from elite "liberal" institutions to small Catholic colleges—engaged in some form of demonstration. National Guard troops were called out to scores of campuses in sixteen different states. Then on May 14 two more students were killed—black ones this time—at Jackson State College in Mississippi.[42]

In October 1970 a hastily organized presidential commission into the killings at Kent and Jackson State, the Scranton Commission, issued its finding that the actions of the Ohio Guard were "unnecessary, unwarranted, and inexcusable."[43] However, the Nixon administration refused to authorize a federal grand jury to begin the process of prosecuting those involved in the killings. To this day no one—not the governor who called the Guard out, not the head of that Guard, nor any of the guardsmen who shot at the defenseless students—has ever been called to defend himself in a court of law.

Although the actual circumstances surrounding the Kent State tragedy remained unresolved because of political stonewalling, *The Bold Ones* episode provided a fictional closure denied in actuality. The program, broadcast only a month after the release of the Scranton Commission findings, circulated its meanings about the tragedy in the midst of a generationally polarized and volatile state of affairs. In effect the episode attempted to renegotiate Kent State and to provide a resolution that at least one segment of the potential television audience might find satisfying.

From the very beginning of the narrative Senator Stowe was figured as the proverbial "man in the middle." His other two commissioners included a right-wing newspaper editor, whose paper had printed negative stories about protesting students, and a black sociologist openly sympathetic to the disaffected young. Thus Stowe, the white liberal, would function as the site of truth, moderation, and rationality as the discourses of all sides converged around him. The episode's narrative worked to showcase Stowe's position as the final arbiter of truth. Using *Rashomon*-like flashbacks, the narrative treated viewers to the testimony of the governor who called out the Guard, the town mayor who demanded force against the students, the university chancellor defending the students, the head of the Guard, and two guardsmen, one remorseful for what had happened and the other proud of the stand they'd taken.

It should be noted that the Scranton Commission was unable to compel any members of the Ohio National Guard who had engaged in the May 4 action to testify. Only their commander in chief agreed to appear. As well, Ohio governor James A. Rhodes, the man responsible for actually calling out the Guard, did not appear before the commission. Therefore, the fictional Stowe Commission offered viewers what the Scranton Commission could not—a more complete accounting of the event in fictional form.

However, far more important to the narrative was the relationship between Stowe and the students. When he first arrived on campus to begin his work, he met red-armbanded students who chanted at him, "Pigs off campus." As he walked away, he replied that he hadn't realized that included him. He asked a young man, Zach, the student "leader" Stowe would have to attempt to win over, why he (Stowe) was a pig. "Man, if you don't know . . . Dig. The governor orders out the Guard. The Guard murders us, right?" The male student's girl-friend completed the argument: "And then the governor orders out a commission. Now what do you think that commission is going to do to us?" Stowe retorted that he hadn't heard the evidence yet.

In a formula that we have seen recurring from one "relevancy" program to another, Stowe's mission involved convincing the young that he was not a "pig," not part of the murderous institutional machinery that killed students who dared to rebel against authority. Stowe's real mission was to convince the students that he and his commission, along with the very process of the liberal search for truth, was on their side and concerned with their interests.

Zach ended up leading a student noncooperation movement. None of the youths involved in the protests or witnesses to the murders would testify before the commission. Zach's girlfriend, however, served as the weak link in the chain of nonparticipation. In various scenes of confrontation between father-figure Stowe and rebellious son Zach, the girlfriend was consistently portrayed as wavering in her commitment to Zach's unequivocal position. She was caught between an ideological and generational struggle represented as a battle between patriarch and man-child. Typically she would be shown in close-up, lowering her eyes or providing some other visual indicator of malleability. Just like *The Mod Squad*'s "The Guru," the radical political commitments of the female activist were always more questionable. Political struggle was something that went on among men; the woman's position was that of go-between and facilitator of conciliation.

One way to read Zach is as "the bad radical." Certainly this would have been the reading strategy employed by *Distant Drummer* editor Don Demaio, who wrote an article comparing television's crop of radical youth to traditional depictions of Indians. Demaio began his article with the rhetorical query:

Question: What paints signs, demonstrates, mouths arrogant and inane rhetoric, and always acts against his own best interests—i.e., the Establishment?

Answer: To be found any given night on the nearest television set.

Those of us who grew up with John Wayne and Tab Hunter will have no difficulty understanding the new film villain. We are the ones who were supposed to believe that all "redskins" were anti-American, that the average cowpoke was still willing to work things out, as long as the redskins didn't try to drink at the local saloon.

Now there's the new villain and, like his western counterpart, he is a non-conformist. He wears long hair, like the redskin, and he says dirty things about pollution, the establishment, and his parents.[44]

Zach's radical position was depicted as counterproductive to his own interests—that of vindicating the students as innocent victims of official governmental/military brutality and murder. Senator Stowe could be read as a consummate establishment figure trying to show how dominant institutions did have young people's best interests at heart. However, much narrative energy was expended trying to show that Stowe was not an establishment figure but an impartial outsider wanting to hear all sides, especially that of the students. In this way the program appealed to the same liberal pluralist ideals that *Bracken's World* resorted to in its attempt to incorporate the revolutionary bomber as a legitimate political figure to be heard.

In the end, after all the other stories had been told, Zach's girlfriend made an abrupt appearance in the room where the three commissioners had sequestered themselves to come to their verdict. After being assured that they had not yet made up their minds, she provided her flashback account of what she witnessed. In her narrative, unlike those of the guardsmen, the students were not armed and there was no sniper. In her account one black student balled up a leaflet and threw it at the Guard, and another threw a lightbulb that exploded on the ground, precipitating the shooting by the Guardsmen. (In other flashbacks the black student threw a rock and the light bulb metamorphosed into gunfire from the student ranks.) At the end of the young woman's flashback the conservative publisher said he found her story hard to believe. The black sociologist countered that the Guards' stories were also hard to believe. The woman exclaimed that she knew her testimony would make no difference given that they'd already figured it all out: "The students were wrong. The Guard was wrong. And all God's children are wrong. That's your verdict." With this bit of dialogue, the character pointed out a narrative strategy that many critics (including some in *Variety*) accused television writers of belaboring. By seeing all sides as equally extreme, culpable, and at fault, the liberal middle held. No political allegiances or positions needed to be affirmed. No sides were taken. The liberal middle thus became a meaningless, nonplace, signifying no particular commitment to anything beyond a disdain for identifiable ideological stances.

This was not, however, the way "A Continual Roar of Musketry" resolved its narrative dilemma. In the final scene in the hearing room Stowe delivered the unanimous findings of his commission. He proclaimed that it was "men in positions of responsibility and authority" who set in motion the deadly force that resulted in the killings on campus. Using cinematic punctuation there were cuts to close-ups of the state governor, then the general in charge of the Guard, then the gung-ho guardsman (metonymically standing in for the whole regiment) as Stowe repeated three times, over each close-up, that these particular "men in positions of responsibility and authority" must answer in court for their actions. In a total reversal of what actually transpired in the Kent State case, prime-time television judged the institutions of the State and the military to be guilty of the unjustifiable murder of protesting students.

The episode ended with a zoom in on the blank face of the female student who had cooperated. The shot functioned to affirm that Stowe and his commission (another group of men in a position of responsibility and authority) were, finally, not part of some positionless middle but rather aligned with the protesting students. The blankness of the woman's demeanor left suitably undecidable whether such an ideological shift to the position of the young would lead to the rewinning of consent. However, in this popular-culture terrain the attempt had been made—by affirming and validating the truth of the largely despised (fictional) Kent State demonstrators.

Harlan Ellison in the pages of the *Free Press* was wildly enthusiastic about the program and focused particularly on the narrative's refusal to damn all sides. "It did not end with one of those 'we are all at fault' numbers. It said: this one seems guilty, and this one seems guilty, and they must be brought to task for it."[45] For Ellison this uncompromised assertion of a potentially unpopular position (we need to remember the polls indicating 60 percent approval of the Ohio Guard's actions) had definite utility for student activists. He gave the example of a student at a USC panel on television who told the assemblage about her mother's response to the show. The woman had been quite unsympathetic to the youth movement yet, according to the student, had sat through the program, murmuring "right on" as the

narrative developed. Ellison observed, "Now that may not be an indication of radicalization on the part of the Middle American per se,
but it is the kind of acceptable agitprop material we need to see more
of" (316).

Ellison's example provides a tantalizing but solitary clue to reception possibilities among adult viewers of this kind of "relevant" fare.
In this case a piece of popular culture attempted to argue against
a pervasive (White House sanctioned) antiyouth, antidemonstrator
popular opinion. By refusing to maintain Stowe's position as the perpetual "man in the middle" and by asserting that the students *were
right* (even if their leader was no paragon), the program risked alienating its dominant audience. On the other hand, as Ellison hoped,
it may have helped reshape the opinions of those who had initially
condemned the young. Again, the question arose: could this be a
kind of popular propaganda for the movement? In the attempt to lure
a young audience, could entertainment television actually sensitize
the elder generation to the causes and campaigns of their youth in
revolt?

Ironside Sings "The Draft Dodger Rag"

If *The Bold Ones* advocated a generally unpopular position about the
innocence of student demonstrators, *Ironside*'s September 24, 1970,
episode, "No Game for Amateurs," ended up advocating not only an
unpopular radical youth position but an illegal one. The *Ironside* program dealt less overtly with questions of politics and ideology yet
came to a thematic conclusion even more startling than that of "A
Continual Roar of Musketry."

The episode dealt with the issue of draft avoidance and the organized aiding and abetting of young men who tried to flee to Canada
to evade induction.[46] The narrative's law-and-order dilemma focused
not on draft resisters, however, but on a Mob hit man who attempted
to pass himself off as a draft resister in order to use the services of
the antidraft "underground railroad" to whisk him out of the country. The hit man (Martin Sheen) managed to dupe a pregnant young
woman into getting him in touch with other underground draft resistance activists who could negotiate his safe passage to Vancouver.
The young woman was portrayed as a sincere, idealistic, and deeply

committed antiwar activist whose hatred for the war resulted from her husband's recent death in Vietnam.

In attempting to track down the hit man Ironside and his young associates needed to persuade not only the woman but also the organizer of the underground railroad, Phil, and a draft resister who had successfully "railroaded" his way to Canada to reveal their strategies, safe havens, and escape route to Vancouver. Ironside tried to persuade these antidraft activists to cooperate with him by contrasting their pacifism and hatred of killing to the violent nature and murderousness of the hit man they effectively shielded by not cooperating. All three succumbed to this line of reasoning. By juxtaposing the antiwar activists with the hit man the episode legitimized and sanctioned the activists' antidraft work. He was the bad guy, not them. By insisting on the nobility and sincerity of their intentions (they were taking their nonviolent beliefs to their logical conclusion) the episode constructed Phil and the pregnant woman as heroes.[47]

With their plans already underway for escorting over the border the hit man, along with a group of bona fide draft resisters, Phil negotiated with Ironside on how to nab the murderer. Realizing the illegality of his activity, Phil worried about what would happen to the actual draft resisters who would be together with the hit man. Ironside tersely told him to get them away, he was only interested in the hit man. This was a strange comment from a representative of law and order given that the draft resisters were also breaking the law. Later we see Phil driving the hit man, along with another draft resister and Ironside's black assistant, Mark, who impersonated a draft resister. The Sheen character gradually figured out that he was being driven into a trap. Pulling out a gun and disparaging the rest of them as "you non-violent characters," he informed them that he played by different rules. The dialogue reasserted the binary between the courageous, "good guy" antiwar activists aligned with the police force and the evil villain who operated outside the pale of civilized humanity. In part, the antidraft activists were legitimated and sanctioned within this narrative context because they willingly worked together with the forces of law and order. Thus they resembled the young outcasts of *The Mod Squad*. Their youth politics and activity could be rendered acceptable by their connection to a dominant "establishment" institution whose activities they respected and upheld. They were law-abiding at a higher level.

In the end police at a roadblock nabbed the hit man. Phil's fate was handled gingerly with a bit of dialogue between Ironside's assistants, police officer Ed and Mark. Ed asked Mark pointedly, "Was Phil in on this?" Mark, with appropriate disingenuousness, replied, "Phil who?" Again, the narrative showed a pair of law-enforcement officers who were disinclined to bring down the force of their institution on these particular law breakers. For a television prime-time law-and-order show from this period, such a flouting of the rules was unusual if not unprecedented. Then, as if to hammer the message home even more, in the episode's coda Phil and the pregnant woman dropped by Ironside's living/working space. As they entered, Ironside, flanked by his three assistants and a senior police lieutenant, greeted them with the salutation: "Welcome to the halls of the Establishment." The two antiwarriors proclaimed they'd come by to save the police a trip. Ironside asked, "What trip?" "To arrest us." Ironside then turned, with a certain amount of calculation, to each of his assistants and asked for whatever evidence they had against the two. In successive close-ups Ed, Eve, and Mark innocently declared they hadn't anything. Ironside informed the two, "We don't seem to have enough on you to make a charge stick—this time." He said he would have to report their activities to federal authorities. The two said their good-byes, the woman saying, "Peace." Ironside called after them to ask if he could assume they were going to quit railroading. Phil smiled and declared, "No—we're just going to move the station." The episode ended on an unreadable close-up shot of Ironside.

By the latter half of 1970, when this episode aired, the Selective Service System, as we saw in chapter 5, was in crisis and disarray. Resistance to and growing weariness with the war had forced the Nixon administration to pursue a "Vietnamization" policy that, although doing little to end the war, ensured that fewer of the battlefield casualties would be Americans. The sss tinkered with the draft system, instituted a lottery approach, and decreased draft call-ups. Nevertheless, thousands of antiwar activists engaged in draft resistance counseling, and hundreds of centers offering advice on ways and means to avoid the draft operated throughout the nation. Even so, conscription as an institution would not disappear until 1972.[48]

Although the draft was under strong and relentless attack by the antiwar movement, this did not mean that a broad consensus had developed within the American body politic, agreeing that resistance to the draft was socially acceptable.[49] Only a year and a half earlier Joan Baez's words of support to her draft-resisting husband were considered too provocative for prime-time entertainment. As with *The Mod Squad*'s "Peace Now, Arly Blau," here again we can hypothesize that because the *Ironside* episode dealt with a fictional world of draft resistance, the message of the show may have seemed less immediately incendiary. Also, unlike *The Smothers Brothers Comedy Hour* or *The Mod Squad,* this law-and-order program had no particular history as an advocate and mouthpiece for the discourses of insurgent youth. Thus it may have been a "safer" vehicle for tackling this contentious issue. However, from within that seemingly "safe" space the program ended up circulating a remarkably radical position—a position without the negotiating and balancing so fundamental to *The Mod Squad*'s handling of the issue. In the *Ironside* world it was acceptable and proper to engage in draft resistance. It was also acceptable to aid and abet those who wished to avoid the draft. And it was entirely proper for those in law enforcement to find ways to avoid prosecuting those engaged in such activities.

The Apparent Failure of Relevance

Shortly after the Season of Relevance made its debut, industry alarm bells began ringing as it became obvious that the new youth-oriented shows were proving Nielsen duds. However, industry studies hastened to point out that established shows with familiar characters (such as *Ironside*) actually strengthened their ratings positions with their episodes of social relevance. The problem with the new shows was not so much their themes of campus turmoil, drug use, and political polarization—although there was criticism of the unrelenting quality of those themes in the newer shows—but rather the inability of the newer shows to properly develop sympathetic characters in the midst of tackling such monumental themes.[50]

Also of concern was the obvious fact that the young had not come rushing back to television to sample video fare purporting to deal with their interests and political commitments. Suddenly, demographics, as the new theory for audience measurement, was coming under attack. Les Brown pointed out in a *Variety* page-one, banner-headlined article that despite the talk about the importance of demographics, shows continued to sink or swim based on overall ratings and competitive shares of the viewing audience. Demographic profiles might raise or lower the spot price for ads, but no show would survive without sufficiently large bulk audiences, no matter how good the show's demographics.[51]

Although network executives and programmers may have been befuddled and bewildered at the apparent failure of relevancy in prime-time entertainment to lure the young, an examination of the narrative strategies and modes of address used by the shows provides fairly good clues to the problem. The textual analysis of a selection of "relevant" dramas discussed here should indicate that the preferred audience for this fare was not those under twenty-five but rather adults—those at the upper end of the eighteen-to-forty-nine "young adult" demographic. With the exception of *The Mod Squad* the successful programs all had a mature grown-up as the figure of audience identification. Studio head Bracken, Detective Ironside, Senator Stowe, publisher Farrell were all responsible members of the established social order—even as they were portrayed distancing themselves from what that established order meant to disaffected young people. If these programs served as a pop-cultural vehicle for working through the dislocations and traumas provoked by the social change movements of the 1960s, then it is more likely that these transformations were being worked on a generation of adult television viewers, along with child viewers whose political allegiances had not yet been formed. Harlan Ellison's comment about the reaction of the mother watching "A Continual Roar of Musketry" suggests, tantalizingly, that some adult viewers might actually be swept along into accepting a reformulated "common sense" about youthful revolt that was ideologically weighted toward the positions of the young. The networks may have been attempting to rewin the young by selectively incorporating some of their politically contentious perspectives into otherwise safe and familiar generic narratives. However, the hegemonic work of negotiating a new consensual order may have actually been working more on members of the elder generation. This group needed the comforting representations of institutions connoting law and order so that the less comforting representations of social change could be confronted at all. The effect of the plethora of relevant programming inundating viewers during this period attempted to normalize a discourse that had heretofore been constructed as deviant, extreme, and disreputable. However, as Todd Gitlin has argued, even when the media did succeed in disseminating some youth movement messages, the composition and content of those messages were never within the control of that movement.[52] The ability to define youth dissent rested with cultural and social elites. The spate of relevant television programming reveals a process of cultural containment of a threatening, dissenting social formation. The point I would make about this process is that although these dissenting groups may not be in control of the construction of these representations, this lack of control need not be wholly detrimental to their interests. The textual evidence provided by this programming points to an attempt to make some—always selective, always massaged—discourses and political stances of the youth movement acceptable to a wider public. A political revolution that would wipe out the power bases of one hegemonic alliance and substitute another was objectively out of reach despite some revolutionist rhetoric. However, a tentative achievement such as this within the terrain of popular culture suggests a modest discursive victory. Recurring suggestions, bandied about in the underground press, that shows like these might serve as some kind of movement propaganda to those not yet radicalized hint at an understanding among some movement people that these cultural products could serve a politically progressive role.

Comic Relevance

The Season of Social Relevance, of debatable Nielsen success in the 1970/71 season, would reap rewards in the years to come. As CBS's great triumvirate of early seventies comedies, *All in the Family, The Mary Tyler Moore Show,* and *M*A*S*H*, would prove, youth-targeted, socially conscious television flourished when served up with generous helpings of laughter. The story of how these three shows came to dominate prime time and revitalize entertainment television has been told many times.[53] In the conventional narrative CBS television head Bob Wood, the visionary, courageous executive, acquires a sitcom pilot about a lovable bigot—a project weak-kneed ABC is too cowardly to broadcast. Wood is seemingly alone in understanding the demographic predicament facing network television. With clear-eyed chutzpah he shakes up the network, evicts the hayseed shows, and replaces them with a "feminist" sitcom about a single working woman, an "antiwar" sitcom about a land war in Asia, and an urban, sophisticated sitcom about intolerance and prejudice. CBS is remade as the network of the urban, hip, politically disaffected baby boomers, and network television is saved for the 1970s.

Of course, as we've seen in this chapter, the "turn to social relevance" was more complicated than "The Saga of How Bob Wood Brought Reality to Prime Time" might suggest. All three networks were heavily involved in this turn, and all three saw the demographic writing on the wall. The significant point is CBS's decision to shift its concern with relevancy from drama to comedy. This proved to be the winning strategy.

David Marc has pointed out that although the situation comedy was the most popular television genre of the 1960s, it was also the genre most isolated from the turmoil of the era. Crime genres, on the other hand, inevitably needed to grapple with current events in order to update their stock narratives.[54] It should, therefore, come as no surprise that so many of the programs we have looked at, whether they were generic cop shows or not, tended to construct narratives that dealt with challenges to law and order. Sitcoms occupied a different universe. Says Marc: "The aesthetic foundations of TV situation comedy had been built upon consensus representationalism during the fifties" (p. 105). The placid, morally confident, and wholesome, white-bread world of the Cleavers and the Andersons could not survive the shake-ups of the 1960s. One response to the sociopolitical earthquake was "deep escapism." Sitcoms ignored even the most basic forms of verisimilitude and embraced the wackiest forms of magic, from talking horses named Ed, to perky nuns with a habit for flight, to bottled blonde-bombshell genies, to normal families made up of monsters, to suburban housewife witches.[55] Yet the sheer weirdness of sixties sitcoms suggests more than simple escapism. There was something almost hallucinogenic about these "magicoms."[56] And just as dreams take the raw material of our daily lives and turn them into the fantastical stuff of our sleeping states, so the magicoms can be seen as bizarre symptoms of cultural avoidance-response to the turmoil and upheavals of the period. Television producers may have been too uneasy to bring "the sixties" into the family circle directly, but the silly sixties sitcoms indicated that "normality" and the very laws of nature (let alone the laws of the social order) were now up for grabs.

All in the Family clearly departed from the wacky world of the sixties escapist-coms. Like *The Smothers Brothers Comedy Hour,* the show was aggressively topical, courted controversy, and was masterminded (in the figure of Norman Lear) by a creator who embraced the politics and social values of the youth movement. During preproduction CBS head censor William Tankersley, who had been the bane of the Smothers Brothers' televisual existence, threatened to make things equally difficult for Lear. Lear was intransigent about making changes to his scripts to conform to CBS's standards and practices. In a departure from the Smothers scenario, Bob Wood intervened on Lear's side.[57]

CBS is often lauded for its courageousness in airing *All in the Family,* for supporting the series during its shaky beginnings before it found its audience during summer reruns, for standing by Lear and his vision, and for refusing to water down the show's language and politics. However, shortly after the show aired, the network conducted research on audience reception and discovered that audiences in general liked the show, thought it was funny, and, most significant, were not offended by it.[58] During the famous debut of the show, teams of operators manned the switchboards to deal with the potential mass of angry phone calls to the network. The operators for the most part sat idly by as very few irate calls came in. Therefore, from the very beginning CBS realized that the show was not going to be too politically problematic.

Why was *All in the Family* acceptable when *The Smothers Brothers Comedy Hour* was not? Little over a year and a half separated the latter's forced ejection from the air and the Lear sitcom's debut. *All in the Family* targeted the same younger, urban, college-educated audience that the Smothers Brothers' show so successfully brought to television in the years before the networks embraced social relevance. Despite its bigoted main character and the unprecedented use of raw language, *All in the Family* was actually a much safer show than the Smothers Brothers' variety series had been in that the Lear sitcom managed to play the ideological balancing act so well. Norman Lear's politics were fairly close to those of Tommy Smothers. Mike Stivic, bigoted Archie Bunker's college-student son-in-law, was clearly the mouthpiece for Lear's progressive, left-liberal views. However, as a number of empirical audience studies of *All in the Family* viewers indicated, the sitcom was far more open and polysemic than the *Com-*

edy Hour in its latter days. Whereas Tom and Dick were applauded and condemned for turning into New Left propagandists, *All in the Family*'s satirical humor cut in all directions, skewering the pompous, know-it-all "Meathead" almost as much as the know-nothing Archie. Whereas viewers who did not share the Smothers Brothers' antiwar, procounterculture stance found it increasingly difficult to negotiate pleasing or comforting meanings in watching that show, with *All in the Family* both hard hats and longhairs could find discursive room to maneuver.

The empirical audience studies on the series, which began appearing in communications journals in the mid-1970s, anticipated later cultural studies work on viewer decoding strategies.[59] The studies showed that viewers deemed high in prejudice and intolerance tended to admire Archie more, and those judged low in prejudice and intolerance tended to side with Mike. According to Neil Vidmar and Milton Rokeach:

> People who disliked Archie indicated that he is a bigot, domineering, rigid, loud, and that he mistreats his wife. Persons who liked Archie reported he is down-to-earth, honest, hard-working, predictable, and kind enough to allow his son-in-law and daughter to live with him. Persons who liked Mike reported he is tolerant and stands up for his beliefs; those who disliked him reported he is stupid, narrow-minded, prejudiced against the older generation, rebellious, lazy, and a "banner waver."[60]

Complicating the differential readings of the show was the fact that even the highly prejudiced viewers who liked and admired Archie tended to admit that Mike usually made more sense. This contradictory and paradoxical reading strategy provides some clues to the ways audiences were negotiating the ideological struggles of the period —viscerally hanging on to familiar, if increasingly residual, structures of feeling, while intellectually accepting the emergent consensus slowly forming from the various social-change challenges to the old order.

One of the show's most noteworthy characteristics—what made it such a departure from the socially relevant dramas—was its insistence on locating the conflicts of the 1960s not out there in the public realm as the law-and-order shows did but "all in the family." Observes Ella Taylor in her history of prime-time families: "If Lear was not the first to extract humor or drama from social conflict, he was the first to construct a situation comedy around it."[61] Using comedy, and specifically the very familiar and historically "safe" sitcom genre, Lear 'domesticated" the painful, unresolved social and generational conflicts of the period, and contained them within the walls of 704 Hauser Street. But among the show's many innovations to the genre was the occasional denial of closure at the end of an episode, along with a mixing of wrenching drama with comedy. A December 25, 1976, episode, "The Draft Dodger," is a notable example. A friend of Mike's, a draft evader living in Canada, had returned to the United States incognito. (President Jimmy Carter had not yet granted amnesty to these war resisters.) David was welcomed into the Bunker home to share Christmas dinner along with a friend of Archie's, whose son had died in the war. When David admitted that he was a draft dodger, Archie wanted to kick the young man out of the house. Mike jumped up from the dinner table, confronting Archie:

> *Mike:* Look, what David did took a lot of guts!
> *Archie:* Whaddaya mean, a lot of guts. . . . ?
> *David:* My own father doesn't understand. Why should he?
> *Mike:* When are you going to admit that the war was wrong?!
> *Archie:* (Yelling) I'm not talking about the war! I don't wanna talk
>   about that rotten, damn war no more!

Archie launched into a painful, heated rant that was played both for drama and for uncomfortable laughs about why David was wrong to dodge the draft. With his typical tortured logic Archie yelled that you couldn't get a decent war off the ground with young people deciding whether they would go to war and face getting killed. "That's why we leave it to Congress. Cuz them old crocks ain't gonna get killed! And they're gonna do the right thing, and get behind the President and vote 'yes.'" Archie's friend intervened and asked if his opinion was of any importance. Archie, assuming that this "Gold Star Father" would back him up, encouraged the man to tell "these young people here" his opinion. In a speech constructed as a privileged moment, the father of the dead Vietnam soldier said, "I understand how you feel, Arch. My kid hated the war, too. But he did what he thought he had to do. David here did what he thought he had to do. But David's alive to share Christmas dinner with us. And if Steve were here, he'd want to sit down with him. And that's what

Archie hemmed in between antiwar son-in-law,
Mike, and David, the draft dodger. "I don't wanna
talk about that rotten, damn war no more!"

Pinky welcomes the draft dodger back to the family
table, healing the wounds of the war within the
family circle.

I wanna do." To loud applause from the studio audience, the man
clasped David's hand, wished him a merry Christmas, and led him
back to the table. Archie was left speechless and shaken as the episode ended.

Archie's friend played the mediator figure, reaching across the generational divide to heal the rift and bring an antiwar exile back into

the family circle. But the episode ended on an emotionally unstable note given that Archie's outburst was not resolved, nor was it made particularly comic. On the one hand, the episode brought the lingering polarization of the Vietnam era into the private sphere and tried to resolve it around the family table. On the other hand, the episode, because of its lack of closure, indicated that the rifts were still gaping and that no half-hour sitcom, or perhaps any other form of societal process, was going to heal that divide any time soon. Episodes like this one—and they were not unusual in *All in the Family*—displayed how the social turmoils of the 1960s both could and *could not* be domesticated by the comic form.

If *All in the Family* tried to welcome the war resister to the family table, M*A*S*H, debuting in the fall of 1972, brought American television viewers a whole campful of lovable war resisters. With the war in Vietnam winding down in bloody and bomb-filled fashion, the 20th Century–Fox production was quite unreservedly, nonnegotiably antiwar and antimilitarist. Most of the show's heroes were draftees—such as Hawkeye Pierce, Trapper John McIntyre, and Corporal Klinger—who hated both the war and their "regular army" bosses. Klinger, as the putative draft resister, never suffered criticism or condemnation within the narrative for his dogged attempts to get out of the army by any dress necessary. Most of the villains were military types, such as Head Nurse Hoolihan, the absurdly rigid Colonel Flagg, various buffoonish generals, or supporters like the sniveling Frank Burns. Burns and Hoolihan were bad guys precisely because they supported militarism and the war effort.

The show's producers were apparently somewhat cagey about admitting M*A*S*H's specific relationship to anti–Vietnam War sentiment. Gitlin, in conversation with Larry Gelbart, was able to get the producer only to speak in generalities about the nastiness of war:

> We wanted to say that war was futile . . . to represent it as a failure on everybody's part that people had to kill each other in order to make a point. We wanted to say that when you take people from home they do things they would never do. They drink. They whore. They steal. They become venal. They become asinine, in terms of power. They get the clap. They become alcoholics. They become rude. They become sweet. They become tender. They become loving. We tended to make war the enemy without really saying who was fighting."[62]

Gelbart's vagueness about the show's antiwar stance was fairly typical of prime-time entertainment, which, as we've seen, tended to have difficulties dealing with questions about the specific politics of the Vietnam War or the ideological critiques of youth dissidents.

Using a number of stratagems, M*A*S*H managed to work around the gaping wound left by the war in Vietnam. Unlike Robert Altman's film on which the show was based, CBS's M*A*S*H insisted on its Korea location. References were constantly made to presidents Truman and Eisenhower, General MacArthur, the South Korean capital of Seoul. Except for a couple of quotes displayed during the title sequence, indicating that this was Korea rather than Vietnam, little in Altman's film suggested that Elliot Gould's and Donald Sutherland's Hawkeye and Trapper John were anything but countercultural troublemakers romping through a thinly disguised Vietnam. But if the TV show was set in 1950s Korea, the sensibilities of the characters belonged to the following decade. David Marc has written perceptively about how the attitudes associated with the youth movement thoroughly shaped the show, especially the character of Hawkeye:

> Though living in the fictive fifties, Hawkeye speaks in the tones of a survivor of the sixties. His fear and hatred of the war and of the dehumanizing bureaucracy that wages it create in him a harmony of self-interest and social conscience. The aims of his endless sitcom schemes are not merely to extract privileges for himself from the Army—the Bilko model—but to shelter the psychologically vulnerable, including himself, from the horror and the horror-making apparatus. A sixties hero in a seventies sitcom set in the fifties, Hawkeye's hedonism leads him not toward an obsession with personal material gain, but rather to an ethics-based social sensibility.[63]

Marc's argument suggests one reason why socially relevant comedies like M*A*S*H were so successful, whereas dramas were more problematic. The socially relevant dramas attempted to appeal to sophisticated and disaffected baby boomers by giving them characters of their own age group who mouthed their sensibilities and values. However, as we've seen, these characters were always under the tutelage or paternalistic wing of a Great White Father Figure. *All in the Family* and M*A*S*H differed in that the young protagonists were in active rebellion against the patriarch. Mike and Gloria were in perpetual conflict with intolerant Archie, the fatally flawed patriarch.

Hawkeye and Trapper John were constantly flummoxing the incompetent Colonel Henry Blake, who didn't really want to be a patriarch anyway. These two sitcoms were premised on the theme that in no way did Father-figure Know Best. Authority, whether in the guise of the nuclear family unit or the U.S. military, constantly undermined itself. In targeting the family and the military, these two shows held up to satire two key American institutions that the sixties youth rebellions challenged most. The dramas, on the other hand, wanted to critique institutions, values, and lifestyles associated with "the establishment" and at the same time demonstrate that adults associated with those institutions and lifestyles could be reformed in ways presumably acceptable to the disaffected young.

If Nielsen numbers are any reliable guide, these shows—*M*A*S*H* in particular—were notably successful in reaching the boomer demographic. A November 1972 Nielsen ranking of shows favored among young adults between eighteen and thirty-four found the antiwar comedy the fourth most popular. When compared to the overall ratings for that year, the show did not even break into the top twenty-five.[64] Apparently, older viewers had not yet warmed to the show's irreverence. Not until the 1973/74 season, when American troops were finally out of combat in Southeast Asia, would *M*A*S*H* prove to be a major network hit show.

By 1973 the social turbulence of the 1960s was over, and the youth movements of the era had disintegrated. But on network television sixties values and attitudes dominated all over the dial. In the next chapter we will consider the legacy of the network's attempts to chase the baby boomer audience and how entertainment television was fundamentally changed by its clash with the era's social and cultural revolutionaries.

Conclusion

7 Legacies

By the early 1970s the youth rebellion that had been causing social and cultural mayhem throughout the American body politic
for over half a decade, began to peter out. The largest and most
important campus-based youth organization in history, SDS, lay in
ruins, ripped apart by revolutionism even as membership was exploding to unprecedented numbers. Countercultural meccas like
the Haight-Ashbury had turned into crime-infested death traps for
junkies and hustlers. Hippies, freaks, and exhausted politicos headed
to the countryside, dreaming of respite in communal living experi-
ments. Official but generally covert State repression began taxing
the financial and psychological resources of the movement as White
House and FBI "dirty tricks" campaigns disoriented activist groups
and organizations.[1] Underground newspapers began folding under
the strains of faction fights, disillusionment, burnout, and paranoia
over Nixon administration subversion. The antiwar movement continued producing huge mobilizations of citizens to express their outrage at the continuing carnage in Vietnam despite White House
assurances that it was winding down the war. But the May 1970
outcry against the Kent State massacre and the Cambodia invasion
served as the last organized, coordinated, and coherent expression of
youth rage against the system. Demonstrations and dissent continued
against the war and against other manifestations of dominant power,
but the movement had begun to lose its always tenuous sense of unity.
Internal contradictions could no longer be suppressed. Many female

radicals could no longer deal with the cognitive dissonance of experiencing their own gender-oriented subordination within a movement that purported to be about liberation and empowerment of the socially disenfranchised. By 1971 and 1972 "the sixties" were over.

But just as the movements of the sixties were marching off into the sunset, with jingling bells and chants of "Hell no, we won't go" fading into the night, many of the values and discourses of those movements were getting entrenched into popular culture. In the aftermath of network television's attempts to grapple with the youth rebellion and entice disaffected baby boomers back to the magic box, the medium had changed in some profound ways.

Into the 1990s broadcast television still struggled with the legacy of 1960s social relevance. For some media commentators that legacy meant entertainment TV programming that, in general, adopted a left-liberal, left-populist common sense. S. Robert Lichter, Linda S. Lichter, and Stanley Rothman, politically conservative mass-media researchers, argue that the socially relevant era of programming — beginning with shows like *The Smothers Brothers Comedy Hour, The Mod Squad,* its imitators, and the Norman Lear sitcoms — serves as a dividing line between the social ideology predominant in television entertainment before and the ideology that predominates in the aftermath of the late 1960s. In their book *Watching America* they assert that "television started as an agent of social control but became an agent of social change. Once the servant of the status quo, it now fosters populist suspicions of traditional mores and institutions. A medium that originally helped legitimize authority today tries to demystify it."[2] Using traditional communication studies quantitative methods of coding characters and storylines, along with simple, mostly descriptive textual analysis, the research trio help to bolster the arguments made in this book for a profound shift in what Raymond Williams would call the "structure of feeling" or what Gramscian theorists would call hegemonic common sense. For instance, using quantitative methods, they coded portrayals of prime-time's view of "the establishment" — by which they mean institutions associated with the government, the military, and religion. For television shows produced before 1975 they found that 47 percent of the randomly sampled episodes indicted the system, whereas 53 percent exonerated it. Prime-time productions produced after 1975 condemned establishment institutions 70 percent of the time, upholding

them only 30 percent of the time (pp. 290–291). Of all the institutions they analyzed, the military took the hardest hit. "In the early
years, TV lauded soldiers of all stripes. After 1965, it began to distinguish sharply between the virtues of enlisted men and officers. . . .
Since 1965, military officers have taken their place in prime-time's
rogue's gallery" (p. 275). *M*A*S*H* institutionalized an antiwar stance
in prime time and tarnished the military's brass for over a decade. Despite the series' astonishing success, few shows with a military theme
have proven to be ratings winners in the post-Vietnam era, however.
Lichter, Lichter, and Rothman discuss the late eighties realist dramas
that, unlike *M*A*S*H*, attempted to grapple with the experience of
the Vietnam War directly: *Tour of Duty* and *China Beach*. "The military is no joke here, as it often was in *M*A*S*H*. But military authority
is upheld more often than it is respected" (p. 274).

Other authority figures suffered as well. In their coding of various
professions Lichter, Lichter, and Rothman discovered that business-
men were consistently disparaged and demonized in the aftermath of
the 1960s. In the world of post-sixties prime time to be a business-
man meant being greedy, nefarious, and often downright criminal.
J. R. Ewing is, of course, the quintessential example of capitalist greed
running gleefully amok. Portrayals of those in the so-called helping professions (doctors, teachers, social workers, and the like) were
consistently laudatory, and since the 1960s storylines involving such
characters focused less on individual issues and far more on issues of
the larger society. "Since the mid 1960s, they have become far more
socially aware and enmeshed in social problems" (p. 177). The heroic
doctors and nurses of Chicago's inner-city public hospital in NBC's
top-rated 1990s drama *ER*, to use a recent example, do not just patch
together bullet-ridden bodies but grapple with the social ills that lead
to gang violence and with their own institutionalized racism in treat-
ing young black patients. Socially relevant issues from the stigma associated with living with AIDS to the effects of chronic underfunding
of public hospitals all find their way onto *ER*'s medical charts. A world
away from *Dr. Kildare*, *ER* and *Chicago Hope*, another recent hospital drama, owe more to their failed Season of Social Relevance pro-
genitor, *The Interns*, at least in their preoccupation with interrogating
social problems.

Lichter, Lichter, and Rothman are not unusual as social conservatives preoccupied with the alleged leftward lurch of mass media and

popular culture since the 1960s. Right-wing politicians from Newt Gingrich to Bob Dole to Dan Quayle have lambasted the entertainment industry for its sick, sixties values. The *Watching America* authors are at least evenhanded and cool headed in their assessments, for instance in pointing out that although prime time portrays great skepticism toward authority figures, it is nevertheless reluctant to grapple with the institutions themselves. Entertainment television may be unwilling to uphold the traditional missions of the political system, religion, or the military, but it doesn't call for their dismantlement either (p. 285). But although they argue that prime-time television has turned into a reformist, left-populist medium, rather than a radical left medium, they end their study with understated anxiety about what all these decades of social relevance and leftist political messages have done to TV viewers:

> The potential cumulative impact of such messages should not be underestimated. Scholars know that news media coverage of social issues can gradually alter public opinion very substantially, even when the coverage diverges from expert opinion or objective indicators of reality. Even those who downplay the media's ability to reshape attitudes concede its power in reinforcing existing beliefs and forging new ones on unfamiliar topics. . . . George Comstock [concludes] . . . in his text *Television in America,* "given the continuing exposure of viewers to unfamiliar experiences and the inculcation of new generations that grow up with television, its influence in a liberalizing direction has probably been profound." [3]

Left-wing media analysts are, in general, more dubious about the argument that prime time is a bastion for progressive politics. Grounded in more nuanced and complex theoretical paradigms than are most conservative critics, left media analysts such as Kellner and Gitlin recognize a definite liberalizing trend in American television in the 1970s, with the airing of progressive discourses never before seen on network television. [4] However, as good Gramscians, they see the medium as a site of ideological contestation, as do I. Kellner sees American television in the seventies up to the election of Ronald Reagan as a particularly "contested terrain," where liberal and conservative forces battled discursively to make sense of the challenges and shocks of the previous decade. Television programming was both more conservative and more aggressively liberal with such new forms as the miniseries, which, in this period, frequently explored "issues hitherto excluded from network television, such as class conflict, racism and anti–Semitism, imperialism, and the oppression of the working class and blacks while presenting capitalists and right wingers as oppressors and exploiters."[5] African Americans could enjoy a form of "popular revenge" against centuries of white racism in the phenomenally successful miniseries *Roots*. Victims of right-wing political oppression could take revenge over the FBI and Joseph McCarthy in numerous docudramas that explored that dark period of American recent history. "In all these programs," says Kellner of the spate of realist miniseries and docudramas, "the oppressed were portrayed in positive images and the oppressors in negative ones, thus providing a critical perspective on political institutions and on views previously presented positively" (p. 58). In this assessment the left-progressive Kellner is in remarkable agreement with his right-wing colleagues, Lichter, Lichter, and Rothman, although the latter three are blind to the principle of ideological struggle in popular culture.

It may be more difficult to see the legacy and continuing influence of "the sixties" in eighties television. In her book *Seeing through the Eighties* Jane Feuer argues that the period was "incredibly hegemonic," a time in which right-wing Reaganite ideology appeared to have won a decisive victory.[6] However, as her work shows, television programming was shot through with contradictions and audience subversions. It is also worth noting that, although the networks attempted to catch the ostensible right-wing wave overtaking the American body politic by creating politically conservative programming, almost every one of those efforts ended up a ratings loser, if the project even got past the development stage.[7] And much to the chagrin of the *Watching America* authors, capitalists and business people continued to be portrayed in less than flattering ways. *Dallas* and *Dynasty*, prime-time soap operas that epitomized eighties TV, figured the capitalist class in excessively, hyperbolically, and campy ways as evil, conniving, pathetic, and generally out of control. Although these globally popular series may have seemed the very embodiment of Reaganism, the shows were far more open to critical readings by American and worldwide audiences who frequently read the series in anticapitalist ways.[8]

Other high-profile eighties television series manifested overt preoccupations with the 1960s. University-educated baby boomers, who continued to be the networks' most desirable audience, began entering their middle years, and prime time featured a spate of shows aimed at boomer middle-aged angst. *The Wonder Years* softened the turmoil of the sixties by nostalgically representing the period through the experiences of a prepubescent boy living in generic suburbia-land. Kevin Arnold's world was more preoccupied with his unrequited puppy love for classmate Winnie than with the war raging in Vietnam. The political and social turmoil so fundamental to America in the 1960s seldom intruded on the gentle world of the Arnold family. The series attempted to merge the lost innocence of *Leave It to Beaver* with sixties music and fashion. But we can also see the show as a symptomatic text. For white, middle-class boomers the pain and dislocations of the 1960s remained so great, the sense of soaring idealism so unfulfilled, that childish nostalgia was one of the few ways the era could be remembered and negotiated as those boomers left youth irrevocably behind. *Family Ties,* a hugely popular family sitcom, also renegotiated the sixties by taking the premise of *All in the Family* and turning it upside down. Parents Steven and Elyse Keaton were old "sixties people," whereas elder children Mallory and Alex were, respectively, an empty-headed, socially unaware shopping machine and an unapologetically supply-sider Reaganite (but lovable). Sixties social values were never at the center of the show's comedy as they were in the Lear sitcom, but they subtly structured the series and the representation of Alex, the yuppie-in-training. *Thirtysomething* extended *Family Ties'* preoccupation with how one—or whether one—could maintain "sixties values" in a reactionary political climate. Like the other series, this one emphasized family life and seemed excessively preoccupied with the minutiae of everyday life—almost as if the turmoil of the sixties that presumably formed the Steadmans, the Westons, and their single friends was too painful to bring into the foreground of their life stories. But the specter of "the sixties" made itself felt in the show's famously annoying "yuppie guilt" themes. The characters were all supposed to have participated in some vague way in the sixties youth movement (although, as Feuer points out, the show appeared confused about actual ages and whether the characters were a tad young to have really participated in antiwar demonstrations and Woodstock). As careerists and homebodies in the 1980s, the show's characters, especially advertising man and sensitive guy Mike Steadman, along with seemingly perfect wife, Hope, felt terribly guilty about their comfortable material lives.[9]

In the 1990s the "ABC/NBC/CBS" oligarchy was displaced by the "hundred-channel universe" of specialty channels, cable networks, and niche programming. New channels like Fox and MTV proved largely uninterested in catering to baby boomers, making their fortunes chasing the new youth demographic: the postboomers, busters, and Gen-Xers. But if the era of three-network supremacy is over, the three webs appear to be in no danger of disappearing. Their programming, although no longer commanding the massive audience numbers taken for granted in the sixties and seventies, still functions as North America's televisual common culture. The media hoopla that surrounded the retirement from the air of NBC's *Seinfeld* in 1998 showed just how powerful a hold the traditional networks wield over North American popular imagination.[10] But to what extent do the programming preoccupations and social relevance themes inaugurated in the late sixties and early seventies still reverberate? Is prime time, at least the ABC/NBC/CBS corner of it, still influenced by those "sixties values" that became so entrenched by the early seventies?

The summer of 1998 provides a useful vantage point from which to examine this question. In that summer three of the most significant network comedies of the nineties met their prime-time demise: *Seinfeld, Murphy Brown,* and *Ellen.* All three, in differing ways, were a response to that legacy. *Murphy Brown* continued CBS's tradition of the Lear sitcoms, featuring the sixties survivor and feminist Murphy as a tough-as-nails network news reporter with a photo of Ronald Reagan on her office dartboard. Her sixties-inspired cultural preferences, along with her progressive politics, clashed with youthful philistines like producer Miles and bubble-headed reporter Corkey. However, the show became a media event and reached an apotheosis of social relevance when the fictional Murphy decided to have a baby out of wedlock and the (presumably) real Republican vice president Dan Quayle condemned her for it. Suddenly the series became a site of heated contestation over the keystone to the Republican political platform: "family values." Much of that platform was a direct challenge to 1960s-influenced social values of alternative family structures, feminism, gay rights, and cultural heterogeneity. In the realm of prime time Murphy, as the middle-class feminist and independent woman, prevailed over Quayle and soon-to-be-ex-president George Bush. If eighties television, as Feuer argues, was a period of "complicitous critique" of Reaganism and its reactionary politics, nineties television, in the figure of *Murphy Brown,* signaled that politics to be in residual mode and a renewed left populism to be emergent. The success of Murphy's battle with Quayle suggested a new shift in the structure of feeling that would be further heralded in electoral politics with the victory of the first baby boomer president, Bill Clinton, six months after the Murphy-Quayle debate began.[11] Clinton, the draft-avoiding, pot-smoking (but not inhaling) president with the feminist wife, carried numerous sixties signifiers. In 1992 his presidency promised (but rarely delivered) a political entrenchment of 1960s social values in the electoral arena that so many conservative commentators saw as already accomplished in the entertainment arena.

Whereas *Murphy Brown* continued the socially relevant sitcom tradition, *Seinfeld,* the comedy about "nothing," emphatically and quite self-consciously turned away from that legacy. Not only did the show refuse the time-honored convention of providing lovable characters, but it also dispensed with hugs, lessons learned for the week, and moral homilies. In its preoccupation with the minutiae of daily life, from trying to avoid masturbation, to getting lost in a parking lot, to debating the value of muffin stumps, *Seinfeld* had more in common with *thirtysomething* than creator Larry David might have cared to admit. Both shows featured middle-class baby boomers obsessively involved in the mundanity of their everyday lives, thoroughly divorced from the larger social and political realm. Whereas *thirtysomething* allowed the memory and a resultant guilt about the sixties to inform how its characters made sense of their current lives, *Seinfeld* thoroughly eradicated any such memory. Jerry, Kramer, George, and the younger Elaine were in no way touched by movements for social change. They lived in a hermetically sealed universe in to which political and social questions never entered. If *Seinfeld* was so noteworthy about its lack of significant social content, this may tell us something about the convention of prime-time comedy following the Lear years, in which sitcoms often *were* about something socially significant.[12] In turning its back so hyperbolically on socially relevant comedy, *Seinfeld* indicated how hegemonic that approach to prime-time programming was. Social and political relevance were *Seinfeld*'s structured absence.

Ellen, a less successful but highly visible sitcom, was an ideological world away from *Seinfeld* and, in fact, bears comparison with *The Smothers Brothers Comedy Hour* in both its handling of the politics of gay visibility in prime time and its struggle with parent network ABC. The show became a flashpoint for controversy and ideological struggle when gay comic Ellen DeGeneres decided to have her character Ellen Morgan come out as gay on the struggling series in April 1997. Although prime time had flirted with gay supporting characters in recent years, *Ellen* would be the first series to feature a gay character in the starring role. Although DeGeneres did not encounter the heavy-handed censorship and repression that the Smothers faced with CBS, DeGeneres went public with her complaints that the Disney-owned ABC was unsupportive of the show, refused to advertise it appropriately, and, most galling, forced the show to carry a humiliating network message warning audiences about the content. As had been the case with the Smothers Brothers, the political agenda of a performer who was connected with a movement for social change clashed with the more conservative sensibilities of the network, with the battle between the two serving as a terrain for television viewers to struggle over the meanings of normalizing homosexuality. Similarly to *The Smothers Brothers Comedy Hour, Ellen* was taken off the air at the end of her coming-out season. DeGeneres's approach to bringing gay rights politics into popular television also bears comparison with the Smothers Brothers' attempts to bring sixties youth movement politics into prime time. In both cases the performers were serious and devoted to the project of making their little area of prime time a liberated zone for a lifestyle and politics that threatened dominant social mores and interests. In both cases opponents accused the performers of turning entertainment television into propaganda for their causes. Both were accused of no longer being funny. One of the criticisms of *Ellen* came from the most unlikely source, Gay and Lesbian Alliance against Defamation spokesperson Chastity Bono, whose observation in *Variety* was disseminated throughout the major and alternative media: "[*Ellen*] is so gay, it's excluding a large part of our society. A lot of the stuff on [the show] is somewhat of an inside joke. It's one thing to have a gay character, but it's another when every episode deals with pretty specific gay issues." Although Bono's comment generated much outrage from both DeGeneres and other gays and lesbians, her observation acknowledges the problem when an at best "progressive" medium is used for "radical" purposes.[13] The polysemy so necessary to popular culture goes out the window. Episode after episode dealt with Ellen's gayness, with numerous didactic speeches about tolerance and gay normality. Both DeGeneres and the Smothers thirty years earlier found themselves narrowing their appeal, although there were no recorded instances of youth movement commentators critiquing the Smothers Brothers for being too antiwar or too procounterculture. But it was precisely their disinclination to play the ideological balancing act that helped pave the way for their prime-time dismissal. Regretably, a similar fate awaited Ellen DeGeneres.[14]

That a show like *Ellen* could play at all on American prime time is still a legacy of the opening up of the medium sparked by the liberation movements of the 1960s and early 1970s. *Ellen's* lack of success resulted largely from the fact that it followed in *The Smothers Brothers Comedy Hour* tradition of social relevance rather than *The Mod Squad* and Norman Lear models of ideological balancing that have proven so powerful and long-standing as popular television narrative forms. Although social relevance and even a kind of left populism are alive and well on prime time, they are largely divorced from any coordinated, activist movements for social change. *Ellen* was a notable exception. That very fact made the show threatening and deeply discomforting to network executives, advertisers, and other culture industry power brokers. It may be no accident that social relevance and attitudes distrustful of establishment institutions became so predominant on prime time only as the protest movements that sparked this new structure of feeling were disappearing. Popular culture is never in the avant-garde of social change. It mediates that change as it is occurring and helps entrench it after the sociopolitical terrain has settled. But then the battles at the level of cultural meaning start all over again.

Although this book has focused on the impact of the 1960s youth movements on popular television, the political, social, and cultural upheavals of the period transformed other arenas of the culture industry in profound ways also. Plenty has been written about the music and motion picture industry, but who would think to argue that the advertising industry was fundamentally changed by the six-ties counterculture? Thomas Frank, in his work on Madison Ave-nue in the wake of the youth movement, comes to conclusions about the advertising industry that echo arguments made in this book about entertainment television.[15] Frank challenges co-optation theo-ries that assume that the advertising industry in the 1960s cynically appropriated the empty signifiers of the counterculture in order to sell to baby boomers. Business culture did not see the counterculture as a threat or an enemy but rather as a healthy and hopeful movement against conformity, dullness, and the "mass society" so famously cri-tiqued by 1950s social analysts David Reisman and William Whyte. "Like the young insurgents, people in more advanced reaches of the American corporate world deplored conformity, distrusted routine and encouraged resistance to established power. They welcomed the youth-led countercultural revolution not because they were secretly planning to subvert it or even because they believed it would allow them to tap a gigantic youth market (although it was, of course, a fac-tor), but because they perceived in it a comrade in their own struggles to revitalize American business and the consumer order generally."[16]

Throughout *Groove Tube,* but especially in the last chapter, we saw exactly this philosophy moving television executives and pro-ducers in their attempts to remake prime-time television. Elton Rule, at ABC, extolled unconventionality; Aaron Spelling ballyhooed his support for rebel youth; CBS showed its disdain for the old, estab-lished way of doing prime time by ditching its long-standing suc-cessful "hayseed" shows. Madison Avenue marketers embraced the mass-culture critique and saw the counterculture as a much-needed remedy to the stultifying gray-flannel world of conform-or-die capi-talism. Likewise in prime time the old formulas were getting stale —how many times could Granny Clampett and her hillbilly clan flummox banker Drysdale? How often could Darrin get zapped into another member of the animal kingdom by his mother-in-law, En-dora? Prime time embraced both countercultural style, in shows like *The Monkees* and *Laugh-In,* and some degree of youth movement sociopolitical criticism, in the socially relevant dramas and comedies. More often than not, prime time's embrace of sixties youth was great for ratings.

But unlike the advertising industry during this period, prime time's dance with youth rebellion was fraught with more danger.

Frank mentions a few ad campaigns that fell flat because the ad agencies tried to incorporate psychedelic and countercultural images without any of the movement's values evident in the ads' content, but he doesn't document any cases of "hip" ad campaigns generating protest, industry or public outrage, or any particular contestation. As we've seen in these pages—from *The Monkees* to coverage of the Chicago Democratic Convention protests, *The Smothers Brothers Comedy Hour,* and *The Mod Squad*—network television did not have an easy time bringing the counterculture and youth rebellion into its purview. The process of cultural co-optation and incorporation was a heated, difficult, disruptive business. Hegemonic procedures that work best when hidden were stumbling around, at times badly, out there in the open, allowing the disaffected to point out the workings of the system—and giving them more ammunition against it.

If advertising had an easier time with youth rebellion, it may be because of the differences between advertising and entertainment television as mediums, as well as the ways Madison Avenue and network television represented youth rebellion. As a medium, advertising emphasizes imagery, simple emotional appeals, with little, if any, narrative or character development. Thus, "hip" ad campaigns didn't have to engage in any complicated ways with youth movement politics. Countercultural nonconformity and rebellion against the Organization Man's world was one thing; antiwar politics was something else. Prime time, as a narrative medium requiring conflict, found itself inevitably engaging in explosive political issues around Vietnam, drug use, and other aspects of youth rebellion that the ad agencies could easily ignore. Madison Avenue could selectively appropriate what it wanted from the hippie counterculture and ignore the more threatening New Left. There was no way that student rebellion and anti-imperialist politics could sell VW Beetles or Pepsi-Cola. Entertainment television could also have tried to ignore the more combustible phenomena of youth rebellion, but it did not. Prime time needed to revitalize its narrative arsenal, and trucking with threatening political discourses, at times, was the price that had to be paid.

John Fiske has noted that the sixties and seventies were the heyday of a brand of cultural theory that argued American society (unlike European) operated with pluralist impulses, resulting in a social sys-

tem of difference within consensus. The United States was "a vast
tribe whose national media and national sports acted as community-
building rituals."[17] Certainly the strategies used by the television industry to give mediated voice to the perspectives of insurgent sixties
youth might suggest the robustness of pluralist consensus. However,
such a model cannot account for the incredible amount of struggle
also documented in these pages. The representations of youth dissent that emerged onto prime time were the result of conflict, not
consensus. Movement commentators regularly struggled with and
against their mass-mediated images, only grudgingly accepting certain representations as possibly of propaganda value. In the case of
the entertainment industry the apparent embrace of selected bits of
antiestablishment youth politics resulted only in part because entertainment industry executives and producers actually accepted those
positions. Some, like Aaron Spelling and Norman Lear, certainly did.
Whether executives like Robert Wood or Elton Rule did, or whether
they saw the embrace of youth-movement values as a necessary ex-
pedient, is debatable. Cutting-edge ad agency personnel may have
accepted countercultural values and attitudes, but whether their corporate clients did, or whether they merely accepted them as desirable
tools to move product, is debatable. That network television needed
middle-class, upwardly mobile baby boomers to constitute a quality
audience is not debatable. If embracing rebellious youth concerns
could begin the process of rewinning consent and lessening disaffection, then the bottom line demanded accommodation with those
concerns. The bottom line was still the bottom line. Capitalist industries had to make themselves over into "das hip capital," making consumerism and the market economy compatible with countercultural
and some New Left values. Although the economic base changed
little, the cultural superstructure—the politics of everyday life—had
changed profoundly.

    This lived experience and taken-for-granted common sense of
many who had come of age during the period of the cold war, the
civil rights movement, the Vietnam War, and—finally—the women's
movement needed to be incorporated into a new social order. Had
the rebellions of the 1960s not been generally successful in forcing
some fundamental shifts in the cultural politics of everyday life, then
the New Right and Reaganite "culture wars" of the late 1970s and
1980s would not have been quite so virulent. As many commentators

have noted, the main impulse galvanizing much New Right activism was a reactionary disgust at "sixties-inspired" reconceptualizations of family, gender, sexuality, patriotism, racism, and other social institutions and values that came under such attack from the young during that decade. However, although the Reagan and Bush administrations proved fairly successful in asserting their economic agenda and, to a lesser extent, their foreign policy goals, they largely failed to shift social and cultural common sense away from the tolerance and "permissiveness" that were the fallout of the social-change movements of the 1960s. Battles over "political correctness" are but the latest attempt by these forces to struggle against the legacy of the sixties. It is rather fitting that the central site for this struggle was college campuses. Arguably, the institution of higher education was the most fundamentally transformed by the youth movement of the 1960s.

This book has traced the ways in which the entertainment industry was compelled to disseminate generally sympathetic representations of antiwar and countercultural positions because of its economic need to woo the huge numbers of American young to its products. We have seen how entertainment television struggled with the cultural handling of a threatening social and political rebellion during a specific historical conjuncture. These pages have attempted to examine a delimited moment in which popular culture functioned as a terrain for contestation, transformation, and struggle for meaning. Cultural studies theorists have asserted the importance of exploring this process. I have also tried to insist on the importance of situating such struggles within historical contexts of social change and of recognizing the crucial role played by mobilized, active movements for social change in precipitating such contestations. I have tried to insist on the enormous cultural power generated by the youth movements of the 1960s, even as I would acknowledge the ways in which the power of self-definition was denied them in mass-mediated representations.

Jazz performer Gil Scott-Heron declared in a musical piece released in 1970, "The revolution will not be televised." In the late sixties and early seventies prime time may not have been awash in revolution. However, prime time was not televising the status quo either. The television networks, despite their own elite interests, disseminated certain amounts of antiestablishment discourse that assisted in the process of fundamentally changing the American social and cultural landscape. We continue to live with those transformations.

Appendix

A *Groove Tube*

Selective Chronology

of the Years 1966 to 1971

Chronologies tend to be fixtures in many books about the 1960s. Usually tucked into an appendix at the back, these time lines provide month-by-month, year-by-year testament to the overwhelming volume of momentous "Events" exploding one after the other in dizzying rapidity within the span of an impossibly small number of years. Although these chronologies may not explain much about what these "Events" might mean, they certainly give a palpable sense of the intensity, deliriousness, chaos, and sheer tumultuousness of the period. History becomes a roller-coaster ride of one "Wow!" moment after another.

Todd Gitlin has pointed out the problem of seeing the 1960s in this way. As history appeared to "come off the leash," social and political contexts also spun away from any kind of grounding. Writes Gitlin: "Movement events conditioned the experience of time: one marked one's life experience by 'Chicago,' which signified *this,* by 'People's Park,' which signified *that.* Life came to seem a sequence of tenuously linked exclamation points. But what were the sentences between?"[1] These "exclamation points" or "Wow!" moments were typically also highly telegenic, rendering the 1960s in popular memory as a roller-coaster ride of dramatic peaks of action and spectacle. "March on the Pentagon!" "Summer of Love!" "Columbia!" "Chicago!" "Kent State!" Such exclamation points tend to evoke colorful and gripping visual images but tell us little about what these events meant and how they might have been historically connected or significant. This roller-coaster approach to the past tends to decontextualize such moments from a complicated field of forces and currents, pulling our attention away from the less thrilling exploration of underlying causes.

Having presented this big caveat about the historical utility of chronologies, I (perversely, perhaps) now present a narratively detailed one of my own for the period under consideration in this book. The "Wow!" moments are itemized here but with at least a schematic attempt to account for their context and significance. The point is to give the reader a sense of the flow of events that swirled around and had some impact on the issues discussed in the preceding chapters. Because this book focuses on the middle-class, white, youth movement in its various manifestations from hippie counterculture to the (often contentious) evolution of the campus New Left, antiwar, anti-imperialist movements, this chronology is similarly selective. It charts the rise and fall of the hippies — focusing on the highly visible phenomenon of the Haight-Ashbury. It also charts the growth and major protests associated with the antiwar movement, along with a tracking of the slow escalation of the war in Vietnam under the Johnson administration and the even slower (and bloodier) deescalation under the Nixon administration. The chronology also tries to give a sense of the growing militancy of the youth movement as splintered factions embrace revolutionism and armed struggle. Also included here are citations of the various television shows discussed in the following chapters so that the reader can contextualize the shows within the flow of tumultuous events that these examples of popular culture were mediating.[2]

1966

January 3   Thelin brothers open up the Psychedelic Shop on Haight Street near Ashbury in San Francisco to serve the reading, socializing, and meditational needs of young bohemians in the neighborhood.

January 21–23   Novelist Ken Kesey and his LSD-proselytizing band of Merry Pranksters organize a Trips Festival in San Francisco. Blowing people's minds with lighting effects, Grateful Dead music, electronics, strobes, film loops, plentiful amounts of still legal LSD, the festival serves as an early inauguration of the burgeoning hippie counterculture.

January 28–February 18   Dovish Senator William Fulbright (D.-Ark.), through his Senate Foreign Relations Committee, holds televised hearings on the war. Taking testimony from military and foreign affairs personnel, the hearings convince many TV viewers to begin questioning the war. General Maxwell Taylor, when asked about civilian casualties, breezily replies, "I would doubt if we would find many of the [B-52 strikes] hitting exactly where we would like them to . . . but the over-all effect has been very helpful." Napalmed babies were an "unhappy concomitant" to the war.

January 31 The United States resumes bombing of North Vietnam. Bombing had been halted on Christmas to encourage negotiations. By year's end American troops in Vietnam will number almost 400,000.

June Formation of the Underground Press Syndicate (UPS), an article-sharing, resource-pooling clearinghouse for the burgeoning alternative newspapers servicing youth movement readers throughout the United States.

June 30 Three army privates (called the "Fort Hood Three") refuse orders to serve in Vietnam: "We want no part of a war of extermination." Convicted by a military court, they serve two years behind bars.

July Students for a Democratic Society, the major campus-based New Left organization, embraces the concept of "revolution" to describe the kind of radical social change necessary in the universities and required to end the war in Vietnam.

July–August Large influx of young, psychedelically inclined residents to the Haight-Ashbury. Hip merchants open establishments like the I/Thou Coffeeshop, Far Fetched Foods health food store, and Blushing Peony boutique to serve this new turned-on clientele. Most of the young residents make pocket money by panhandling and by dealing in small quantities of marijuana and LSD.

September 12 *The Monkees* joins the NBC prime-time lineup.

September 20 The *Oracle*, a psychedelically oriented underground newspaper for the Haight-Ashbury community begins publication. It is notable for its use of intense, swirling color washes and trippy, difficult-to-read layouts.

October 6 Use of LSD, which had been legal until this date, is outlawed. The Haight-Ashbury community organizes a "Love Pageant Rally" in response. A "Declaration of Independence" is circulated by the Psychedelic Rangers, stating: "We hold these experiences to be self-evident, that all is equal, that the creation endows us with certain inalienable rights, that among these are: The freedom of body, the pursuit of joy, and the expansion of consciousness. . . . We declare the identity of flesh and consciousness; all reason and law must respect and protect this holy identity."

Mid-October A group of "life actors" called the Diggers (Haight-Ashbury's political conscience and Salvation Army) begins doling out free food in the Panhandle. To the Diggers this is not charity: "It's free because it's *yours*." The Diggers also deliver broadsides against the community's merchants for engaging in the moneyed economy. They establish headquarters in a garage. Outside the door is an eight-foot yellow frame, "the Free Frame of Reference," through which people pass when entering. Visitors can outfit themselves with free clothes and are encouraged to "assume freedom." Anyone asking "Who's in charge here?" would be answered, "*You* are!"

November 7 Harvard SDSers and a thousand protesters surround and trap Secretary of Defense Robert McNamara during his visit to campus. Agreeing to field questions, McNamara answers "I don't know" when asked how many civilian casualties have been incurred in South Vietnam. To the shouts of "Murderer!" and "Fascist!" McNamara is freed by police.

November 15 Police raid the Psychedelic Shop for selling obscene literature, specifically hippie poet Lenore Kandel's collection of erotic poems, *The Love Book*. The busting of the book becomes a cause célèbre —an attack on the burgeoning counterculture.

Early December President Johnson resumes air strikes on Hanoi in North Vietnam, resulting in massive civilian casualties.

December 17 Haight-Ashbury community and the Diggers throw a street party to "Celebrate the Rebirth of the Haight and the Death of Money Now." The festivities result in the arrest of two members of the Hell's Angels, who have formed a bizarre alliance with the resident hippies.

December 26 *Time* magazine chooses as "Man of the Year" those who are "twenty-five and under." The magazine describes them as "well educated, affluent, rebellious, responsible, pragmatic, idealistic, brave, 'alienated' and hopeful."

1967

January 12 Jack Webb's *Dragnet* premieres with the episode entitled "The Big LSD."

January 14 Hippies and campus politicos stage a "Gathering of the Tribes for a Human Be-In" in San Francisco's Golden Gate Park. Thousands gather as poet Allen Ginsberg chants "OMmmmmmmm" and "We Are One." Timothy Leary chants, "Tune in, turn on, drop out." Berkeley politico and future Yippie Jerry Rubin is (for once) at a loss for words. Lenore Kandel reads her "obscene" poems. Jefferson Airplane and the Grateful Dead play. The Hell's Angels provide security.

February 5 *The Smothers Brothers Comedy Hour* begins broadcasting Sunday nights on CBS, opposite NBC's *Bonanza.*

March Formation of antidraft organization the Resistance. One of its leaders is David Harris, future husband of folksinger Joan Baez. Revealing the fissures and disunities within the youthful New Left, some SDSers accuse Resistance organizers of "bourgeois moralism" for engaging in acts of individual refusal rather than organizing mass-based political struggle. Campus-based protest around the Selective Service System points to the class-based nature of the system: student deferments protect middle-class youth and work to channel them into managerial and specialized fields resulting from an extended university education. Protest also points to university complicity: "Class ranking" system threatens students with low grades with induction into the military. Universities must make student records available to SSS, thus directly implicating institutions of higher learning in the war policies of the Johnson administration.

March 6 Canadian media theorist Marshall McLuhan is featured on the cover of *Newsweek.*

April 4 Martin Luther King Jr. delivers a strong antiwar speech, pointing out that blacks are dying in extraordinarily high numbers relative to the rest of the population.

April 5 Haight-Ashbury organizations announce the formation of a Council for a Summer of Love. Expecting a deluge of perhaps one hundred thousand young people to descend on the neighborhood, the council appeals to the city of San Francisco for help. The mayor declares a mass hippie invasion officially "unwelcome." The parks are off limits to overnight camping, and intensive health inspections are stepped up in the Haight. Improbably named city health director Ellis D. Sox claims that along with sexually transmitted diseases, epidemic meningitis and even bubonic plague are possible. Gray Line Bus Company begins running a tour bus through the Haight-Ashbury: the "Hippie Hop Tour."

April 15 Spring Mobilization against the War in Vietnam gathers three hundred thousand people—many first-time protesters—in Central Park for the largest antiwar demonstration to date. The first organized public draft-card burnings occur as about 170 young men illegally destroy their draft cards. Many come forth spontaneously to deposit their cards into a burning coffee can. Later, marchers led by luminaries like Dr. Benjamin Spock, Harry Belafonte, and Dr. Martin Luther King Jr. head to the United Nations to rally.

April 16 A leaflet is distributed in the Haight about the drugging and gang rape of a sixteen-year-old newcomer to the neighborhood: "Rape is as common as bullshit on Haight Street."

May The *Chicago Seed,* an underground paper serving a psychedelic as well as politicized readership, begins publication

May 2 Forcefully suggesting a shift from the politics of nonviolent protest, members of the Black Panther Party invade the State Capitol in Sacramento, California, brandishing rifles, shotguns, and pistols in protest of a bill to restrict the carrying of firearms. The Panthers, with their politics of black self-defense against white law enforcement, become a potent symbol of black-power.

May 13 Council for a Summer of Love releases an announcement: "This summer, the youth of the world are making a holy pilgrimage to our city, to affirm and celebrate a new spiritual dawn."

End of May Marijuana supply drying up in the Haight. More and more newcomers use amphetamines as their drug of choice. As crowded conditions swell, vibes turn aggressive and tense. Many longtime Haight residents leave for communes. Diggers Feeds and crashpads close down.

June Haight-Ashbury Free Medical Clinic opens with doctors volunteering their time.

June 16–19 Monterey Pop Festival. A dazzling array of the top rock performers plays before a turned-on crowd of over fifty-five thousand. Mysterious and revered acid chemist Augustus Stanley Owsley III scatters "Purple Haze" LSD to the festival goers.

August San Francisco General Hospital reports that the number of drug abuse cases it handles has risen from 150 in February to 750 in July. Half of its psychiatric beds are occupied by patients suffering "toxic drug reaction."

August 3 A well-known LSD dealer is brutally murdered in the Haight-Ashbury. A day later another prominent dealer, a man named "Superspade," also turns up dead.

August 4 Johnson agrees to send forty-five thousand to fifty thousand additional troops to Vietnam, far fewer than the one hundred thousand requested by General Westmoreland. Johnson fears fueling antiwar sentiment. He also worries that a too-rapid escalation will fuel ultraright hawkishness and the demand for an invasion of North Vietnam, Laos, and Cambodia, which in turn could provoke the Chinese and lead to the ultimate use of nuclear weapons.

August 22   CBS News Special, "The Hippie Temptation" airs.

September   The Summer of Love is over. Scores of young kids can be seen hitchhiking, presumably back home. According to Charles Perry, "Haight Street had the tawdry, exhausted air of a beach town at the end of summer. Peace and love, however, had not returned to the battered neighbourhood. On the contrary, amphetamine and heroine [*sic*] were bigger problems than ever, and the Haight was a restless, fearful place."[3]

September 10   CBS censors folk singer Pete Seeger's antiwar song "Waist Deep in the Big Muddy" from *The Smothers Brothers Comedy Hour*'s second-season premiere.

October   The United States bombs Haiphong harbor in North Vietnam.

October 6   Haight-Ashbury Diggers and hippies organize a "Death of Hippie" ceremony to protest the mass media's distortion of the community. To the playing of "Taps," participants cast into a fire mass-media emblems of hippiedom.

October 16   The Resistance organizes "Stop the Draft Week" demonstrations. Over twelve hundred young men around the country illegally turn in their draft cards. Thousands of draft protesters attempt to shut down the Oakland induction center. An antidraft poster begins circulating that carries the (sexist) message: "Girls say 'yes' to boys who say 'no.'"

October 18   A *Beverly Hillbillies* episode has Jethro suspected of draft evasion when he shows up crippled and deaf for his physical prior to induction—the result of Granny's doctoring.

October 21   National Mobilization to End the War in Vietnam organizes fifty thousand people for a March on the Pentagon. The protesters are a mixed group, from militants wanting to provoke confrontation to moderates demanding only that the administration begin negotiations with North Vietnam. Kept from getting close to the Pentagon by hundreds of military police, protesters appeal to the young soldiers guarding the perimeter to "Join us!" "You are our brothers!" Some protesters insert flowers into the troops' rifle barrels, creating a famous media moment. Future Yippies Abbie and Anita Hoffman copulate before the troops, graphically illustrating the slogan "Make love, not war." A small group of activists, including Hoffman and Jerry Rubin, attempt to levitate the Pentagon (according to poet Ed Sanders, a pentagon being a five-sided symbol of evil) in order to cast out its evil spirits. Presumably the building does not rise. The stunt serves as an early example of Yippie media-oriented antics. Secretary of Defense McNamara and other Pentagon officials watch from their windows. Said McNamara, "It was terrifying. Christ, yes, I was scared. You had to be scared. A mob is an uncontrollable force." By nightfall only a few thousand protesters are left. They are removed with great violence by the MPs. In the aftermath of the protest some activists are concerned about the increasingly militant forms of confrontation adopted by some protesters. Others, especially in SDS, believe that nonviolent protest is having no effect. Active resistance is now needed.

November 30 Minnesota senator Eugene McCarthy, having come out against the war, announces his candidacy for the presidency.

December 31 The "Yippies" are created by a group of activists gathered in Abbie and Anita Hoffman's apartment in a planning meeting about how to disrupt the 1968 Democratic National Convention in Chicago. According to Paul Krassner: "What a perfect media myth that would be—the Yippies! And then, working backward, it hit me. Youth International Party! Of course! *Youth*—this was essentially a movement of young people involved in a generational struggle. *International*—it was happening all over the globe, from Mexico to France, from Germany to Japan. And *Party*—in both senses of the word. We would *be* a party and we would *have* a party."[4] The Yippies begin to organize a "Festival of Life" to combat the Democrats' "Convention of Death."

1968

January 5 Johnson administration indicts five prominent advocates of draft resistance for conspiracy to "counsel, aid and abet young men to violate the draft laws." One of the alleged conspirators is Dr. Benjamin Spock.

January 31 Beginning of the Tet Offensive, a massive, full-scale assault by Viet Cong guerrillas on targets throughout South Vietnam, including the American embassy. Although U.S. and South Vietnamese troops eventually beat back the offensive, the Johnson administration's "credibility gap" with the American public widens. Just a few months earlier the administration was touting its positive prospects in Vietnam. General Westmoreland traveled to the United States, proclaiming that the end was in sight and that the United States was winning.

February 25 CBS permits Pete Seeger to return to *The Smothers Brothers Comedy Hour* and to sing "Waist Deep in the Big Muddy."

February 27 Walter Cronkite, CBS anchorman, flies to Vietnam to do a series of reports. He delivers a momentous editorial stating that the war is hopelessly stalemated and that the United States should negotiate an end to it as "honorable people."

March 4 The *New York Rat,* a New Left–oriented underground paper, begins publication.

March 12 Eugene McCarthy almost beats President Johnson in the first presidential primary in New Hampshire.

March 16 Robert Kennedy announces his candidacy for president.

March 21 Airing of *Ironside* episode, "Trip to Hashbury."

March 31 In a televised address to the nation President Johnson announces a partial bombing halt over North Vietnam, then concludes the broadcast by stating, "I shall not seek, and will not accept, the nomination of my party for another term as your president."

April During a bombing halt North Vietnam unexpectedly agrees to begin peace talks, which start the next month in Paris. Johnson refuses General Westmoreland's request for 206,000 more troops, deploying only 13,500. This will be the last new deployment. The United States begins its slow, violent, bloody retreat.

April 4 Martin Luther King Jr. is assassinated. Riots and arson break out in 110 cities as seventy-five thousand National Guardsmen are called out. Guardsmen are deployed around the White House and Capitol as black demonstrators spread throughout the city, and smoke wafts toward Pennsylvania Avenue. Thousands are injured, thirty-nine killed.

April 23–30 Students at Ivy League Columbia University, under the leadership of Students for a Democratic Society, occupy five campus buildings to protest the university's connection to the war effort and its racist land grabs into the surrounding Harlem neighborhood. After constructing "participatory democracy" communes in the seized buildings for a week, Columbia president Grayson Kirk, on April 30, makes the fateful decision to bring New York City police onto campus to remove the students. The police do their work with extreme violence. Black students occupying a separate building are treated much more gingerly. Shock and rage at the beatings and clubbings galvanize the majority of the student body, which shuts down the campus for the rest of the semester in a student strike. A subsequent seizure of campus buildings leads to further police force and a university community in shambles. The charismatic, macho, blue-eyed, big-jawed Columbia SDS leader, Mark Rudd, becomes an instant media celebrity in part because of his use of inflated and bombastic rhetoric.

May Columbia University strikers and other youth-movement activists are removed by police force from the *Alan Burke Show,* a New York City television talk show.

May The FBI launches COINTELPRO, a program of dirty tricks to discredit the New Left and antiwar movement and to sew division and disarray within the movement's ranks.

June 5 Robert Kennedy is assassinated immediately after winning the California Democratic primary.

June 25 A group of youth protesters invade New York public television station WNDT-TV and take over a live talk show. Police are called to remove the protesters as the proceedings are broadcast.

August 18–30 Chicago Democratic Convention. Only between five thousand and ten thousand demonstrators show up for what many fear (and some militants hope) will be a bloody confrontation. Mayor Daley withholds demonstration permits and the right of protesters to stay overnight in city parks. This leads to running, televised battles between blue-collar police and mostly young middle-class protesters wanting to camp in Lincoln Park. When protesters attempt a march to the Hilton Hotel, National Guard troops fire tear gas at them. Some are shoved through the hotel's plateglass window. Democratic candidate Hubert Humphrey, high above the mêlée in his room, is overcome by the tear gas. Police invade McCarthy's headquarters, roughing up his "Clean for Gene" young campaign workers, instantly radicalizing many of them. Chicago police invade the convention floor and club CBS correspondent Dan Rather. Demonstrators chant, "The Whole World Is Watching," as images of the confrontations are broadcast live to an estimated U.S. television audience of fifty million. Eventually the actions of the Chicago police are deemed a "police riot."

September The syndicated late-night television talk show the *Les*

Crane Show is canceled because the host is deemed too sympathetic to the youth movement.

September 24   *The Mod Squad* premieres on ABC.

September 29   *The Smothers Brothers Comedy Hour* third-season premiere airs.

October 15   *CBS Playhouse* broadcasts the J. P. Miller drama "The People Next Door."

October 31   Johnson stops all bombing of North Vietnam.

November 5   Republican Richard Nixon narrowly defeats Democrat Hubert Humphrey in the presidential election.

December 31   *The Mod Squad* episode "The Guru," about the bombing of an underground newspaper, is broadcast.

1969

Winter/Spring   The "youth problem" starts to become a preoccupation in the White House as Nixon is increasingly concerned about social disorder. The president's mania for intelligence on the antiwar movement begins as his paranoia about political enemies grows. This paranoia ends in Watergate.

February 21   *Star Trek* airs its "hippies-in-the-twenty-third-century" episode, "The Way to Eden."

Early March   Attorney General John Mitchell announces that the Justice Department will prosecute "hard-line militants" who cross state lines to cause trouble on campuses. There is talk in the administration of setting up what could be viewed as concentration camps of student activists as the White House devises plans to deal with domestic insurrection.

March 9   *The Smothers Brothers Comedy Hour*'s scheduled episode with folksinger Joan Baez is pulled by CBS. She makes mention of her husband David Harris's imprisonment for draft resistance.

March 29   Justice Department indicts eight organizers and participants of the protests at the Chicago Democratic Convention on charges of conspiracy to incite a riot. Among the eight are Yippies Abbie Hoffman and Jerry Rubin, a number of SDS leaders, Bobby Seale of the Black Panthers, and noted pacifist David Dellinger. The trial of the "Chicago Eight" becomes a rallying point for the antiwar movement.

April 3 The Smothers Brothers are "fired" by CBS president Robert D. Wood.

April 4 *The Mod Squad*'s episode "Peace Now—Arly Blau," about a draft resister, airs.

April–May A group of students, hippies, and community organizers takes over an abandoned lot owned by the University of California, Berkeley. They sod it; plant trees, flowers, and a vegetable garden; and call it "People's Park." It becomes a pleasant gathering place for the community. Asserting the university's property rights, the UC Berkeley chancellor dispatches flak-jacketed police, with tear gas to fence off the park and plow it over. Rage from the community leads to massive street battles with police who use tear gas and buckshot against protesters. One young man is killed, and many are wounded by the gunfire. California governor Ronald Reagan fumes, "If there's going to be a bloodbath, let's get it over with. No more appeasement." In the end People's Park reverts back to a weed-infested, abandoned lot.

June 8 Beginning a campaign of "Vietnamization" of the war, Nixon starts withdrawing U.S. troops from Vietnam.

June 18 At its national convention, Students for a Democratic Society splinters between a Maoist faction (chanting "Mao, Mao, Mao-Tse-Tung") and a "revolutionary youth movement" faction (chanting "Ho, Ho, Ho-Chi-Minh"). The Maoist faction believes the student movement needs to organize the working classes as the only group who can really cause revolution. The "RYM" faction wants to organize street kids and work with the Black Panthers. The latter faction takes over and kicks the Maoists out. The RYM faction benefits from drawing its leadership from among SDS's celebrities—Mark Rudd and Bernardine Dohrn, one of the very few females in New Left leadership. Sporting miniskirts and proclaiming herself a "revolutionary communist," Dohrn devolves her splintered SDS into "Weatherman," an urban guerrilla–terrorist outfit. The New Left effectively dies, replaced by revolutionary vanguardism and extremism.

August 15–17 Almost half a million hippies and rock fans close the New York State Thruway on their way to "An Aquarian Exposition—3 Days of Peace & Music," otherwise known as "Woodstock." Braving rain, mud, overflowing portable toilets, and bad LSD, the young people manage to practice their communal, nonviolent beliefs.

October 8–11 The Weathermen organize a national action called "Days of Rage" in Chicago. Rampaging through the streets, scores of militants sporting crash helmets and clubs smash car windows and attack police. Many are arrested, and felony indictments are brought down on its high-profile leaders, including celebrities Mark Rudd and Bernardine Dohrn.

October 15 Over two million Americans, many first-time demonstrators, participate in a nationwide "Moratorium"—a one-day no-business-as-usual action against the war. Organized by middle-of-the-road (not SDS) antiwarriors, the protest develops into a huge media event as these "moderate" elements of the antiwar movement become a sphere of "legitimate controversy"—Daniel Hallin's term to describe news events that receive journalistic strategies of balanced reporting. Moratorium garners lots of establishment support, including the endorsement of sixty-four congressmen. Both NBC and CBS broadcast ninety-minute special reports on the protest in prime time.

November 13 Public revelation that U.S. troops cold-bloodedly massacred over 350 unarmed civilians—mostly women, children, babies, and old people—in the South Vietnam hamlet of My Lai. First substantiation that American soldiers were engaging in war crimes.

November 13 Vice President Spiro Agnew delivers a speech accusing the media of biased coverage of the White House. Cowed, the three networks all carry the speech live.

November 13–15 Half a million protesters converge on Washington, D.C., for a Mobilization against the war. Nixon's dirty tricks attempt to decrease the numbers, but this is still the largest protest to date. Military units and a barricade of buses ringing the White House keep the protesters at bay. Forty-five thousand participate in a March against Death, a forty-hour procession past the guarded White House. When an individual marcher gets to the White House, he or she calls out the name of a dead American soldier. In a more militant action demonstrators protesting the Chicago Eight trial as well as the war, descend on the Justice Department. Police spray them with tear gas. Attorney General Mitchell comments that it all looks like the Russian Revolution.

November 26 In an attempt to defuse antidraft protest Nixon changes the draft laws to a lottery system.

December 9 The Rolling Stones organize a free concert at California's Altamont Speedway. Ballyhooed as a West Coast Woodstock, the concert attracts similar numbers of longhairs. The vibes are terrible, however, as bad drugs and violence predominate. The Hell's Angels, who provide "security," beat up concert goers, slug the Jefferson Airplane's

Marty Balin, and then, in front of the performing Stones, stomp a young black man to death. To many Altamont signifies the "end of the age of Aquarius."

1970

February Women's liberationist members of the *New York Rat* take over the paper and run it as an all-women collective. Robin Morgan's manifesto announcing a feminist break with the New Left, "Goodbye to All That," makes waves. "Goodbye to the WeatherVain, with the Stanley Kowalski image and theory of free sexuality but practice of sex on demand for males. . . . Goodbye to Hip Culture and the so-called Sexual Revolution, which has functioned toward women's freedom as did the Reconstruction toward former slaves—reinstituted oppression by another name. . . . Goodbye, goodbye forever, counterfeit Left, counterleft, male-dominated cracked-glass-mirror reflection of the Amerikan Nightmare. Women are the real Left."[5]

Spring A flurry of bombings of ROTC buildings, banks, and corporate headquarters by the Weathermen and other groups such as "Vanguard of the Revolution" and "Revolutionary Force 9."

March 6 An elegant townhouse in Greenwich Village that was serving as a Weatherman bomb factory explodes. Three Weathermen are killed. Surviving members go underground.

March 27 Abbie Hoffman is visually censored when he appears on the *Merv Griffin Show* wearing a shirt made from an American flag.

April 10 Nixon administration organizes a day-long conference at the White House on the horrors of the youthful drug culture for television producers, urging them to flood the airwaves with messages about the harmfulness of drugs. This leads to a plethora of TV dramas with drug addiction themes in the 1970/71 season.

April 20 Nixon announces the withdrawal of 150,000 U.S. troops from Vietnam. Over 100,000 troops have already been removed.

April 30 President Nixon announces the invasion of neutral Cambodia by American troops in order to destroy Viet Cong headquarters supposedly stationed there.

May 1 Hundreds of protests rock the country. A national student strike takes shape. Within a few days hundreds of campuses are on strike.

Numerous ROTC buildings go up in flames, including one at an obscure public university in Kent, Ohio.

May 4 In the midst of a protest against the Cambodia incursion, Ohio National Guardsmen are called onto the campus of Kent State University. Shooting at unarmed students, they kill four and injure nine. Hundreds of colleges strike in anguished rage — 536 campuses are shut down, 51 for the rest of the academic year. Half of the nation's students participate in protests. More ROTC buildings go up in flames, and more National Guard with bayonets and live ammo are called onto campuses.

May 8 Hundreds of hard-hatted construction workers attack nonviolent young demonstrators in New York City. Police officers cheer them on. Seventy youths are injured, some badly.

May 9 Another Mobilization protest in Washington, D.C. Again buses form a barricade around the White House. Federal buildings are filled with troops in full combat gear. Fear of another Kent State leads officials to emphasize use of nonlethal force on demonstrators. Over one hundred thousand turn out for a demonstration that was organized in only one week's time.

May 14 White police open fire on unarmed black students at Jackson State College in Mississippi. Two students are killed, twelve injured. These killings receive much less attention than the massacre of the white students at Kent State.

May Henry Kissinger writes of this period, "The very fabric of government was falling apart."[6] Those around Nixon fear he is suffering a nervous breakdown. He begins to drink heavily.

June 30 Congress starts passing legislation to defund the war effort.

July 27 The Weathermen bomb a branch of the Bank of America in New York City.

August 23 An antiwar terrorist group, the New Year's Gang, bombs the Army Mathematics Research Center at the University of Wisconsin-Madison. A graduate student is killed in the blast.

Fall Television networks CBS, NBC, and ABC inaugurate a season of "socially relevant" dramatic programming in an attempt to capture a more youthful, politicized and "antiestablishment" audience.

September 24 Broadcast of *Ironside* episode "No Game for Amateurs," about draft evasion and those who aid and abet draft evaders.

September 27 *Bonanza* airs its "post–Civil War hippies" episode, "The Weary Willies."

October 3   Broadcast of *Bracken's World* episode "Jenny Who Bombs Buildings," a fictionalized account of a Weatherman-type terrorist.

November   Nixon intensifies bombing campaigns over North Vietnam.

November 17   *The Mod Squad* episode "A Far Away Place So Near," a fictionalized treatment of the My Lai massacre, airs.

November 22, 29   Broadcast of *The Bold Ones* two-part episode, "A Continual Roar of Musketry," a fictionalization of the Kent State massacre.

1971

January 12   *All in the Family* joins the CBS lineup as a midseason replacement.

February 8   Nixon administration begins invasion of Laos. Antiwar protest is modest in size, reflecting the growing weariness and despair of the movement.

March 1   Protesting the Laos invasion, the Weathermen detonate a bomb in a lavatory in the Capitol building.

April 19–23   Spring demonstrations by Vietnam veterans opposing the war. Washington, D.C., sees protest actions by vets who camp out on the Mall and march to the Arlington Cemetery and to the Pentagon. Because of the public support the vets garner, the White House decides not to have any of them arrested for illegally camping out. In a major media event vets take the medals they received for services in Vietnam and dramatically hurl them over a fence erected around the Capitol to barricade it from demonstrators.

June 13   *New York Times* begins publishing the "Pentagon Papers," a top-secret study of American decision making about the war commissioned by Secretary of Defense Robert McNamara in 1967. The papers are illegally "liberated" by Daniel Ellsberg, a Defense Department analyst at the RAND Corporation, who has turned against the war. He hopes publication of the papers will discredit the war and discourage Nixon from escalating and actually trying to win the war.

September   Nixon administration dirty tricks squad, "the Plumbers," breaks into Ellsberg's psychiatrist's office, hoping to find information to discredit the activist. This, and the more famous break-in at the Democratic Party headquarters in the Watergate Hotel in June 1972, begins the downfall of the increasingly paranoid Nixon presidency. Facing impeachment, Nixon resigns from office August 8, 1974.

October–November Wave of Weatherman bombing and underground communiqués. Bernardine Dohrn, who issues the communiqués, ends up on the FBI's Ten Most Wanted list.

December Having seen another one hundred thousand troops withdrawn, American combat forces in Vietnam now number 184,000. Bombing of North Vietnam is intensified. Throughout 1972 more troops are pulled out, but the air war intensifies. By August the last American ground troops leave Vietnam. Just before signing the Paris Peace Accords with the North Vietnamese in January 1973, the Nixon administration launches a massive, hugely destructive "Christmas bombing" of Hanoi and Haiphong in December 1972. On April 30, 1975, North Vietnamese and NLF troops march into Saigon, and the Vietnam War is finally over for the Vietnamese. It is arguable whether the war is yet really over for the Americans.

Notes

Introduction Turning on the Groove Tube

1 James Baughman, *The Republic of Mass Culture: Journalism, Filmmaking, and Broadcasting in America since 1941* (Baltimore: Johns Hopkins University Press, 1992), p. 92.

2 See John Fiske, *Understanding Popular Culture* (Boston: Unwin Hyman, 1989).

3 For discussions about the relationship between the rock music industry and 1960s youth, see, for instance, Steve Chapple and Reebee Garofalo, *Rock 'n' Roll Is Here to Pay* (Chicago: Nelson Hall, 1977); Simon Frith, *Sound Effects: Youth, Leisure, and the Politics of Rock 'n' Roll* (New York: Pantheon, 1981); and George Lipsitz, "Who'll Stop the Rain? Youth Culture, Rock 'n' Roll, and Social Crisis," in *The Sixties: From Memory to History,* ed. David Farber (Chapel Hill: University of North Carolina Press, 1994).

4 Landon Y. Jones, *Great Expectations: America and the Baby Boom Generation* (New York: Coward, McCann, and Geoghegan, 1980), p. 21. For more on the postwar baby boom see chapter 1. Arthur Marwick in his comparative history of the 1960s in the United States, Britain, France, and Italy attributes a great deal of significance to the increase in the postwar number of youths in the three European countries he examines. See Marwick, *The Sixties: Cultural Revolution in Britain, France, Italy, and the United States, c.1958–c.1974.* New York: Oxford University Press, 1998.

5 Ibid., p. 80.

6 See George Katsiaficas, *The Imagination of the New Left: A Global Analysis of 1968* (Boston: South End Press, 1987).

7 Ibid., pp. 38–39. The author reprints a map showing sites of major student disruptions around the world between 1968 and 1969. Australia and New Zealand experienced a total of four. Canada, another baby boom nation, apparently experienced only three.

8 John Clarke, Stuart Hall, Tony Jefferson, and Brian Roberts, "Subcultures, Cultures, and Class: A Theoretical Overview," in *Resistance through Rituals: Youth Subcultures in Post-War Britain,* eds. Stuart Hall and Tony Jefferson. London: Hutchinson, 1976.

9 Clayborne Carson, *In Struggle: SNCC and the Black Awakening of the 1960s* (Cambridge: Harvard University Press, 1981). The removal of white activists from SNCC was the heralding of Black Power. Activists like Stokely Carmichael believed that blacks could only empower themselves by working separate from whites, whose educational training tended to make black activists feel less competent and assured—even in their own organizations.

10 For an analysis of the relationship between the counterculture and Madison Avenue ad agencies, see Thomas Frank, *The Conquest of Cool: Business Culture, Counterculture, and the Rise of Hip Consumerism* (Chicago: University of Chicago Press, 1997). Paul Lyons discusses baby boomers who did not participate in the political and social activism of the era in *New Left, New Right, and the Legacy of the Sixties* (Philadelphia: Temple University Press, 1996).

11 For instance, Todd Gitlin's work is brilliant and absolutely indispensable to anyone who wants to understand the youth rebellion of the sixties. However, as an SDS "Old Guard" leader, Gitlin tends to attack the more militant and revolutionary directions the New Left took in the later 1960s. He tends to overvalorize the small, highly intellectualized, East Coast, privileged, early SDSers and to demonize the more action-oriented, mass-movement New Left that replaced his "beloved community." See *The Whole World Is Watching: Mass Media in the Making and Unmaking of the New Left* (Berkeley: University of California Press, 1980) and *The Sixties: Years of Hope, Days of Rage* (New York: Bantam, 1987).

12 Abe Peck, *Uncovering the Sixties: The Life and Times of the Underground Press* (New York: Pantheon, 1985), p. 183. Peck was a former staff writer for the *Chicago Seed*.

13 David Armstrong, *A Trumpet to Arms: Alternative Media in America* (Boston: South End Press, 1981), p. 46. Armstrong was a former editor of the *Berkeley Barb*.

14 Lynn Spigel, *Make Room for TV: Television and the Family Ideal in Postwar America* (Chicago: University of Chicago Press, 1992), p. 8.

15 Atlanta's *Great Speckled Bird* was a notable exception. The editorial staff seems to have comprised a number of heterosexual couples who articulated politics of gender and racial equality quite overtly in the pages of the paper. It was one of the few underground papers (and the only one of the sample I examined closely) that refused to publish anything considered sexist or demeaning to women. Thus there were no sex ads or ads for pornographic films—both staples in many other such papers. For me, as a researcher, the *Bird* was a welcome relief from the blithe misogyny of so much of the fare in other papers I studied.

16 Peck, *Uncovering the Sixties*, pp. 208, 212.

17 See Stuart Hall, "Notes on Deconstructing 'The Popular,' " in *People's History and Social Theory,* ed. Raphael Samuel (London: Routledge and Kegan Paul, 1981).

18 Ibid., p. 228.

19 Ibid., pp. 232–233.

20 Todd Gitlin, "Prime Time Ideology: The Hegemonic Process in Television Entertainment," in *Television: The Critical View,* ed. Horace Newcomb, 4th ed. (New York: Oxford University Press, 1987), p. 527.

21 This book is enormously indebted to Gitlin's work, especially *The Whole World Is Watching,* but my approach to Gramscian hegemony theory is quite different from his. Gitlin's work tends to emphasize the mechanisms whereby hegemonic elites manage to defeat, circumvent, and neutralize any attempts by subordinated groups to transform dominant ideology and structures of power. Gitlin's narrative depicts hegemonic alliances among the media and political power as fairly monolithic and as not significantly discomfited by challenges posed by the antiwar movement. His book tends to depict the New Left as largely unable to force its discourses into popular circulation. He emphasizes the strength of media elites to frame those discourses within their own hegemonic parameters.

22 Raymond Williams, *The Long Revolution* (New York: Columbia University Press, 1961), p. 49. Williams also elaborates on structures of feeling in *Marxism and Literature* (New York: Oxford University Press, 1977), pp. 128–135.

23 Hegemony considers how power relations operate not only within such "coercive" state apparatuses as government, law, and military but also within "consensual" civil institutions such as the family, the church, cultural and political associations, and institutions of popular entertainment. According to Gramscian hegemony theory, hegemony is perpetuated by a "power bloc," a shifting alliance of groups that exert various kinds of political, economic, intellectual, social, and cultural power. During periods of hegemonic stability, their ideological interests mesh fairly harmoniously. Hegemony persuades disempowered groups that the current distribution of power benefits all. A "common sense" results by which those within the social order make sense of social reality in such a way that the interests of the power bloc are maintained. See Roger Simon, *Gramsci's Political Thought: An Introduction* (London: Lawrence and Wishart, 1982), for a good, general introduction to Gramsci's work.

24 Antonio Gramsci, *Selections from the Prison Notebooks,* ed. and trans. Quintin Hoare and Geoffrey Nowell Smith (New York: International Publishers, 1971), p. 276.

25 Some readers may be interested in how I chose the various television programs that will be discussed in these pages. I systematically scanned

through capsule descriptions of television programs written up in *TV Guide* between the years 1966 and 1971. I found this a particularly fruitful means for getting a sense of programming flow and content over the period. I ended up with a list of almost two hundred prime-time shows, mostly episodic drama and comedy, along with some documentary news reports, made-for-TV movies, and a few talk show installments. All dealt in some way with rebellious youth. I was then able to locate approximately fifty of the programs at the Library of Congress, Division of Motion Picture, Broadcasting and Recorded Sound. A few other programs that are easily available in syndication I was able to study in the comfort of my own living room. All episodes of *The Smothers Brothers Comedy Hour* (which I did not include on the above mentioned list) were viewed at the UCLA Archive Study and Research Center. Wherever possible I tried to locate specific programs mentioned by writers in the underground press and privileged those for analysis.

Chapter One "Clarabell Was the First Yippie": The Television Generation from *Howdy Doody* to Marshall McLuhan

1 Donald Bowie, *Station Identification: Confessions of a Video Kid* (New York: M. Evans, 1980), p. 20. Thanks to Mary Ann Watson for drawing my attention to this book.

2 Ibid., pp. 16, 22.

3 Annie Gottlieb, *Do You Believe in Magic? The Second Coming of the Sixties Generation* (New York: Times Books, 1987), p. 30.

4 James N. Miller, "TV and the Children," *The Nation*, July 22, 1950, p. 87.

5 Robert Lewis Shayan, "The Pied Piper of Video," *Saturday Review of Literature*, Nov. 25, 1950, pp. 49–50.

6 For a study of the ways in which the U.S. government and the women's magazine industry worked together to first encourage women to enter nontraditional work for the war effort and then to eject them from those fields, see Maureen Honey, *Creating Rosie the Riveter: Class, Gender, and Propaganda during World War II* (Amherst: University of Massachusetts Press, 1984).

7 Elaine Tyler May, *Homeward Bound: American Families in the Cold War Era* (New York: Basic Books, 1988), p. 14.

8 Cobbett S. Steinberg, *TV Facts* (New York: Facts On File, 1980), p. 142.

9 Leo Bogart, *The Age of Television* (New York: Frederick Ungar, 1972 [1956, 1958]), p. 19. First published in 1956, this book was a compendium of contemporary social science research studies of television and its viewers.

Bogart revised the book in 1958 to include the findings of new research studies. In 1972 he added endnotes to bring his material up to date.

10 Ibid., p. 96–97.

11 See Spigel, *Make Room for TV.*

12 James Gilbert, *A Cycle of Outrage: America's Reaction to the Juvenile Delinquent in the 1950s* (New York: Oxford University Press, 1986), p. 15.

13 Spigel, *Make Room for TV,* p. 105. From a 1948 DuMont ad.

14 Douglas Edwards, "The One World of Television," *Parents,* Mar. 1951, p. 160.

15 Bogart, *Age of Television,* p. 246.

16 Ibid. Spigel has also examined this particular method of advertising television sets. See Spigel, *Make Room for TV,* pp. 59–60.

17 Spigel, *Make Room for TV,* p. 41.

18 Ibid., p. 45.

19 Dorothy Barclay, "Calmer Attitudes toward Television," *New York Times Magazine,* Nov. 2, 1952, p. 50.

20 For an analysis of the development of a youth culture in the 1920s, see Paula Fass, *The Damned and the Beautiful: American Youth in the 1920s* (New York: Oxford University Press, 1977).

21 Jones, *Great Expectations,* p. 45.

22 Gilbert, *Cycle of Outrage,* p. 138.

23 Bogart, *Age of Television,* pp. 254–255.

24 For older children, teenagers in particular, there was a great moral panic about the link between violence on certain television shows, such as crime shows and many westerns, and a perceived rise in juvenile delinquency. The 1954 Estes Kefauver Senate Subcommittee hearing on juvenile delinquency heightened these fears. See Gilbert, *Cycle of Outrage.*

25 Dorothy Barclay, "The TV Generation's Growing Pains," *New York Times Magazine,* May 23, 1954, p. 54.

26 Many of these themes about the relationship between children and television have been examined in a theoretically nuanced way by Joshua Meyrowitz, *No Sense of Place: The Impact of Electronic Media on Social Behavior* (New York: Oxford University Press, 1985), pp. 226–267. See also Neil Postman, *The Disappearance of Childhood* (New York: Delacorte Press, 1982).

27 Dorothy Barclay, "Making the Most of Television," *New York Times Magazine,* Feb. 21, 1954, p. 34.

28 Ibid.

29 Leo Bogart introduced Klapper's phrase and his concerns into the 1958 edition of his book. See Bogart, *Age of Television* (1958 edition), p. 287.

30 Joseph T. Klapper, *The Effects of Mass Communication* (New York: Free Press,

1960), p. 213. See also Meyrowitz, *No Sense of Place,* esp. p. 246, for a more contemporary analysis of how television "exposes the 'Secret of Secrecy'" of adulthood.

31 Klapper, *Effects,* pp. 213–214.

32 Bogart, *Age of Television,* p. 287.

33 Quoted in Peck, *Uncovering the Sixties,* p. 27.

34 The civil rights and black-power movements seemed a civil war of race, and the women's liberation movement of the early seventies seemed a civil war of gender. The point is that a manufactured consensus that normalized white, middle-class, patriarchal familial values had unraveled, exposing the ideological origins of those values. They served a particular group. In the 1960s and early 1970s numerous subordinated and disempowered social formations—youth, women, African Americans, Latinos, gays, and lesbians—began to recognize this and rebelled.

35 It is important to emphasize that large numbers of baby boomers did not embrace the counterculture, join SDS, participate in protests against the Vietnam War, experiment with hallucinogenic drugs, and otherwise engage in rebellious activity, but it was the actions and demeanor of those who did that defined this generation in public discourse. And although many baby boomers were not white, not of the middle classes, not college bound, and not from suburban neighborhoods, this particular segment of the cohort stood in to define the entire baby boom. They do to this day. See my introduction for more on this issue.

36 Quoted in Jerry Rubin, *Do It: Scenarios of the Revolution* (New York: Simon and Schuster, 1970), p. 79. The Yippies were a small coterie of activists who attempted to bridge the perceived gap between countercultural hippie youth and the more overtly political New Left–oriented campus activists. Yippie media celebrities such as Abbie Hoffman and Jerry Rubin were particularly interested in the possibilities of using mainstream media, especially television, to radicalize young people. See chapter 3.

37 As discussed in the introduction, discourse that emphasized masculine imagery was rampant during this period. Although young women participated in numbers equal to those of young men, their presence was continually erased through the movement's rhetoric. Even the famous "Port Huron Statement," the founding document of SDS and a major early New Left manifesto, was riddled with rhetorical exclusions: "We regard *men* [emphasis in original] as infinitely precious. . . ." "Men have unrealized potential for self-cultivation. . . ." "Personal links between man and man are needed. . . ." See James Miller, *"Democracy Is in the Streets": From Port Huron to the Siege of Chicago* (New York: Simon and Schuster, 1987), for full text. For an examination of how this exclusionary atmosphere within the New Left and civil rights movements fostered the women's

liberation movement, see Sara Evans, *Personal Politics* (New York: Vintage Books, 1979).

38 For a study on the ways that television journalists and news organizations tried to legitimize themselves as authoritative storytellers of the Kennedy assassination, see Barbie Zelizer, *Covering the Body: The Kennedy Assassination, the Media, and the Shaping of Collective Memory* (Chicago: University of Chicago Press, 1992).

39 Jones, *Great Expectations,* pp. 65–66.

40 Jeff Greenfield's article "A Member of the First TV Generation Looks Back" appeared in the *New York Times Magazine* on July 4, 1971. It was reprinted in his book, *No Peace, No Place: Excavations along the Generational Fault* (Garden City, N.Y.: Doubleday, 1973). Greenfield is now a well-known television news broadcaster, having been a commentator on Ted Koppel's *Nightline* and on CNN.

41 Greenfield, *No Peace,* pp. 107, 119.

42 Eric Bonner, "Echoes of Interzone," *Great Speckled Bird,* Apr. 26, 1968, p. 13.

43 Ibid.

44 Greenfield, *No Peace,* p. 121.

45 A number of video collectives sprang up in the late sixties and early seventies with the marketing of relatively light-weight videotape decks and recorders. Some had exhibition spaces to show their works. The rise of cable television opened up more exhibition possibilities to these groups, who saw themselves as determinedly grassroots, decentralized, and interactive. They were deeply distrustful of the mainstream mass media (as were many within the movement) as a means for dissemination of their views and actions. This movement of "video guerrillas" will be discussed in more depth later in this chapter. For a detailed history of guerrilla television, see Deirdre Boyle, *Subject to Change: Guerrilla Television Revisited* (New York: Oxford University Press, 1997).

46 Michael Shamberg and Raindance Corporation, *Guerrilla Television* (New York: Holt, Rinehart, and Winston, 1971), p. 9. Shamberg's book became a veritable bible for the alternative video movement of the 1970s, and Shamberg headed a high-profile outfit called TVTV discussed at length by Deirdre Boyle in *Subject to Change.* Shamberg eventually went Hollywood, producing such notable baby boomer film fare as *The Big Chill* and *Pulp Fiction.*

47 Erik Barnouw, *Tube of Plenty* (New York: Oxford University Press, 1990), pp. 443–445. All three networks carried the speech, which was written by Patrick J. Buchanan.

48 Miller Francis Jr., "Medium Rare, Thank You," *Great Speckled Bird,* Nov. 24, 1969, p. 4.

49 Greenfield, *No Peace,* p. 113.

50 The only deeply critical examination I found in my survey of numerous underground papers was in the Madison, Wisconsin, paper *Connections.* See David Gross, "McLuhan," *Connections,* Apr. 1, 1967, pp. 4–5. This short-lived paper was far more intellectually and theoretically oriented than most other underground papers. (Stuart Ewen was a contributing writer.) Whereas other underground press articles I came across more or less took McLuhan's theories as given truth, the *Connections* article scoffed at them.

51 Robert Roberts, "New Size," *East Village Other,* Aug. 13, 1969, p. 4.

52 Charles Perry, *The Haight-Ashbury: A History* (New York: Vintage Books, 1984).

53 Roberts, "New Size," p. 4.

54 Marshall McLuhan and Quentin Fiore, *The Medium is the Massage: An Inventory of Effects* (New York: Bantam Books, 1967), p. 100. It should be pointed out that although most counterculturists assumed McLuhan approved of their values and activities, he, in fact, was personally quite conservative, devoutly Catholic, and no promoter of television. As a theorist and cultural analyst he felt it inappropriate to pass judgment on the new media environment he was probing. See W. Terrence Gordon, *Marshall McLuhan: Escape into Understanding* (Toronto: Stoddart, 1997).

55 Shamberg, *Guerrilla Television,* p. 1.

56 A McLuhan "probe" from *The Medium is the Massage:* "Electric circuitry is Orientalizing the West. The contained, the distinct, the separate—our Western legacy—are being replaced by the flowing, the unified, the fused" (p. 145). Quentin Fiore, the book's graphic designer, placed the probe over an image of a Vietnamese Buddhist monk immolating himself in protest against the war.

57 See Martin A. Lee and Bruce Shlain, *Acid Dreams: The CIA, LSD, and the Sixties Rebellion* (New York: Grove Press, 1985), and Jay Stevens, *Storming Heaven: LSD and the American Dream* (New York: Harper and Row, 1987), for examinations of the formative influence of hallucinogenic drugs on the sixties youth movement.

58 "The Message of Marshall McLuhan," *Newsweek,* Mar. 6, 1967, p. 53.

59 According to McLuhan, all media are extensions of some human function. The wheel is an extension of the foot, the book (print) is an extension of the eye, clothing is an extension of the skin. (A poster I have in my possession illustrates the pervasiveness of McLuhan's impact. The poster, printed in 1967, is an advertisement for a clothing shop in the Haight-Ashbury. Along the top, in psychedelic print, it reads: "An extension of your skin.") The sense of touch brings together all the senses. Touching is, thus, more involving than seeing or hearing.

60 Francis, sidebar to "Medium Rare," p. 10.

61 Roberts, "New Size," p. 4.

62 Dennis Jarrett, "How to Get With It," *Great Speckled Bird,* June 7, 1968, p. 5.

63 Roberts, "New Size," p. 4.

64 Neil Hickey, "What Is Television's Most Critical Failure?" *TV Guide,* Jan. 23, 1971, p. 8. This article was the first installment of a five-part series on television's coverage of campus unrest.

65 Kirkpatrick Sale, *SDS* (New York: Vintage Books, 1973), pp. 517–518. Sale's book is still the definitive history of Students for a Democratic Society, the most important New Left student organization of the period. It is impossible to overestimate the impact of this group within the youth movement.

66 See editorials "As We See It," *TV Guide,* Nov. 15, 1969, p. 2, Apr. 18, 1970, p. 2.

67 "As We See It," *TV Guide,* Nov. 15, 1969, p. 2.

68 "As We See It," *TV Guide,* Jan. 17, 1970, p. 2.

69 Spiro T. Agnew, "Another Challenge to the Television Industry," *TV Guide,* May 16, 1970, p. 8.

70 Eliot Daley, "What Produced Those Pot-Smoking, Rebellious, Demonstrating Kids—Television," *TV Guide,* Nov. 7, 1970, p. 7.

71 "As We See It," *TV Guide,* Apr. 18, 1970, p. 2.

72 Daley, "What Produced," p. 10.

73 "As We See It," *TV Guide,* Nov. 15, 1969, p. 2.

74 Spigel, *Make Room for TV,* p. 51.

75 Agnew, "Another Challenge," p. 8.

76 Harlan Ellison, *The Glass Teat: Essays of Opinion on the Subject of Television* (New York: Ace Books, 1983 [1970]), p. 47. All of Ellison's columns from the *Free Press* were compiled into this book and into its companion, *The Other Glass Teat* (New York: Pyramid Books, 1975).

77 See chapter 4.

78 Roberts, "New Size," p. 4; D. A. Latimer, "Channel One," *East Village Other,* July 15, 1967, p. 10.

79 Katzman E. Bowart, "Sgt. Pepper's Lonely Hearts Political Club and Band," *East Village Other,* July 1, 1967, p. 5. "We now return control of your set . . ." was an announcement used at the end of the mid-1960s science fiction anthology series *The Outer Limits.*

80 Robert Higgins, "TV Is Groovy, Man," *TV Guide,* Nov. 18, 1967, pp. 7–8.

81 Latimer, "Channel One," p. 10.

82 Ibid.

83 Patricia Mellencamp, *Indiscretions: Avant-Garde Film, Video, and Feminism* (Bloomington: Indiana University Press, 1990), p. 45.

84 Allan Katzman, "Poor Paranoid's Almanac," *East Village Other,* Dec. 31,

1969, p. 10. A detailed account of the Freex flirtation with network television is presented in Deirdre Boyle, *Subject to Change*, pp. 14–25.

85 Shamberg, *Guerrilla Television*, p. 33.

86 William Boddy, "Alternative Television in the United States," *Screen* 31, no. 1 (spring 1990): 92.

87 Mellencamp, *Indiscretions*, p. 52. Mellencamp quotes from an article in *Design Quarterly* (1978/1979): 6–18.

88 Ibid., p. 53. Mellencamp quotes from Linda Burnham, "Ant Farm Strikes Again," *High Performance* 24 (1983): 27.

89 "Video Project," *Great Speckled Bird*, Sept. 6, 1971, n.p.

90 Benhari, "TV or Not TV," *Good Times*, Oct. 15, 1970, p. 10.

91 Alex Gross, "Taping the Universe," *East Village Other*, Dec. 3, 1969, n.p.

92 "Cable TV: Big Business Crushes Democratic Potential," *Los Angeles Free Press*, Oct. 30, 1971, p. 1. The article acknowledged material used from the Washington, D.C., underground paper *Quicksilver Times* and from the *Chicago Journalism Review*.

93 Boddy, "Alternative Television," p. 95. See also, Thomas Streeter, "Blue Skies and Strange Bedfellows: The Discourse of Cable Television," in *The Revolution Wasn't Televised: Sixties Television and Social Conflict* (New York: Routledge, 1997), pp. 221–242.

Chapter Two Plastic Hippies: The Counterculture on TV

1 This is one explanation for the origin of the term. The etymology of the word *hippies* is contested. Some trace its origins to *San Francisco Chronicle* columnist Herb Caen.

2 David Farber, *The Age of Great Dreams: America in the 1960s* (New York: Hill and Wang, 1994), pp. 168–169.

3 "The Hippies," *Time*, July 7, 1967, p. 22.

4 Thomas Frank, in his provocative book on the counterculture and American business culture, argues that hippie values were embraced by advertising agencies who quite sincerely agreed with countercultural critiques of American mass society. But those ad agencies found nothing incompatible between countercultural values and consumerism. I discuss Frank's work in more detail in my conclusion. See Frank, *Conquest of Cool*.

5 John Fiske explores this argument in *Power Plays, Power Works* (London: Verso, 1993).

6 For an in-depth discussion of representations of the counterculture in the Hollywood motion picture industry and the response by members of the hip community, see Aniko Bodroghkozy, *Groove Tube and Reel Revolution:*

The Youth Rebellions of the 1960s and Popular Culture (Ph.D. diss., University of Wisconsin-Madison, 1994), pp. 101–133.

7   See chapter 6 for industry studies on the demographic breakdown of television audiences.

8   "TV Gains Young Set at Expense of Viewers over 35 This Season," *Variety*, Jan. 12, 1966, p. 34.

9   Jack Pitman, "Demon Demographics Key to CBS Massive Surgery on Winning Sked; Out to Slough Geriatric Stigma," *Variety*, Mar. 1, 1967, p. 25. Received wisdom in broadcast history, influenced to a large extent by the work of Todd Gitlin in *Inside Prime Time* (New York: Pantheon Books, 1983), is that these concerns only materialized in 1969/1970. Gitlin credits new CBS president Bob Wood with recognizing the problem of the network's elderly viewership and steering the network toward the more desirable young demographics by junking the network's so-called hayseed shows and programming youth-oriented socially relevant shows such as *All in the Family.* Clearly these concerns predate Wood. For a fuller examination of these issues see chapter 6.

10 Jack Pitman, "New 'TV Orphans'—Old Folks: All Webs Eager to Serve Youth," *Variety*, Mar. 8, 1967, p. 1.

11 "The Doan Report," *TV Guide*, Mar. 25, 1967, p. 12.

12 They went on to produce the much acclaimed star vehicle for Jack Nicholson, *Five Easy Pieces,* after their Monkees film disaster, *Head,* written by Nicholson and Rafelson.

13 "Prefab Four" was a pun on the popular moniker for the presumably more authentic "Fab Four"—the Beatles.

14 Quoted in Eric Lefcowitz, *The Monkees Tale* (San Francisco: Last Gasp, 1989), p. 12.

15 "Critics Views of Hits, Misses," *Broadcasting*, Sept. 19, 1966, p. 64.

16 "Consensus," *Television*, Nov. 1966, p. 68.

17 "Romp! Romp!" *Newsweek*, Oct. 24, 1966, p. 102.

18 Dwight Whitney, "The Great Revolt of '67," *TV Guide*, Sept. 23, 1967, p. 8.

19 Lefcowitz, *Monkees Tale*, p. 13. See also Whitney, "Great Revolt," p. 8.

20 "New Shows Have Male Appeal: TvQ," *Variety*, Oct. 26, 1966, p. 28. TvQ was an alternative means to measure audience familiarity and preference in television shows. Random viewers were contacted by telephone and asked to rate their favorite performers and shows. Proponents of the TvQ approach argued that it was a better means to gauge audience attention to particular shows and thus was of added value to sponsors.

21 See chapter 4.

22 "Romp! Romp!" p. 102.

23 Lefcowitz, *Monkees Tale,* pp. 12–13.

24 Quoted in Lefcowitz, *Monkees Tale,* p. 12.

25 Leslie Raddatz, "More Fun Than . . . a Barrel of the Originals," *TV Guide,* Jan. 28, 1967, p. 19.

26 Timothy Leary, *The Politics of Ecstasy* (New York: Putnam, 1968), p. 174.

27 J. Fred MacDonald, *Television and the Red Menace: The Video Road to Vietnam* (New York: Praeger, 1985), p. 195.

28 Kenneth J. Bindas and Kenneth J. Heineman, "Image Is Everything: Television and the Counterculture Message in the 1960s," *Journal of Popular Film and Television* (spring 1994): 25.

29 The Monkees mined this theme further in their 1968 film, *Head,* which targeted a counterculture audience. The film failed but later attained cult-classic status.

30 I was able to view a 16mm version of this program at the Library of Congress, Motion Picture, Broadcasting, and Recorded Sound Division.

31 Roland Barthes discusses "anchorage" as verbal text that attempts to limit the polysemy of images, "to *fix* the floating chain of signifieds in such a way as to counter the terror of uncertain signs." See Barthes, "Rhetoric of the Image," in *Image-Music-Text,* ed. and trans. Stephen Heath (London: Fontana, 1977), p. 39.

32 I viewed the episode at the Library of Congress. It also has appeared regularly on the cable channel Nick at Nite. This particular episode, known to Nick fans as "Blue Boy," is apparently considered a favorite among current viewers.

33 "Television Review: Dragnet '67," *Variety,* Jan. 18, 1967, p. 42.

34 Lawrence Lipton, "Radio Free America," *Los Angeles Free Press,* Jan. 20, 1967, p. 2.

35 The law-and-order genre became a particularly useful popular cultural space for working through anxieties and concerns about youth rebellion. For more on this see chapter 6.

36 I was able to view this program at the Library of Congress.

37 See "Close-Up" capsule description of program in *TV Guide,* Oct. 12, 1968.

38 Ellison, *Glass Teat,* pp. 39–40. This column ran in the *Los Angeles Free Press* on Oct. 25, 1968.

39 This episode is available at the Library of Congress.

40 This episode is available at the Library of Congress.

41 I'd like to thank John Fiske for pointing these issues out to me.

42 This episode, entitled "Uptight" (airdate undetermined), is available at the Library of Congress.

43 John Fiske has discussed the contradictory aspects of this form of "masculine" narrative structure. Anxieties about phallic power are worked

through both by depicting the feminine as victim of that power and as saved by that power. See Fiske, *Television Culture* (London: Methuen, 1987), pp. 198–223.

44 The implications of gendering the counterculture as feminine will be discussed in more detail below.

45 See Roland Barthes, *Mythologies* (London: Paladin, 1973), p. 150: "One immunizes the contents of the collective imagination by means of a small inoculation of acknowledged evil; one thus protects it against the risk of a generalized subversion."

46 "Letters," *TV Guide*, Dec. 2, 1967, pp. A-4–5. The letter was written by Alfred S. Brand of Culpepper, Va.

47 *TV Guide*, Sept. 26, 1970. I was able to view this episode at the Library of Congress.

48 For a somewhat more self-conscious and possibly subversive figuring of the hippie chick, see the discussion on Goldie O'Keefe in chapter 4.

49 I was able to view this episode at the Library of Congress.

50 I was able to view this episode at the Library of Congress.

51 One of the signifiers of the female hippie in visual representations is long, straight blonde hair parted in the middle. Whiteness—a *Nordic* whiteness—is an overdetermined feature of this representation.

52 For an examination of how this movement affected at least one popular-culture representation of African Americans, see my article " 'Is This What You Mean by Color TV?' Race, Gender, and Contested Meanings in NBC's *Julia*," in *Private Screenings: Television and the Female Consumer*, ed. Lynn Spigel and Denise Mann (Minneapolis: University of Minnesota Press, 1992), pp. 143–167.

53 I began noticing some early feminist pieces printed in New Left–oriented underground papers by 1968. Hippie-oriented papers such as the *East Village Other* were almost entirely oblivious to the first stirrings of the movement and were frequently quite hostile by the very late sixties and early seventies when they could no longer ignore it. For the still definitive history of the ways in which the women's liberation movement came out of the New Left and civil rights movements, see Sara Evans, *Personal Politics* (New York: Vintage Books, 1979).

54 See Perry, *Haight-Ashbury*, pp. 242–243. See also Peck, *Uncovering the Sixties*, p. 53.

55 Perry, *Haight-Ashbury*, p. 243.

56 "Letters," *East Village Other*, Mar. 1, 1967, p. 2. The letter was from Michael Rapp, Swarthmore, Pa.

57 Stephen Shapiro, "Hippy Dippy Bread," *Connections*, Oct. 3, 1967, p. 10.

58 Herbert Marcuse, *One-Dimensional Man: Studies in the Ideology of Advanced Industrial Society* (Boston: Beacon Press, 1964), p. 14.

59   Lawrence Lipton, "Radio Free America," *Los Angeles Free Press,* Oct. 10, 1969, p. 4.

60   Tommy Tinker, "Image Media as a Cultural Medium," *Los Angeles Free Press,* Apr. 4, 1969, p. 36.

61   Todd Gitlin, *The Whole World Is Watching: Mass Media in the Making and Unmaking of the New Left* (Berkeley: University of California Press, 1980).

62   See, for instance, the controversy surrounding the "Build, Not Burn" position put forth by SDS president Paul Booth to counter the negative representations of the organization in the press. See Gitlin, *Whole World,* pp. 104–109.

63   Lawrence Lipton, "Radio Free America," *Los Angeles Free Press,* Oct. 27, 1967, p. 4.

64   Gitlin admits as much in his introduction, where he points out that his study ignores the movement's own media. He goes on to emphasize, "*I never mean to suggest that the movement's interior culture was purely the creature of media images, or that movement people were wholly or even largely dependent on them for information and bearings*" (p. 16 [italics in original]). The underground press assisted in giving the movement its bearings. Gitlin's failure to pay attention to media discourse in that venue results in a somewhat one-sided and impoverished picture of the movement.

Chapter Three: "Every Revolutionary Needs a Color TV":
The Yippies, Media Manipulation, and Talk Shows

1   Jerry Rubin, "Do It!," *Seed,* vol. 4, no. 11, n.d., p. 18. The article was reprinted in Rubin's book *Do It* under the title "Every Revolutionary Needs a Color TV."

2   Jerry Rubin, *We Are Everywhere* (New York: Harper and Row, 1971).

3   Paul Krassner, *Confessions of a Raving, Unconfined Nut: Misadventures in the Counter-Culture* (New York: Simon and Schuster, 1993), pp. 156–157.

4   See Rubin, *Do It,* and Abbie Hoffman [Free], *Revolution for the Hell of It* (New York: Dial Press, 1968).

5   John Fiske, *Television Culture,* pp. 94–95. Fiske describes the producerly text in relation to popular television. The concept is derived and extended from Barthes's distinctions between the readerly and writerly text. The readerly text is easily accessible, providing a singular meaning, requiring little if any active work on the part of the reader. The writerly text, on the other hand, is complex, full of contradictions, resists easy consumption, and requires the active work of the reader to construct meanings. In Barthes's conception the writerly text is inevitably avant-garde. The producerly text, by comparison, is popular.

6 Rubin, *Do It,* p. 83.

7 Hoffman, *Revolution,* p. 27.

8 Abbie Hoffman, "Violence and the Commuter Protest," *Seed,* vol. 4, no. 9, n.d., p. 23.

9 Gitlin, *Whole World,* p. 176.

10 Rubin, "Do It!" *Seed,* p. 18.

11 Hoffman had studied psychology at Brandeis and the University of California at Berkeley. Despite his clownish televised persona, Hoffman was a widely read intellectual. See his autobiography, *Soon to Be a Major Motion Picture* (New York: Perigee Books, 1980).

12 Hoffman, *Revolution,* p. 133.

13 This will be discussed in more detail below.

14 William Small, *To Kill a Messenger: Television News and the Real World* (New York: Hastings House, 1970), p. 90.

15 Hoffman, *Revolution,* p. 134.

16 Shamberg, *Guerrilla Television.* Of course, Shamberg was using an establishment publishing company to pump out his vision of an alternative, movement-based video system.

17 David Farber, *Chicago '68* (Chicago: University of Chicago Press, 1988), p. 212.

18 See Colin MacCabe, "Realism and Cinema: Notes on Brechtian Theses," and Colin MacCabe, "*Days of Hope,* a Response to Colin McArthur," both in *Popular Television and Film,* ed. Tony Bennett, S. Boyd-Bowman, C. Mercer, and J. Woollacott (London: British Film Institute/Open University, 1981). See also John Fiske's discussion of the *Days of Hope* debate in *Television Culture,* pp. 33–36.

19 Fiske, *Understanding Popular Culture,* p. 188. See also Fiske, *Television Culture,* pp. 45–47.

20 Rubin, "Do It!," *Seed,* p. 18.

21 "TV's Top Rated Events of 1960—," *Variety,* Aug. 27, 1969, p. 39. According to the article, 90.1 percent of the population watched some of the convention coverage.

22 David Farber quotes poll results that indicated only 10 percent of all whites thought too much police force had been used, whereas 25 percent of all respondents thought not enough force had been used. On the other hand, 63 percent of all blacks believed that too much force had been used. Among those who opposed the war in Vietnam, 50 percent reacted negatively to the protests, and 23 percent reacted with extreme hostility. Only 12 percent of those opposed to the war indicated extreme sympathy to the protests. See Farber, *Chicago '68,* p. 206. The sympathy felt by large numbers of black respondents indicates a potential alliance of interests between the predominantly middle-class, white, young people and

African Americans as a group. That such an alliance never actually materialized in spite of civil rights and antiracist discourse within the youth movement speaks volumes about the intractability of racial divisions in American society.

23 Lawrence Lipton, "Radio Free America," *Los Angeles Free Press,* Sept. 27, 1968, p. 4.

24 Robert Gabriner, "Back to You, Walter," *Connections,* Sept. 2, 1968, p. 10.

25 Actually it was Senator Ribicoff who, in his nominating speech for George McGovern, referred to the Chicago police as "gestapo."

26 Louis Althusser, "Ideology and Ideological State Apparatuses," *Lenin and Philosophy and Other Essays,* trans. Ben Brewster (New York: Monthly Review Press, 1971), p. 146. Althusser goes on to note, "Ideological State Apparatuses may be not only the *stake,* but also the *site* of class struggle, and often of bitter forms of class struggle. The class (or class alliance) in power cannot lay down the law in the ISAs as easily as it can in the (repressive) State apparatus" (p. 147). Althusser's focus on class relations may be a bit too rigid for our purposes, but clearly the communications ISA became both a stake and a site of ideological struggle between social formations aligned with the youth movement and those of the established power bloc.

27 Gabriner, "Back to You, Walter," p. 10.

28 Allan Katzman, [Untitled], *East Village Other,* Sept. 17, 1969, p. 3.

29 Allan Katzman, "Bandages and Stitches Tell the Story," *East Village Other,* Aug. 30, 1968, p. 5.

30 Dennis Frawley, [Untitled], *East Village Other,* Aug. 30, 1968, p. 9.

31 The report was published in paperback as *Rights in Conflict: "The Chicago Police Riot"* (New York: Signet Books, 1968).

32 Richard Doan, "The Doan Report," *TV Guide,* Dec. 14, 1968, p. A-1.

33 Richard Nixon won by one of the smallest margins of victory in American presidential history. Nixon's percentage of the popular vote was 43.4, whereas Hubert Humphrey's was 42.7. See William H. Chafe, *The Unfinished Journey: America since World War II* (New York: Oxford University Press, 1991), p. 378.

34 David Bodie, "A Night at the Opera," *East Village Other,* Oct. 4, 1968, p. 12.

35 Richard Warren Lewis, "Crazy George and Friends Run Wild in Downtown Burbank," *TV Guide,* Mar. 8, 1969, p. 27.

36 For further discussion of *Rowan and Martin's Laugh-In,* see chapter 4.

37 "Too Live for Live TV?!?" *Rat,* Aug. 23, 1968, p. 9.

38 For a more recent analysis of how the politically weak can use talk shows to disseminate their discourses, see Joshua Gamson, *Freaks Talk Back: Talk Shows and Sexual Nonconformity* (Chicago: University of Chicago Press, 1998).

39   John Wilcock, "Other Scenes," *East Village Other*, Feb. 15, 1966, p. 4.

40   "Alan Burke Show Taken Over by Guerrillas," *East Village Other*, May 3, 1968, p. 19.

41   Allan Katzman, "Poor Paranoid's," *East Village Other*, June 28, 1968, p. 4.

42   Jeff Shero, [untitled], *Rat*, July 1, 1968, p. 10.

43   Chapter 4 will examine in more depth the playing out of exactly these same power relations in CBS's treatment of *The Smothers Brothers Comedy Hour*, an entertainment program that found itself in difficulty when it began taking up positions and perspectives associated with youth rebellion.

44   Elliot Mintz, "Looking Out," *Los Angeles Free Press*, June 28, 1968, n.p.

45   Paul Eberle, "Les Crane Fired—Why?" *Los Angeles Free Press*, Sept. 13, 1968, p. 2.

46   Paul Eberle, "KHJ Cancels Discussions of Revolution, Bohrman out," *Los Angeles Free Press*, Sept. 27, 1968, p. 21.

47   Popular comedian and social commentator Mort Sahl, who also hosted a television talk show, found himself censored and canceled in short order as well.

48   Renfreu Neff, "CBS Proves Abbie Hoffman Is True Blue," *East Village Other*, Apr. 1, 1970, pp. 15, 19.

49   Hoffman, *Revolution*, p. 82.

50   Meridee Merzer, "FCC: Message to Garcia," *Distant Drummer*, Apr. 16, 1970, p. 8.

51   "We've Had Enough," *East Village Other*, Apr. 1, 1970, p. 10.

52   For an account of the picketing at CBS, see Allan Katzman, "Poor Paranoid's Almanac," *East Village Other*, Apr. 7, 1970, p. 4.

53   "We've Had Enough," p. 10.

54   The networks and advertisers increasingly agreed, as we will see in chapter 6.

55   Quoted in Farber, *Chicago '68*, p. 216.

Chapter Four Smothering Dissent: *The Smothers Brothers Comedy Hour* and the Crisis of Authority in Entertainment Television

1   All episodes of *The Smothers Brothers Comedy Hour* have been deposited by the Smothers Brothers at the UCLA Film and Television Archive. All shows referred to in this chapter were viewed on half-inch video copies at the UCLA Archive Research and Study Center. Final draft scripts for all episodes are also available at the UCLA Arts Library, Special Collections Division. My description of the "Outside Agitators" sketch is drawn from both a reading of the script and a viewing of the episode.

2 "Snippers v. Snipers," *Time,* Feb. 2, 1968, p. 57.

3 "Mothers Brothers," *Time,* June 30, 1967, p. 41.

4 Opening dialogues between the brothers occasionally had Tom proclaiming that he wanted to do "pungent social commentary." Predictably the scatter-brained and verbally maladroit Tom would be cut down by sharp-witted brother Dick.

5 This verse apparently refers to a police assault against hippies congregated on Los Angeles' Sunset Strip.

6 Dialogue quoted from script for episode broadcast Mar. 12, 1967, at UCLA Arts Library, Special Collections Division.

7 A copy of the lyric sheet is included in the uncatalogued papers of the Smothers Brothers at their Los Angeles office. The song's chorus itemizes a fairly accurate list of situations, maladies, and activities that would render one ineligible for the draft. Thanks to Jan Levine Thal for pointing this out to me.

8 Episode aired Nov. 19, 1967.

9 The lyric sheet and memo are in the Smothers Brothers papers, Los Angeles. The memo from Sam Taylor Jr. to Thomas Downer was dated Feb. 26, 1968. Four letters of complaint were not necessarily a major problem. Also mentioned in the memo was an episode that aired originally on Mar. 11, 1968, and contained some political jibes at President Johnson. That material resulted in 110 complaint letters.

10 Todd Gitlin, "Prime Time Ideology," p. 526.

11 For a good overview of the Seeger controversy, see Bert Spector, "A Clash of Cultures: The Smothers Brothers vs. CBS Television," in *American History/American Television,* ed. John E. O'Connor (New York: Frederick Ungar, 1983), pp. 159–183.

12 Lyrics quoted in the chapter "The Smothered Brothers," in Robert Metz, *CBS: Reflections in a Bloodshot Eye* (Chicago: Playboy Press, 1975), p. 298.

13 CBS memorandum, Sept. 20, 1967, Smothers Brothers papers, Los Angeles. Tankersley's misspelling of the name of counterculture drug guru Timothy Leary gives some support to Tom Smothers's later claims that the CBS censors were entirely out of touch with youth culture and values.

14 Todd Gitlin, "Prime Time Ideology," p. 526.

15 CBS to Mr. Clifford A. Botway, Jack Tinker, and Partners, Inc., Jan. 19, 1968, Smothers Brothers papers, Los Angeles.

16 CBS to Mr. E. H. Lunde, Chicago, Ill., Mar. 25, 1968, Smothers Brothers papers, Los Angeles. I have not been able to determine on what program "Open Letter to a Teenage Son" was aired. It does not appear to have been featured on *The Smothers Brothers Comedy Hour* based on my survey of *TV Guide* capsule descriptions of episodes.

17 Thanks to Michael Curtin for suggesting this argument. For analysis of

the relationship between growing antiwar sentiment among elites and critical media coverage of the war, see Gitlin, *Whole World,* and Daniel C. Hallin, *The "Uncensored War": The Media and Vietnam* (New York: Oxford University Press, 1986). For an in-depth examination of when and how governmental elites turned against the war and of the influence wielded by the antiwar movement, see Tom Wells, *The War Within* (Berkeley: University of California Press, 1994).

18 See videotape entitled "Smothered Sketches," UCLA Film and Television Archives collection of *The Smothers Brothers Comedy Hour.*

19 Episode aired Sept. 27, 1967.

20 Episodes aired, respectively, Dec. 22, 1968, and Feb. 2, 1969.

21 Episode aired Nov. 3, 1968.

22 Episode aired Feb. 2, 1969.

23 William Kloman, in his in-depth article on the Smothers-CBS controversy, "The Transmogrification of the Smothers Brothers," *Esquire,* Oct. 1969, noted that the segments were "never cut or drastically censored . . . in spite of the drug-oriented nature of her act. The reason was that nobody at CBS could figure out what she was talking about. For a period of two months, the Smothers writers called Miss French "Goldie Kief" — both words are marijuana references — on the air and nobody at CBS batted a corporate eyeball" (p. 148).

24 CBS memo, Mar. 1, 1969, Smothers Brothers papers, Los Angeles.

25 CBS memo, May 2, 1969, Smothers Brothers papers, Los Angeles.

26 According to Tom Smothers, 75 percent of the show's episodes were subjected to censorship in the second and third seasons.

27 See Carson, *In Struggle,* for an excellent analysis of the shift from integrationist civil rights to black-power.

28 See Charles DeBendetti with Charles Chatfield, *An American Ordeal: The Antiwar Movement of the Vietnam Era* (Syracuse: Syracuse University Press, 1990).

29 See Tom Bates, *Rads: The 1970 Bombing of the Army Math Research Center at the University of Wisconsin and Its Aftermath* (New York: HarperCollins, 1992), pp. 81–92.

30 Todd Gitlin argues vehemently in both of his books on the 1960s, *The Whole World Is Watching* and *The Sixties: Years of Hope, Days of Rage,* that there was no — even potentially — revolutionary situation in the offing in the late sixties and early seventies. Clearly state power was not about to be seized. Weatherman rhetoric was obviously inflated, and urban guerrilla groups such as them had practically no popular base on which to draw. However, we should not minimize the extent of social, cultural, and political chaos that rippled through so many different sectors of the social order. It was the depth and breadth of the crisis of authority that

indicated an utter breakdown of hegemonic control—thus the possibility of a counterhegemonic position's prevailing. The capture of state power, as Gramsci has pointed out, must be the final achievement, after ideological victories have been won throughout the institutions of civil society. The fear or hope that revolution was possible in this period was not all that naive for those who found themselves in the midst of the chaos.

31 This is Antonio Gramsci's phrase for a period in which the ruling classes are no longer able to naturalize their power, no longer able to lead. During such a crisis hegemonic forces can only dominate, using coercive means rather than consensual methods attributable to a smoothly functioning hegemonic order. Subordinated groups no longer participate in validating the ruling classes in their positions as rulers. Dominant ideology is no longer accepted as common sense. See Gramsci, *Selections from the Prison Notebooks.*

32 Dick Smothers would keep his moustache, which he wears to this day. Tom shaved his off after a couple of episodes.

33 Episode aired Sept. 29, 1968. See also final draft script, UCLA Arts Library, Special Collections Division.

34 *TV Guide,* Aug. 31, 1968, p. A-2. The magazine printed numerous letters with this theme in its letters section.

35 The number is included in the tape "Smothered Sketches," UCLA Film and Television Archives. The lyrics for the entire song are in the final draft script for airdate Sept. 29, 1968, UCLA Arts Library, Special Collections Division.

36 CBS memo, Sam Taylor Jr. to "File," Sept. 23, 1968, Smothers Brothers papers, Los Angeles.

37 For an insider's view of the coverage of the Chicago demonstrations, see the account by head of CBS News in New York, William Small, *To Kill a Messenger.*

38 The phrase "doily for your mind" comes from resident Smothers Brothers staff writer Mason Williams's "The Censor's Poem." Scheduled for the never-aired Apr. 6, 1969, episode, Williams's poem went as follows:

> The censor sits
> somewhere between
> the scenes to be seen
> and the television sets
> with his scissor purpose poised
> watching the human stuff
> that will sizzle through
> the magic wires
> and light up

like welding shops
the ho-hum rooms of America
and with a kindergarten
arts and crafts concept
of moral responsibility
snips out
the rough talk
the unpopular opinion
or anything with teeth
and renders
a pattern of ideas
full of holes
a doily
for your mind.

See final draft script, UCLA Arts Library, Special Collections Division and tape "Smothered Sketches," UCLA Film and Television Archives.

39 The episodes of *The Smothers Brothers Comedy Hour* collected in the UCLA Film and Television Archives all contain at least some commercial spots.

40 Thomas Frank devotes considerable attention to the groundbreaking VW ad campaign and its connections to countercultural critiques of the "mass society." See Frank, *The Conquest of Cool.*

41 Carl E. Lee, Fetzer Broadcasting Company, to William B. Lodge, Vice President of Affiliate Relations, CBS, Mar. 8, 1968, Smothers Brothers papers, Los Angeles.

42 "Smothers and Others Rub 'Main St.' TV Wrong Way; Topeka's WIBW among Stations in Midwest Beefing to CBS," *Variety,* Mar. 26, 1969, p. 63.

43 "Video Top 20. 2nd Round," *Variety,* Oct. 16, 1968, p. 35.

44 [Untitled], *Variety,* Jan. 15, 1969, p. 43.

45 "Top 50 Primetime Shows," *Variety,* Apr. 2, 1969, p. 42. The Smothers Brothers' variety show rival, *Laugh-In,* was firmly entrenched as the number-one show in the country.

46 Episode aired Oct. 13, 1968.

47 Episodes aired, respectively, Nov. 17, 1968, and Mar. 23, 1969.

48 The tapes deposited by the Smothers at UCLA contain two versions of Baez's introduction. In the other one she says, "And the reason he's going to jail is because he refused to have anything to do with the Armed Forces or Selective Service. As a gift to him, I made this album." See episode scheduled to air Mar. 9, 1969, broadcast Mar. 30, 1969.

49 Metz, *Bloodshot Eye,* p. 301.

50 Robert Lewis Shayan, "Smothering the Brothers," *Saturday Review,* Apr. 5, 1969, p. 48.

51 This sketch is featured in *Rowan and Martin's Twenty-Fifth Anniversary Special.*

52 Episode aired Oct. 27, 1968.

53 See script for airdate Feb. 2, 1969, UCLA Arts Library, Special Collections Division; and episode in UCLA Film and Television Archive.

54 Ellison, *Glass Teat,* pp. 113–114. The book reprints all of Ellison's columns from the *Los Angeles Free Press.* This one ran in the *Free Press,* Feb. 21, 1969.

55 Ellison, *Glass Teat,* p. 111.

56 CBS press release, Apr. 4, 1969, Smothers Brothers papers, Los Angeles. The press release reprinted the text of three wires from Wood to Smothers dated Apr. 3, Mar. 25, and Mar. 27.

57 For a Bourdieu-influenced examination of the debate over taste in the Smothers Brothers–CBS controversy, see Steven Alan Carr: "On the Edge of Tastlessness: CBS, the Smothers Brothers, and the Struggle for Control," *Cinema Journal* 31, no. 4 (summer 1992): 3–24.

58 This apparent draft of a letter was addressed to a Mr. Conlon, who seems to have been affiliated with the Democratic Study Group in Washington, D.C., which Tom Smothers had recently addressed. See undated letter, Smothers Brothers papers, Los Angeles.

59 See typescript on CBS letterhead, entitled "THE GENERAL CONFERENCE OF CBS TELEVISION NETWORK AFFILIATES. Remarks of Richard W. Jencks, President of CBS/Broadcast Group, New York Hilton, May 20, 1969," Smothers Brothers papers, Los Angeles.

60 Nat Hentoff, "The Smothers Brothers: Who Controls TV?" *Look,* June 24, 1969, p. 29.

61 "Smothered Out: A Wise Decision," *TV Guide* (special editorial), Apr. 19, 1969, p. A-1. In a thorough survey of the magazine from 1966 to 1971 I came across no other editorials beyond the regular "As We See It" feature.

62 See regular feature of news blurbs, "Roaches," *Seed,* vol. 3, no. 8, p. 18. The blurb provided readers with the address of the Smothers Brothers' Los Angeles business offices.

63 Ellison, *Glass Teat,* p. 111.

64 Allan Katzman, "Poor Paranoid," *East Village Other,* Sept. 10, 1969, p. 6. Katzman, a notably bad writer, was a regular contributor to *EVO,* and this was his featured column.

65 "An Open Letter to C.B.S." from R. W. Black, Bell Gardens, *Los Angeles Free Press,* Apr. 18, 1969, p. 42.

66 "Classifieds," *Los Angeles Free Press,* Apr. 18, 1969, p. 49. *Freep* classifieds were infamous for their sexually explicit personal ads, a feature pioneered by the paper and taken up by many other underground papers. The prac-

tice, along with the publication of ads for pornographic films, became one rallying site for movement women who pointed out the sexist and misogynist nature of these ads.

67 "Classifieds," *Los Angeles Free Press,* May 9, 1969, p. 22.

68 Rudnick/Frawley, "Kokaine Karma," *East Village Other,* Apr. 23, 1969, p. 16.

69 Alice Embree, "Pollution Smothers: Tom Smothers vs. Smog of CBS," *Rat,* Sept. 24, 1969, p. 14.

70 Ibid.

71 Lawrence Lipton, "Radio Free America," *Los Angeles Free Press,* May 23, 1969, p. 4.

72 Leonard Brown, "Censorship Hits Smothers Brothers: Show Will Run without Joan Baez Segments," *Los Angeles Free Press,* Mar. 21, 1969, p. 21.

73 Press release dated Apr. 9, 1969, printed on *The Smothers Brothers Comedy Hour* letterhead, Smothers Brothers papers, Los Angeles.

74 Kloman, "Transmogrification," p. 199. Tom Smothers had made an initial trip to Washington in March, shortly before the cancellation, to see if he could find governmental ammunition to fight the network's censorship. It is important to point out that at the time Senator John O. Pastore's Subcommittee on Communications was receiving wide publicity as the latest manifestation of a moral panic over television sex and violence. Pastore was calling for industry codes of self-censorship, a proposal that had the networks very nervous.

75 Typescript for speech entitled, "Remarks by Tom and Dick Smothers at the Annual Banquet of the American Society of Newspaper Editors—Shoreham Hotel, April 18, 1969," Smothers Brothers papers, Los Angeles.

76 Hentoff, "Who Controls TV?" p. 29.

77 Embree, "Pollution Smothers," p. 14.

78 "The Brothers Smothered—A Slap at Youth Audience?" *Senior Scholastic,* Apr. 25, 1969, n.p.

79 Hall, "Deconstructing 'the Popular,'" p. 239.

80 John Fiske, *Understanding Popular Culture,* p. 159.

Chapter Five Negotiating the Mod: How *The Mod Squad* Played the Ideological Balancing Act in Prime Time

1 The phenomenon of social relevance as a prime time programming strategy is discussed in the next chapter.

2 Stuart Hall, Chas Critcher, Tony Jefferson, John Clarke, Brian Roberts, *Policing the Crisis: Mugging, the State, and Law and Order* (New York: Holmes

and Meier, 1978), p. 221. The authors quote from Karl Marx in an 1859 newspaper article on "Population, Crime, and Pauperism."

3 Aaron Spelling, *Aaron Spelling: A Prime-Time Life* (New York: St. Martin's Press, 1996), p. 62.

4 Ibid., pp. 65–66.

5 See ABC interdepartmental correspondence, Marcia Barrett to Leonard Goldberg, Apr. 9, 1968, on the subject of "ASI In Depth Test Results for Mod Squad," Tony Barrett Collection, box 39, folder 1, UCLA Theatre Arts Collection.

6 See ASI test results, Aug. 22, 1968, Tony Barrett Collection, box 39, folder 3, UCLA Theatre Arts Collection.

7 Dick Hobson, "The Show with a Split Personality," *TV Guide,* July 3, 1971, p. 24.

8 Ibid.

9 Dick Hobson, "Big A Is Triple T: Tremendous Television Tycoon," *TV Guide,* Dec. 13, 1969, p. 42.

10 The ways in which this motif worked out in many storylines of "relevant" shows will be discussed further below.

11 Hall, "Deconstructing 'the Popular,' " p. 228.

12 Hobson, "Split Personality," p. 24.

13 Christine Gledhill, "Pleasurable Negotiations," in *Female Spectators: Looking at Film and Television,* ed. E. Deidre Pribram (London: Verso, 1988). Gledhill refers to another cop-show hybrid, *Cagney and Lacey.* That show, in attempting to woo female viewers sympathetic to the women's movement, needed to engage with "codes of recognition" (the women's film, the independent heroine, etc.) not traditionally associated with the cop genre. The show, therefore, could not ignore questions of gender conflict if it wished to be "realistic" on its own narrative terms.

14 [Untitled], *Seed,* vol. 3, no. 3 [Nov. 1968?], p. 13. *Narc* was countercultural slang for undercover police narcotics agents, understandably considered a particular menace to drug-oriented hip communities.

15 "Letters to the Editor," *Los Angeles Free Press,* Nov. 15, 1968, p. 9. The letter was signed Gilbert Simon.

16 Meridee Merzer, "Television," *Distant Drummer,* Oct. 3, 1969, p. 10.

17 This episode is part of a "Collectors Edition" of *Mod Squad* episodes put out by Nu Ventures Video. The episode was directed by Richard Rush, who at the time was known for directing youth-oriented projects. He had directed the hippie exploitation film *Psych-Out,* which starred Bruce Dern, Susan Strasberg, Dean Stockwell, and the still unknown Jack Nicholson. He also directed the campus-revolt film *Getting Straight.* Rush went on in 1978 to direct the highly acclaimed, cinematically self-reflexive film *The Stunt Man* with Peter O'Toole.

18   Lawrence Lipton, "Radio Free America," *Los Angeles Free Press,* Jan. 24, 1969, p. 4.

19   Paul Eberle, "Mod Squad Hype Bombs Out," *Los Angeles Free Press,* Jan. 10, 1969, p. 5.

20   Lawrence M. Baskir and William A. Strauss, *Chance and Circumstance: The Draft, the War, and the Vietnam Generation* (New York: Knopf, 1978), pp. 26–27.

21   Ibid., p. 6.

22   See script, "Peace Now—Arly Blau," Tony Barrett Collection, UCLA Arts Library, Special Collections Division.

23   The script contains no coda, although I would assume that some final, wrap-up sequence would have been filmed. Unfortunately, I have not been able to find a copy of the screened episode for analysis.

24   Ellison, *Glass Teat,* pp. 190–191. The column ran in the *Free Press,* June 6, 1969.

25   Hobson, "Split Personality," p. 23. Note that Bennett uses the antidraft movement's preferred phrase "draft resister" rather than "draft dodger" or "evader."

26   William L. O'Neill, *Coming Apart: An Informal History of America in the 1960s* (New York: Quadrangle, 1971), p. 401.

27   Seymour Hersh, *My Lai 4: A Report on the Massacre and Its Aftermath* (New York: Random House, 1970), p. 151–153.

28   See Linda Dittmar and Gene Michaud, eds. *From Hanoi to Hollywood: The Vietnam War in American Film* (New Brunswick, N.J.: Rutgers University Press, 1990). The anthology includes a very useful chronological filmmography of fiction and documentary films that contain material about the war in Vietnam, its veterans, its impact, etc.

29   Michael Klein, "Historical Memory, Film, and the Vietnam Era," in Dittmar and Michaud, *Hanoi to Hollywood,* pp. 20–21.

30   My analysis of this episode is based on both a reading of the final-draft script, located in the Tony Barrett Collection, UCLA Arts Library, Special Collections Division, and on a viewing of the episode available in the UCLA Film and Television Archives. All dialogue extracts are taken from the final draft script and checked against the videotape.

31   Hobson, "Split Personality," p. 23.

32   Hersh, *My Lai 4,* p. 18.

33   Audience testing data showed Linc to be the most popular character; Julie was the least favored. See ASI Test Results, Tony Barrett Collection, box 39, folder 3, UCLA Theatre Arts Collection. Anecdotal reminiscences from a range of respondents also suggests that baby boomer viewers found Linc to be "cool" and, in memory at least, one of the key reasons they engaged with the series.

34 For a discussion about the response to Julia's blackness and gender in the context of later 1960s race politics, see Bodroghkozy " 'Is This What You Mean,' " pp. 143–167.

35 For historical analyses of black images and representations in American television and cinema, see J. Fred MacDonald, *Blacks and White TV* (Chicago: Nelson-Hall, 1983), and Ed Guerrero, *Framing Blackness: The African American Image in Film* (Philadelphia: Temple University Press, 1993).

36 In Tony Barrett Collection, box 39, folder 2, UCLA Theatre Arts Collection.

37 John Riley, "Clarence Williams III on 'How I Feel Being Black and Playing a Cop and Blah, Blah, Blah,' " *TV Guide,* Feb. 28, 1970, n.p.

38 Ibid.

39 Thanks to my colleague Susan Smith in the history department, University of Alberta, for suggesting this argument.

40 My analysis of this episode is based on both a reading of a revised script of the show, Harve Bennett Collection, box 18, UCLA Arts Library, Special Collections Division, and on a viewing of the aired episode, UCLA Film and Television Archive.

41 For complete Nielsen rankings, see Tim Brooks and Earle Marsh, *The Complete Directory to Prime Time Network Shows 1946–Present* (New York: Ballantine, 1981), p. 928.

Chapter Six Make It Relevant: How Youth Rebellion
Captured Prime Time in 1970 and 1971

1   Les Brown, "Elton's Rule: Be Different: ABC-TV Prez Puts Accent on Youth," *Variety,* Apr. 3, 1968, pp. 33, 52.

2   "New TV Must Be Willing to Mix Issues, Entertainment: ABC's Rule," *Variety,* May 13, 1970, pp. 32, 48.

3   "Bring us together" was one of the campaign slogans for Richard Nixon's 1968 presidential race.

4   "More TV 'People' Numbers in Offing," *Variety,* Oct. 30, 1968, p. 33.

5   Les Brown, "Video at Blue-Pencil Point: Fear Loss of Youth Audience," *Variety,* Mar. 19, 1969, pp. 1, 86.

6   Les Brown, "TV's Old Math for New Myth: Wooing of Youth Proves a Fizzle," *Variety,* Dec. 31, 1969, p. 21.

7   Ibid., p. 32.

8   For a brief history of television ratings and the ways ratings companies have consistently counted only audiences considered good consumers, see Eileen Meehan, "Why We Don't Count: The Commodity Audience," in

Logics of Television, ed. Patricia Mellencamp (Bloomington: Indiana University Press, 1990).

9 George Swisshelm, "CBS' Mass Numbers through Rube Show Could Hurt on Price Front," *Variety,* Oct. 29, 1969, pp. 35, 52.

10 Bill Greeley, "Gotham TV vs. Nat'l Rating: 'Sticks Nix Hicks Pix' Turnabout," *Variety,* June 5, 1968, pp. 23, 40.

11 Richard K. Doan, "Demographics," *TV Guide,* July 18, 1970, p. 20. It may have been more accurate to say that the eighteen-to-thirty-four demographic constituted over half the *potential* television audience. But to put it that way would be much less attractive to youth-chasing advertisers.

12 Ibid., p. 21.

13 "As We See It," *TV Guide,* Dec. 13, 1969, p. 2.

14 "As We See It," *TV Guide,* May 2, 1970, p. 2.

15 For an analysis of how the Hollywood studios attempted to lure the under-twenty-five cohort in the late sixties and early seventies, see "Reel Revolutionaries," in Bodroghkozy, *Groove Tube and Reel Revolution.*

16 Richard K. Doan, "The Doan Report," *TV Guide,* July 18, 1970, p. A-1.

17 Steve Knoll, "Myth of TV as Youth Medium: Dominant Accent on Older Crowd," *Variety,* Sept. 30, 1970, p. 142.

18 As discussed in great length in the introduction, I am not arguing that the politicized, movement-oriented young of the 1960s spoke for or represented all members of the baby boom. However, the perspectives of culture industry executives quoted through this book indicate that they did perceive the more radicalized, activist young as the leading edge of the cohort.

19 Les Brown, in a front-page banner headline in *Variety* on September 16, 1970, labeled the new season the "year of transition." A year later he published a book on this relatively tumultuous period in network broadcasting: *Television: The Business behind the Box* (New York: Harcourt Brace Jovanovich, 1971).

20 Steve Knoll, "Eye's Got It (Youth) On Mind: CBS July Bally 'Putting It All Together,'" *Variety,* June 10, 1970, p. 50.

21 "CBS Producers Tell It Like It Will Be Next Fall: 'More Like Real Life,'" *Variety,* Mar. 11, 1970, p. 54.

22 *Variety,* July 8, 1970, pp. 36–37.

23 The UCLA Arts Library, Special Collections Division, has a large selection of *Room 222* scripts, including responses from the network's Department of Standards and Practices. See, for instance, the Robert Mintz Collection.

24 Richard Doan, "The Doan Report," *TV Guide,* June 20, 1970, p. A-1.

25 Cleveland Amory, "The Young Rebels" [review], *TV Guide,* Nov. 21, 1970, p. 52.

26 "Letters," *TV Guide,* Oct. 24, 1970, p. A-4. This letter was juxtaposed to another asking, "What is the new kick with TV that so many of its new, so-called actors are long-haired creeps? Aren't there any clean-cut young actors around any more?"

27 Many episodes of *The Young Rebels* are available for viewing at the Library of Congress.

28 Thomas Schatz, *Hollywood Genres* (Philadelphia: Temple University Press, 1981), p. 74.

29 I viewed this episode at the Library of Congress.

30 I viewed this episode at the Library of Congress.

31 Sale, *SDS,* p. 639.

32 Her serious breakthrough into weighty roles wouldn't come until nine years later in 1979, when she played a committed union organizer in the film *Norma Rae.*

33 In 1975, prime-time television again tackled the Diana Oughton story in fictionalized format. The made-for-TV movie *Katherine,* starring Sissy Spacek, was a very sympathetic, sensitive, and politically astute exploration of a young woman's radical odyssey from Peace Corps volunteer to urban terrorist.

34 I viewed this episode at the Library of Congress. Bochco would go on to greater fame as the producer of such 1980s and 90s prime-time mainstays as *Hill Street Blues, LA Law,* and *NYPD Blue.*

35 Edith Efron, " 'Alert America to the Drug Peril!' " *TV Guide,* Mar. 13, 1971, p. 9.

36 Ibid., p. 12.

37 Edith Efron, "Who's the Heavy?" *TV Guide,* Mar. 20, 1971, p. 25.

38 Ibid., p. 31.

39 I viewed this program at the Library of Congress.

40 This was Harlan Ellison's assertion in his Dec. 18, 1970, column on the program. He noted that the second episode was broadcast immediately after "John Wayne's flag waving special." For more on Ellison's response to the program see below.

41 Material presented here on the Kent State massacre is derived largely from Peter Davies and the Board of Church and Society of the United Methodist Church, *The Truth about Kent State: A Challenge to the American Conscience* (New York: Farrar Straus Giroux, 1973). See also Sale's *SDS.*

42 For more statistics and information on the May 1970 national student strike, see Sale, *SDS,* pp. 636–638.

43 Sale, *SDS,* p. 641. For a detailed discussion of the Scranton Commission findings, see Davies and the Board, *Truth about Kent State,* pp. 143–151.

44 Don Demaio, "The T.V. Radical: A New Indian," *Thursday's Drummer* [re-

named from the former *Distant Drummer*], Oct. 8, 1970, p. 15. Demaio refers to the figure of Rick in "The Guru" episode of *The Mod Squad* and Jenny in the episode of *Bracken's World,* along with a number of other examples from *Dan August* and *The Name of the Game,* arguing that they all are instances of the radical as new Indian.

45 Ellison, *Glass Teat,* p. 316. This was from a review that appeared in the Dec. 18, 1970, issue of the *Los Angeles Free Press.* Because the review postdated the show's initial broadcast, Ellison urged his readers to look for it in summer reruns. The episodes did run again in the summer.

46 I viewed this program at the Library of Congress.

47 According to the program's scriptwriter, there was no resistance from the network about the "attitude of the Underground railroaders." See Sy Salkowitz Papers, box 17, folder 1, State Historical Society of Wisconsin, Manuscript Division. This comment is from a loose-leaf page entitled "Retrospective on Ironside," which accompanied various script versions of "No Game for Amateurs" (previously titled "Ten Drummers Drumming"). Interestingly, the initial script treatment for a proposed two-part episode painted a much harsher picture of the antidraft "railroaders." The story was entirely different and involved the attempts by two antidraft militants to slander the head of Selective Service by making it look like he had sold draft deferments for large sums of money. The man's son, who was unsure about whether he would enlist or not, became the victim of the militants' scheme. In the end they were caught, and the son, in Vancouver, elected to stay put until he could make up his mind about how he felt about serving and possibly having to kill. There was also a subplot revolving around flashbacks about police officer Ed and his first recruitment by Ironside. Ed, having served one tour of duty in Vietnam, was refusing to sign on for another because he'd determined he hated war. Ironside eventually persuaded him to do his second tour by convincing him: "What better kind of soldier to have . . . than one who hates war."

I cannot account for the radical difference between the initial treatment and the episode that finally aired. The version in the treatment would have been politically much, much safer—and would have completely alienated and outraged antiwar young people.

48 DeBenedetti and Chatfield, *An American Ordeal,* pp. 308–309.

49 One need only consider the political controversy surrounding U.S. president Bill Clinton's record of draft evasion and the furor it generated during the 1992 presidential campaign to be reminded that resistance to the Vietnam War continues as an unresolved issue in the American social and political order.

50 " 'Relevant' Themes Do Fine in TV's Established Series, Says B & B Media

Savants, Citing New Look of Top Ten," *Variety,* Dec. 30, 1970, p. 23. The study was conducted by Benson and Bowles's media programming department.

51 Les Brown, "Video's Old-Age Insurance: Geriatric Hypo for the Medium," *Variety,* Oct. 21, 1970, pp. 1, 144.

52 Gitlin, *Whole World,* esp. p. 242.

53 The seminal narrative is provided by Todd Gitlin in his chapter "The Turn toward Relevance" in *Inside Prime Time.* Other scholars who have examined this period tend to base their analyses heavily on Gitlin's work. See, for instance, Ella Taylor's chapter "Prime-Time Relevance: Television Entertainment Programming in the 1970s," in *Prime-Time Families: Television Culture in Postwar America* (Berkeley: University of California Press, 1989).

54 David Marc, *Comic Visions: Comedy and American Culture,* 2d ed. (Oxford: Blackwell, 1997), pp. 104–105.

55 See, for instance, *Mister Ed* (1961–1965), *The Flying Nun* (1967–1970), *I Dream of Jeannie* (1965–1970), *The Addams Family* (1964–1966), *The Munsters* (1964–1966), and *Bewitched* (1964–1972).

56 The term is David Marc's.

57 Richard P. Adler, ed. *All in the Family: A Critical Appraisal* (New York: Praeger, 1979), p. xxiv.

58 Ibid., p. xxix.

59 See, for instance, Neil Vidmar and Milton Rokeach, "Archie Bunker's Bigotry: A Study in Selective Perception and Exposure," *Journal of Communication* (winter 1974); John C. Brigham and Linda W. Giesbrecht, " 'All in the Family': Racial Attitudes," *Journal of Communication* (autumn 1976); and G. Cleveland Wilhoit and Harold de Bock, " 'All in the Family' in Holland," *Journal of Communication* (autumn 1976). All are reprinted in Adler, *Critical Appraisal.*

60 Vidmar and Rokeach, "Archie Bunker's Bigotry," p. 133.

61 Taylor, *Prime-Time Families,* p. 67.

62 Gitlin, *Inside Prime Time,* p. 217.

63 Marc, *Comic Visions,* 160.

64 The eighteen-to-thirty-four Nielsen rankings were listed in a 20th Century–Fox research bulletin filed in the Larry Gelbart Papers, box 91, folder 6, UCLA Arts Library, Special Collections Division. Overall rankings for every season of network television since 1950 are available in Brooks and Marsh, *The Complete Directory to Prime Time Network TV Shows.* A comparison between the eighteen-to-thirty-four rankings for November 1972 and the year's overalls reveal another interesting discrepancy. *Room 222,* the socially relevant high school comedy-drama, which never

charted in the top twenty-five overall ratings, ranked fourteen with these younger adults. *All in the Family* was far and away the most popular show, with two million more viewers than the second most popular, *Maude.* The forgotten medical comedy, *Temperature's Rising,* slotted in third place.

Chapter Seven Conclusion: Legacies

1 J. Edgar Hoover's FBI instituted a highly elaborate counterintelligence program, commonly known as COINTELPRO, to harass the New Left and the Black Panther Party.

2 S. Robert Lichter, Linda S. Lichter, Stanley Rothman, *Watching America* (New York: Prentice-Hall, 1991), p. 4. Their research received support from such conservative organizations as the John M. Olin Foundation and the American Enterprise Institute.

3 Ibid., p. 299. See George Comstock, *Television in America* (Beverly Hills, Calif.: Sage, 1980), p. 141.

4 See Douglas Kellner, *Television and the Crisis of Democracy* (Boulder, Colo.: Westview Press, 1990), and Gitlin, *Inside Prime Time.*

5 Kellner, *Crisis of Democracy,* p. 57.

6 Jane Feuer, *Seeing through the Eighties: Television and Reaganism* (Durham, N.C.: Duke University Press, 1995), p. 16.

7 See Gitlin's discussion of network executives' perception of a rightward swing in the American population in 1980 and the resultant programming flops, *Inside Prime Time,* pp. 221–246.

8 See Feuer, *Seeing through the Eighties;* Ien Ang, *Watching Dallas* (London: Methuen, 1985); Tamar Liebes and Elihu Katz, *The Export of Meaning* (New York: Oxford University Press, 1991); Alessandro Silj et al., *East of Dallas* (London: BFI, 1988); Jostein Gripsrud, *The Dynasty Years* (London: Routledge, 1995).

9 Feuer, *Seeing through the Eighties,* pp. 70–71.

10 *Seinfeld*'s Nielsen numbers could not quite rival those of M*A*S*H's finale, but then the CBS comedy did not have the cable and specialty channel and video rental competition with which contemporary network offerings now battle. That *Seinfeld*'s numbers were as high as they were indicates that the traditional networks are still capable of commanding bulk audiences—and that audiences still crave communal mass experiences through their engagement with television. The wholesale fragmentation of the mass audience by the hundred-channel universe has not yet happened—and may not come to pass any time soon.

11 For an analysis of the political and popular cultural significance of the *Mur-*

phy Brown–Dan Quayle media event, see John Fiske, *Media Matters* (Minneapolis: University of Minnesota Press, 1996), pp. 21–74.

12   *The Cosby Show,* the most successful sitcom of the 1980s, in which gentle lessons about race and gender equality were often ladled out to the Huxtable children, is the most notable example of post-1970s socially relevant comedy on the old-line networks. Significantly, the upstart network Fox successfully appealed to post–baby boomers with its sitcom, advertised as "*not* the Cosbys," *Married with Children.* Following on the heels of the Bundy family was Fox's other huge Gen-X hit, *The Simpsons.* The latter series, however, frequently deals with socially relevant themes and, in fact, is one of the most politically left and subversive shows on television. The political and social sensibilities that structure *The Simpsons* are thoroughly grounded in the oppositionality of the movements of the 1960s. The show's huge success may be a testament to its ability to appeal both to educated, middle-class baby boomer and buster audiences.

13   In *Understanding Popular Culture* John Fiske argues that popular culture is potentially progressive and populist but not radical.

14   Thanks to students in my course "American Film and Television in the 1960s," at the University of Alberta, especially Pooneh Forooghi, for helping me work out this argument.

15   See Frank, *Conquest of Cool,* and Thomas Frank, "Liberation Marketing and the Culture Trust," in Erik Barnouw et al., *Conglomerates and the Media* (New York: New Press, 1997).

16   Frank, *Conquest of Cool,* p. 9.

17   Fiske, *Power Plays,* p. 40.

Appendix

1   Gitlin, *Whole World,* p. 234.

2   Volumes that have been particularly useful in constructing this chronology include the following: Tom Wells's magisterial and definitive (for the moment) book on the antiwar movement and its impact on the Johnson and Nixon administrations' abilities to wage war. See *The War Within: America's Battle over Vietnam* (Berkeley: University of California Press, 1994). The still definitive history of the Haight-Ashbury is Charles Perry, *The Haight-Ashbury: A History.* The most useful book on the evolution of Students for a Democratic Society is Kirkpatrick Sale, *SDS.* A good accessible history of the Vietnam War is Stanley Karnow, *Vietnam: A History* (New York: Viking, 1983). On the development of the underground press, see Abe Peck, *Uncovering the Sixties.* A good synthesis history of the sixties

is David Farber, *The Age of Great Dreams: America in the 1960s* (New York: Hill and Wang, 1994).

3 Perry, *The Haight-Ashbury,* p. 237.
4 Krassner, *Confessions,* pp. 156–57.
5 Robin Morgan, "Goodbye to All That," *Rat,* Sept. 23, 1970, pp. 6–7.
6 Wells, *War Within,* p. 430.

Bibliography

Adler, Richard P., ed. *All in the Family: A Critical Appraisal*. New York: Praeger, 1979.

Althusser, Louis. *Lenin and Philosophy and Other Essays*. Trans. Ben Brewster. New York: Monthly Review Press, 1971.

Anderson, Terry H. *The Movement and the Sixties*. New York: Oxford University Press, 1995.

Ang, Ien. *Watching Dallas*. London: Methuen, 1985.

Armstrong, David. *A Trumpet to Arms: Alternative Media in America*. Boston: South End Press, 1981.

Balio, Tino, ed. *Hollywood in the Age of Television*. Boston: Unwin Hyman, 1990.

Baughman, James. *The Republic of Mass Culture: Journalism, Filmmaking, and Broadcasting in America since 1941*. Baltimore: Johns Hopkins University Press, 1992.

Barnouw, Erik. *Tube of Plenty*. New York: Oxford University Press, 1990.

Barthes, Roland. *Image-Music-Text*. London: Fontana, 1977.

———. *Mythologies*. London: Paladin, 1973.

Baskir, Lawrence M., and William A. Strauss. *Chance and Circumstance: The Draft, the War, and the Vietnam Generation*. New York: Knopf, 1978.

Bates, Tom. *Rads: The 1970 Bombing of the Army Math Research Center at the University of Wisconsin and Its Aftermath*. New York: HarperCollins, 1992.

Bindas, Kenneth J., and Kenneth J. Heineman. "Image Is Everything: Television and the Countercultural Message in the 1960s." *Journal of Popular Film and Television* (spring 1994), pp. 22–37.

Boddy, William. "Alternative Television in the United States." *Screen* 31, 1 (spring 1990), pp. 91–101.

Bodroghkozy, Aniko. *Groove Tube and Reel Revolution: The Youth Rebellions of the 1960s and Popular Culture*. Ph.D. diss., University of Wisconsin-Madison, 1994.

———. " 'Is This What You Mean by Color TV?': Race, Gender, and Contested Meanings in NBC's *Julia*." In *Private Screenings: Television and the*

Female Consumer, ed. Lynn Spigel and Denise Mann. Minneapolis: University of Minnesota Press, 1992.

Bogart, Leo. *The Age of Television.* New York: Frederick Ungar, 1972.

Bowie, Donald. *Station Identification: Confessions of a Video Kid.* New York: M. Evans, 1980.

Boyle, Deirdre. *Subject to Change: Guerrilla Television Revisited.* New York: Oxford University Press, 1997.

Brooks, Tim, and Earle Marsh. *The Complete Directory to Prime Time Network Shows 1946–Present.* New York: Ballantine, 1981.

Brown, Les. *Television: The Business behind the Box.* New York: Harcourt Brace Jovanovich, 1971.

Carr, Steven Alan. "On the Edge of Tastelessness: CBS, the Smothers Brothers, and the Struggle for Control." *Cinema Journal* 31, 4 (summer 1992), pp. 3–24.

Carson, Clayborne. *In Struggle: SNCC and the Black Awakening of the 1960s.* Cambridge: Harvard University Press, 1981.

Caute, David. *The Year of the Barricades: A Journey through 1968.* New York: Harper and Row, 1988.

Certeau, Michel de. *The Practice of Everyday Life.* Berkeley: University of California Press, 1984.

Chafe, William H. *The Unfinished Journey: America since World War II.* New York: Oxford University Press, 1991.

D'Acci, Julie. *Defining Women: Television and the Case of* Cagney and Lacey. Chapel Hill: University of North Carolina Press, 1994.

Davies, Peter, and the Board of Church and Society of the United Methodist Church. *The Truth about Kent State: A Challenge to the American Conscience.* New York: Farrar Straus Giroux, 1973.

DeBendetti, Charles, and Charles Chatfield. *An American Ordeal: The Antiwar Movement of the Vietnam Era.* Syracuse: Syracuse University Press, 1990.

Dittmar, Linda, and Gene Michaud, eds. *From Hanoi to Hollywood: The Vietnam War in American Film.* New Brunswick: Rutgers University Press, 1990.

Douglas, Susan J. *Where the Girls Are: Growing Up Female with the Mass Media.* New York: Times Books, 1994.

Ellison, Harlan. *The Glass Teat.* 1970. New York: Ace Books, 1983.

———. *The Other Glass Teat.* New York: Pyramid Books, 1975.

Evans, Sara. *Personal Politics.* New York: Vintage Books, 1979.

Farber, David. *The Age of Great Dreams: America in the 1960s.* New York: Hill and Wang, 1994.

———. *Chicago '68.* Chicago: University of Chicago Press, 1988.

———, ed. *The Sixties: From Memory to History.* Chapel Hill: University of North Carolina Press, 1994.

Fass, Paula. *The Damned and the Beautiful: American Youth in the 1920s.* New York: Oxford University Press, 1977.

Femia, Joseph V. *Gramsci's Political Thought: Hegemony, Consciousness, and the Revolutionary Process.* Oxford: Clarendon Press, 1981.

Feuer, Jane. *Seeing through the Eighties: Television and Reaganism.* Durham, N.C.: Duke University Press, 1995.

Feuer, Lewis S. *The Conflict of Generations.* New York: Basic Books, 1969.

Fiske, John. "British Cultural Studies and Television." In *Channels of Discourse,* ed. Robert C. Allen. Chapel Hill: University of North Carolina Press, 1987.

———. *Media Matters.* Minneapolis: University of Minnesota Press, 1996.

———. *Power Plays, Power Works.* London: Verso, 1993.

———. *Television Culture.* London: Methuen, 1987.

———. *Understanding Popular Culture.* Boston: Unwin Hyman, 1989.

Frank, Thomas. *The Conquest of Cool: Business Culture, Counterculture, and the Rise of Hip Consumerism.* Chicago: University of Chicago Press, 1997.

———. "Liberation Marketing and the Culture Trust." In *Conglomerates and the Media,* ed. Erik Barnouw et al. New York: New Press, 1997.

Freedman, Carl. "History, Fiction, Film, Television Myth: The Ideology of M*A*S*H." *Southern Review* (winter 1990), pp. 89–106.

Guerrero, Ed. *Framing Blackness: The African-American Image in Film.* Philadelphia: Temple University Press, 1993.

Gilbert, James. *A Cycle of Outrage: America's Reaction to the Juvenile Delinquent in the 1950s.* New York: Oxford University Press, 1986.

Gillis, John R. *Youth and History: Tradition and Change in European Age Relations 1770–Present.* New York: Academic Press, 1981.

Ginzberg, Carlo. "Morelli, Freud, and Sherlock Holmes: Clues and Scientific Method." *History Workshop 9* (spring 1980), pp. 5–36.

Gitlin, Todd. "Fourteen Notes on Television and the Movement." *Leviathan* (July/August 1969), pp. 3–9.

———. *Inside Prime Time.* New York: Pantheon, 1983.

———. "Prime Time Ideology: The Hegemonic Process in Television Entertainment." In *Television: The Critical View,* ed. Horace Newcomb. 4th ed. New York: Oxford University Press, 1987.

———. *The Sixties: Years of Hope, Days of Rage.* New York: Bantam, 1987.

———. *The Whole World Is Watching: Mass Media in the Making and Unmaking of the New Left.* Berkeley: University of California Press, 1980.

Gledhill, Christine. "Pleasurable Negotiations." In *Female Spectators: Looking at Film and Television,* ed. E. Deidre Pribram London: Verso, 1988.

Gordon, W. Terrence. *Marshall McLuhan: Escape into Understanding.* Toronto: Stoddart, 1997.

Gottlieb, Annie. *Do You Believe in Magic? The Second Coming of the Sixties Generation.* New York: Times Books, 1987.

Gramsci, Antonio. *Selections from the Prison Notebooks.* New York: International Publishers, 1971.

Greenfield, Jeff. *No Peace, No Place: Excavations along the Generational Fault.* Garden City: Doubleday, 1973.

Grossberg, Lawrence, et al. *Cultural Studies.* New York: Routledge, 1992.

Hall, Stuart. "Encoding/Decoding." In *Culture, Media, Language,* ed. Stuart Hall et al. London: Hutchinson, 1980.

———. "Notes on Deconstructing 'The Popular.'" In *People's History and Social Theory,* ed. Raphael Samuel. London: Routledge and Kegan Paul, 1981.

Hall, Stuart, Chas Critcher, Tony Jefferson, John Clarke, Brian Roberts. *Policing the Crisis: Mugging, the State, and Law and Order.* New York: Holmes and Meier, 1978.

Hall, Stuart, and Tony Jefferson, eds. *Resistance through Rituals: Youth Subcultures in Post-War Britain.* London: Hutchinson, 1976.

Hallin, Daniel C. *The "Uncensored War": The Media and Vietnam.* New York: Oxford University Press, 1986.

Hayden, Tom. *Reunion: A Memoir.* New York: Random House, 1988.

Hersh, Seymour. *My Lai 4: A Report on the Massacre and Its Aftermath.* New York: Random House, 1970.

Hoffman, Abbie. *Revolution for the Hell of It.* New York: Dial Press, 1968.

———. *Soon to Be a Major Motion Picture.* New York: Perigee Books, 1980.

———. *Woodstock Nation.* New York: Vintage Books, 1969.

Honey, Maureen. *Creating Rosie the Riveter: Class, Gender, and Propaganda during World War II.* Amherst: University of Massachusetts Press, 1984.

Hunt, Lynn, ed. *The New Cultural History.* Berkeley: University of California Press, 1989.

Jones, Landon Y. *Great Expectations: America and the Baby Boom Generation.* New York: Coward, McCann, and Geoghegan, 1980.

Karnow, Stanley. *Vietnam: A History.* New York: Viking, 1983.

Katsiaficas, George. *The Imagination of the New Left: A Global Analysis of 1968.* Boston: South End Press, 1987.

Kellner, Douglas. *Television and the Crisis of Democracy.* Boulder: Westview Press, 1990.

Klapper, Joseph T. *The Effects of Mass Communication.* New York: Free Press, 1960.

Klein, Michael. "Historical Memory, Film, and the Vietnam Era." In *From Hanoi to Hollywood,* ed. Linda Dittmar and Gene Michaud New Brunswick: Rutgers University Press, 1990.

Krassner, Paul. *Confessions of a Raving, Unconfined Nut: Misadventures in the Counter-Culture.* New York: Simon and Schuster, 1993.

LaCapra, Dominick. *History and Criticism*. Ithaca: Cornell University Press, 1985.

Leamer, Laurence. *The Paper Revolutionaries: The Rise of the Underground Press*. New York: Simon and Schuster, 1972.

Lears, T. J. Jackson. "The Concept of Cultural Hegemony: Problems and Possibilities." *American Historical Review* 9, 3 (June 1985), pp. 567–93.

Leary, Timothy. *The Politics of Ecstasy*. New York: Putnam, 1968.

Lee, Martin A., and Bruce Shlain. *Acid Dreams: The CIA, LSD, and the Sixties Rebellion*. New York: Grove Press, 1985.

Lefcowitz, Eric. *The Monkees Tale*. San Francisco: Last Gasp, 1989.

Lichter, Robert, Linda S. Lichter, and Stanley Rothman. *Watching America*. New York: Prentice-Hall, 1991.

Lipsitz, George. *Time Passages: Collective Memory and American Popular Culture*. Minneapolis: University of Minnesota Press, 1990.

Lowenthal, David. *The Past Is a Foreign Country*. New York: Cambridge University Press, 1985.

Lyons, Paul. *New Left, New Right, and the Legacy of the Sixties*. Philadelphia: Temple University Press, 1996.

MacCabe, Colin. "Realism and Cinema: Notes on Brechtian Theses" and "*Days of Hope*, a Response to Colin McArthur." In *Popular Television and Film*, ed. Tony Bennett, S. Boyd-Bowman, C. Mercer, and J. Woollacott London: BFI/Open University, 1981.

MacDonald, J. Fred. *Blacks and White TV*. Chicago: Nelson-Hall, 1983.

——. *Television and the Red Menace: The Video Road to Vietnam*. New York: Praeger, 1985.

Marc, David. *Comic Visions: Comedy and American Culture*. 2d ed. Oxford: Blackwell, 1997.

——. *Demographic Vistas: Television in American Culture*. Philadelphia: University of Pennsylvania Press, 1984.

Marcuse, Herbert. *One-Dimensional Man: Studies in the Ideology of Advanced Industrial Society*. Boston: Beacon Press, 1964.

Marwick, Arthur. *The Sixties: Cultural Revolution in Britain, France, Italy, and the United States, c. 1958–c. 1974*. New York: Oxford University Press, 1998.

May, Elaine Tyler. *Homeward Bound: American Families in the Cold War Era*. New York: Basic Books, 1988.

McLuhan, Marshall. *Understanding Media: The Extensions of Man*. New York: Signet, 1964.

McLuhan, Marshall, and Quentin Fiore. *The Medium Is the Massage: An Inventory of Effects*. New York: Bantam, 1967.

Meehan, Eileen. "Why We Don't Count: The Commodity Audience." In *Logics of Television,* ed. Patricia Mellencamp Bloomington: Indiana University Press, 1990.

Mellencamp, Patricia. *Indiscretions: Avant-Garde Film, Video, and Feminism.* Bloomington: Indiana University Press, 1990.

Metz, Robert. *CBS: Reflections in a Bloodshot Eye.* Chicago: Playboy Press, 1975.

Meyrowitz, Joshua. *No Sense of Place: The Impact of Electronic Media on Social Behavior.* New York: Oxford University Press, 1985.

Miller, James. *"Democracy Is in the Streets": From Port Huron to the Siege of Chicago.* New York: Simon and Schuster, 1987.

Morley, David. *Television, Audiences, and Cultural Studies.* London: Routledge, 1992.

National Commission on the Causes and Prevention of Violence Report. *Rights in Conflict.* New York: Signet, 1968.

O'Neill, William L. *Coming Apart: An Informal History of America in the 1960s.* New York: Quadrangle, 1971.

Peck, Abe. *Uncovering the Sixties: The Life and Times of the Underground Press.* New York: Pantheon, 1985.

Perry, Charles. *The Haight-Ashbury: A History.* New York: Vintage Books, 1984.

Postman, Neil. *The Disappearance of Childhood.* New York: Delacorte Press, 1982.

Radway, Janice. *Reading the Romance: Women, Patriarchy, and Popular Literature.* Chapel Hill: University of North Carolina Press, 1984.

Roszak, Theodore. *The Making of a Counter Culture.* Garden City: Anchor Books, 1969.

Rubin, Jerry. *Do It: Scenarios of the Revolution.* New York: Simon and Schuster, 1970.

Rutstein, Nat. *"Go Watch TV!" What and How Much Should Children Really Watch?* New York: Sheed and Ward, 1974.

Sale, Kirkpatrick. *SDS.* New York: Vintage Books, 1973.

Sassoon, Anne Showstack. *Gramsci's Politics.* Minneapolis: University of Minnesota Press, 1980.

Sayres, Sohnya, et al. *The 60s without Apology.* Minneapolis: University of Minnesota Press in cooperation with *Social Text,* 1984.

Schatz, Thomas. *Hollywood Genres.* Philadelphia: Temple University Press, 1981.

Shamberg, Michael, and Raindance Corporation. *Guerrilla Television.* New York: Rinehart and Winston, 1971.

Simon, Roger. *Gramsci's Political Thought: An Introduction.* London: Lawrence and Wishart, 1982.

Small, William. *To Kill a Messenger: Television News and the Real World.* New York: Hastings House, 1970.

Spector, Bert. "A Clash of Cultures: The Smothers Brothers vs. CBS Television." In *American History/American Television,* ed. John E. O'Connor New York: Frederick Ungar, 1983.

Spelling, Aaron. *Aaron Spelling: A Prime-Time Life.* New York: St. Martin's Press, 1996.

Spigel, Lynn. *Make Room for TV: Television and the Family Ideal in Postwar America.* Chicago: University of Chicago Press, 1992.

Spigel, Lynn, and Michael Curtin, eds. *The Revolution Wasn't Televised: Sixties Television and Social Conflict.* New York: Routledge, 1997.

Steinberg, Cobbett S. *TV Facts.* New York: Facts on File, 1980.

Stevens, Jay. *Storming Heaven: LSD and the American Dream.* New York: Harper and Row, 1987.

Streeter, Thomas. "Blue Skies and Strange Bedfellows: The Discourse of Cable Television." In Spigel and Curtin, *The Revolution Wasn't Televised.*

Taylor, Ella. *Prime-Time Families: Television Culture in Postwar America.* Berkeley: University of California Press, 1989.

Thompson, E. P. *The Making of the English Working Class.* London: Victor Gollancz, 1963.

Turner, Graeme. *British Cultural Studies: An Introduction.* New York: Routledge, 1992.

Watson, Mary Ann. *The Expanding Vista: American Television in the Kennedy Years.* New York: Oxford University Press, 1990.

Wells, Tom. *The War Within: America's Battle over Vietnam.* Berkeley: University of California Press, 1994.

Williams, Raymond. "Base and Superstructure in Marxist Cultural Theory." *New Left Review* 82 (Nov./Dec. 1973), pp. 3–16.

———. *The Long Revolution.* New York: Columbia University Press, 1961.

———. *Marxism and Literature.* New York: Oxford University Press, 1977.

Winn, Marie. *The Plug-In Drug.* New York: Viking Press, 1978.

Zelizer, Barbie. *Covering the Body: The Kennedy Assassination, the Media, and the Shaping of Collective Memory.* Chicago: University of Chicago Press, 1992.

Index

Aniko Bodroghkozy is Assistant Professor of Film and
Media Studies at the University of Alberta.

Library of Congress Cataloging-in-Publication Data

Bodroghkozy, Aniko, 1960–
Groove tube : sixties television and the youth rebellion /
Aniko Bodroghkozy.
p. cm. — (Console-ing passions)
Includes bibliographical references and index.
ISBN 0-8223-2656-6 (cloth : alk. paper) —
ISBN 0-8223-2645-0 (pbk. : alk. paper)
1. Television and youth—United States.   2. New Left—
United States.   3. United States—Social conditions—
1960–1980.   I. Title.   II. Series.
HQ799.2.T4 B63   2000
302.23′45′08350973—dc21   00-061748